MODERN ART

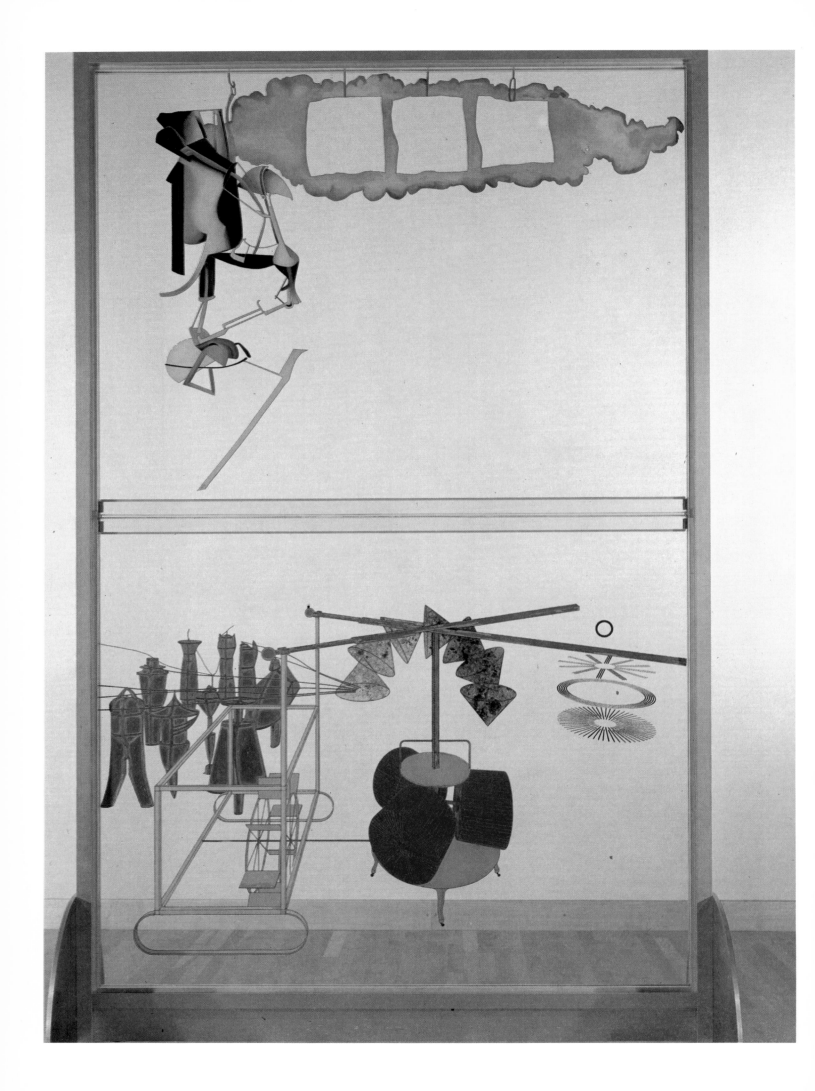

MODERN ART

TREWIN COPPLESTONE

Exeter Books

NEW YORK

Photographic acknowledgments

Albright-Knox Art Gallery, Buffalo, New York 63, 92 top, 183 bottom, 184–185, 190; The Art Institute of Chicago 130 top, 132; Bayerische Staatsgemäldesammlungen, Munich 77 top, 82; Bridgeman Art Library, London 29, 33, 37, 39, 40, 42 top, 46, 48, 90–91, 103, 107, 146, 150, 154 bottom, 159 top, 160, 173, 176, 197, 209, 222 top; Mr and Mrs Gilbert Carpenter, Greensboro, North Carolina 245; Leo Castelli Gallery, New York 238 bottom right; Centre National d'Art Contemporain, Paris 218 top, 218 bottom right; City of Birmingham Museum and Art Gallery 97; The Cleveland Museum of Art 191 top; Colorific, London 240; Trewin Copplestone 92 bottom, 93 bottom, 105, 109 top, 111, 117, 231 top left; André Emmerich Gallery, New York 224 top; Galerie Ariel, Paris 168; Galerie Chalette, New York 116 bottom; Galleria Nazionale d'Arte Moderna, Rome 108; Galleria Schwarz, Milan 201 left; Glasgow Museums and Art Galleries 125; Peggy Guggenheim Collection, Venice 130 bottom; Solomon R. Guggenheim Museum, New York 76, 101 top, 101 bottom, 162, 163, 169 bottom, 171; Calouste Gulbenkian Foundation, Lisbon 203; Joachim Harel Management, Vienna 170; O.K. Harris Gallery, New York 243, 246 bottom; Hatton Gallery, University of Newcastle-upon-Tyne 122 bottom; Hessisches Landesmuseum, Darmstadt 239; Hans Hinz, Basle 121; Michael Holford, Essex 154 top; Sidney Janis Gallery, New York 208; Dr Riccardo Jucker, Milan 85; Kunsthalle Hamburg 72, 73 top; Kunsthalle Tübingen 202; Kunsthaus Zürich 77 bottom; Kunstmuseum, Basle 56, 81; La Jolla Museum of Contemporary Art 223 top; Leicestershire Museums, Art Galleries and Records Service, Leicester 145; Lords Gallery, London 122 top; Los Angeles County Museum of Art 186 top; The Metropolitan Museum of Art, New York 138 left; Musée de l'Annonciade, St Tropez 47; Musée des Beaux-Arts, Algiers 24 top; Musée Gustave Moreau, Paris 35, Musée National d'Art Moderne, Paris 60, 62, 78, 109 bottom, 110 top, 155 top, 159 bottom, 161 left, 164, 166, 220 bottom; Musées Nationaux, Paris 21, 31; Museo dell'Olmo, Como 93 top; The Museum of Modern Art, New York 43, 52, 57, 59, 64, 68, 69, 80 bottom, 86, 87, 88, 89, 104 right, 106 top, 110 bottom, 112 left, 119, 126, 134, 135, 137, 140, 141, 142, 144, 147, 151 bottom, 167, 183 top, 186 bottom, 188, 192–193, 195, 212 top left, 212 bottom, 213, 224 bottom, 226, 227, 228, 229 bottom, 233, 237 top; Museum Von der Heydt, Wuppertal 75; Nasjonalgalleriet, Oslo 71; National Galleries of Scotland, Edinburgh 205 bottom left; National Gallery, London 23, 24 bottom; National Gallery of Victoria, Melbourne 174; Neue Galerie, Aachen 244; Nolde Museum, Seebüll 74; Photographie Giraudon, Paris 153 top; Lauros-Giraudon 66, 67, 151 top; Philadelphia Museum of Art 58, 65, 84, 124; The Phillips Collection, Washington, D.C. 22; Private Collections 27, 61, 115, 128, 165, 201 right, 211, 216, 217 top, 218 bottom left, 222 bottom, 223 bottom, 238 left; Rose Art Museum, Brandeis University, Massachusetts 212 top right; Royal Museum of Fine Arts, Copenhagen 44–45; Sprengel Museum, Hanover 80 top; State Museum Kröller-Müller, Otterlo 36, 116 top, 179, 181 top; Stedelijk Museum, Amsterdam 73 bottom, 102, 118, 129, 234; Stedelijk Museum, Ostende 169 top; Sterling and Francine Clark Art Institute, Williamstown, Massachusetts 38; Peter Stuyvesant Foundation 238 top right; Tate Gallery, London 50 bottom, 55, 79, 95, 96, 98, 99, 106 bottom, 112 right, 123, 152, 153 bottom, 155 bottom, 157 top, 157 bottom, 158 top, 158 bottom, 161 right, 175, 178, 180, 181 bottom, 189, 191 bottom, 194, 196, 205 bottom right, 206, 217 bottom, 220 top left, 220 top right, 230, 231 bottom left, 236 top, 236 bottom, 237 bottom; The 180 Beacon Collection, Boston 204; Van Abbe Museum, Eindhoven 210; Walker Art Gallery, Liverpool 205 top; 207; Wallraf-Richartz Museum, Cologne 219 top, 219 bottom, 229 top, 231 right; Whitney Museum of American Art, New York 136, 138 right, 187, 214, 232, 242, 246 top; Whitworth Art Gallery, University of Manchester 204 top; Woodmansterne Ltd, Watford: Nicholas Servian 156; Yale University Art Gallery, New Haven, Connecticut 104 left, 133; Joseph P. Ziolo, Paris: Circle d'Art 172 top, Faillet 20, 49, G. Nimatallah 172 bottom, Oronoz 148–149, Plassart 50 top, 51

Front cover: *Still-life with Guitar* by Pablo Picasso, 1922. Detail (Rosengart Collection, Lucerne)

Back cover: *Abstract Composition* by Edward Wadsworth, 1915 (Tate Gallery, London). Bridgeman Art Library.

Half title: *M-Maybe* by Roy Lichtenstein. (Wallraf-Richartz Museum, Cologne, Collection Ludwig)

Frontispiece: *The Large Glass or The Bride Stripped Bare by her Bachelors, Even* (1915–1923, replica 1965–1966) by Marcel Duchamp and Richard Hamilton (Tate Gallery, London)

First published in the USA 1985
by Exeter Books
Distributed by Bookthrift
Exeter is a trademark of Simon & Schuster, Inc
Bookthrift is a registered trademark of Simon & Schuster, Inc
New York, New York

Prepared by
Deans International Publishing
52–54 Southwark Street, London SE1 1UA
A division of The Hamlyn Publishing Group Limited
London · New York · Sydney · Toronto

ISBN 0-671-07670-1

Printed in Finland

Contents

(continued overleaf)

(continued from preceding page)

Introduction

Modern art is only the most recent product of an activity that has a very long history. It is well known that men of the Old Stone Age made extraordinarily vivid pictures of the animals they hunted on the walls of their caves, and carved very simple sculptures of female figures. That was ten to twenty thousand years ago, and since then painting and sculpture, drawing, illustration and design – what have come to be called the visual arts – have been part of every society in history.

A great deal of this art has survived, though even more has perished, and it is through the visual arts, more than any other historical evidence, that our understanding of and feelings towards many earlier cultures is formed.

All the evidence suggests that art is an essential activity in human society and, moreover, one that has changed very little through history. Perhaps the most striking aspect of those earliest cave paintings is the sense of affinity anyone who has handled a paintbrush feels with their creators.

We can discover a great deal of information about the physical appearance, clothes, artefacts, architecture, taste and fashion of long-vanished societies through their art, and often gain insight into more obscure subjects, such as beliefs and customs, moral attitudes, social structure and intellectual ideas, through study of artistic style and subject matter. The art of the past tells us a great deal about the past. It also helps to identify our own attitudes to the subjects that have concerned earlier societies and cultures. Art has had a social value even if it has no other.

But it is also generally held to provide another valuable part of the cultural life of later observers. The artefacts of earlier societies have contributed to ideas about wisdom, truth, beauty and other imponderable elements which are lodged in human sensibilities somewhere between the intellect and the spirit. This whole category of interest has given rise to a form of study which is known as aesthetics – the study of the nature of beauty. Aesthetics is concerned with values that go beyond the practical, with abstract speculation about ideas that may differentiate the human from the animal.

Since the study of the art of the past is involved with both the physical evidence and the nature of past societies, it is reasonable to suppose that a study of modern art should be equally involved with these aspects. It is at this point that we begin to encounter the undoubted problems that modern art presents.

It is first necessary to identify what exactly is meant by 'modern' art.

It is not difficult to identify certain differences in attitude, first appearing at the beginning of this century, which clearly distinguish art products of that time from those that preceded them in the 19th century. For us, therefore, 'modern' art is 20th-century art. This is a long period, yet one that could be encompassed in a single human lifetime. But the changes that have occurred in this century – during one lifetime – have no parallel in earlier societies. The pace of change in the development of all aspects of society and culture in this century has been dramatically quicker than earlier centuries and earlier societies ever experienced.

The frequent bewildering problems thrown up by the rapidity of change have given birth to a sense of isolation in the arts and created a gulf between artist and observer. For most people, 20th-century art still remains of dubious justification if not deliberately mystifying. The terms in which the art of all earlier periods can be and is examined or appreciated are apparently of little help in assessing the art of this century.

Naturally, people ask for what reason and to what purpose have these changes taken place? Why did art so suddenly change course? This survey will attempt to establish some at least of the intentions and achievements of the artists concerned, as well as to indicate possible approaches to their work for interested

Half title:
M-Maybe, 1965. Roy Lichtenstein *(Wallraf-Richartz Museum, Cologne. Collection Ludwig).*
Lichtenstein is the most consistently recognizable of the Pop artists and the sources of his imagery are easily identified. After a period as an entirely nonfigurative Abstract Expressionist, he began to use familiar common objects (bubble-gum packs, etc.) as his subject matter, as well as reinterpreting early paintings of the Old West. He became interested in the lack of genuine quality or emotion in popular, mass-produced, merchandizing 'art', represented at its most vulgar by the pulp strip cartoons, execrably printed on poor-quality paper. Enlarging these to reveal the dot structure of the printing method, he has 'fixed' their essential banality and spurious emotional content in such familiar images as this. It suggests the whole span of a commonplace love story by the selection of an appropriate moment.

Frontispiece:
The Large Glass *or* The Bride Stripped Bare by her Bachelors, Even. *Marcel Duchamp. Reconstruction by Richard Hamilton, 1965–66 (Tate Gallery, London).*
The original work was completed in New York after Duchamp settled there in 1915, and, with Nude Descending a Staircase, *is his most important work. Much has been written to aid understanding of its obscurities, but without great effect. The dense imagery is concerned with sexuality, procreation and isolation, and it has been suggested that the Bride can be loosely equated with art. Duchamp's central and continuing influence on a wide range of different art movements in both Europe and America places this work near the centre of the modern revolution.*

observers. There are, however, some preliminary considerations which will occupy the early sections of this book.

The most dramatic break with the past that appears to have been made in the visual arts in this century concerns the representation of the natural world. The art of the West in past centuries – in general, and with many qualifications and caveats – used forms taken from the visible world as the basis for all paintings and sculptures. Sometimes with acute observation, sometimes with deliberate distortion for subjective reasons or for some imaginative end, artists used human figures, landscape, flowers, animals, etc., to fill their creative visual needs. In all cases, except where abstract pattern was used, some relationship with a possible if not actual visual world can be discerned. It gives every observer a rational point of contact; in simple terms, you can see what it is. This enables anyone to make some sense of a picture, sculpture, etc., whether or not it is the kind of sense that concerned the creator of the work. European art seemed through history an available means of expression, open and meaningful to all: except this century!

As the 20th century has advanced, the artists' distortions and rearrangements of the visible world, and even more their tendency to abstraction, which denies all apparent reference to the visible world, have led to a general belief that art is only for an 'aesthetic' elite. (The development of this popular belief is somewhat ironical, since among the motives most often quoted by artists to explain their work is their desire to find a 'universal' language of art, one not restricted by local conditions and customs, an art which is as meaningful to Eastern as to Western minds, to the cultured and the uncultured, the educated and ignorant, even to the sensitive and insensitive.)

However, the effect has been to provoke the question, still asked, 'If art is not necessarily about the representation of visible aspects of the world, what is it about?' The development of modern art suggests that it may be about many things and the pages that follow will indicate some of the most important. But there is one major reason why artists should have turned away from representation. In the past the artist was the only provider of permanent, constructed, visual images. That is very far from the case now. Through photography, cinematography, television, etc., the 20th century has many potent ways of exploiting the visible world for visual images. As we shall see in more detail later, the photograph, at its first appearance, had a disturbing effect on notions of what art was about. Today we recognize that there is never again likely to be a time when the static art image will have the social impact it had in previous ages. It seems equally certain that future students of our own age will turn to photographic evidence, not to paintings or art objects, for historical source material.

It is not surprising that painting and sculpture have been suffering from a loss of identity. The search for a new role in a changed world accounts, at least in part, for the retreat from representation that has been characteristic of a great part of the century's art.

There have indeed been suggestions, and they seem to be growing in force, that the activity itself is doomed, that it has already become a marginal social activity, and is merely, like Charles II, taking an unconscionable time a-dying. The actitivies of artists during the past decade do not, unfortunately, provide much cause for discounting the prophecies of doom. Still, even in the 20th century, a decade is not very long.

The art of any society emerges from the beliefs, attitudes, organization and structure as well as the inherent creativity and energy of that society. The truths and standards generally accepted are also those which underlie all artistic expression – and for that matter all scientific endeavour. To understand 20th-century visual expression, therefore, we are obliged to consider the nature of 20th-century social attitudes and beliefs.

This is hardly the place for a full-scale critique of human society since Victorian times, but the chief features of recent history, depressing as they tend to be, are well enough known. In any case, we cannot jump in conveniently at 1900. The present century is, after all, a continuation of the story of society in the 19th century, and just as we cannot totally ignore the history of society in the previous century when considering our own time, so we cannot account for the dramatic changes in artistic expression in the pre-First World War period without considering a number of developments, some not of immediate and direct relevance, in the 19th century. Thus, the line of retreat from representation can be clearly traced back to the 19th century. As this is vital in establishing the basis for the dramatic changes that begin the story of modern art, some discussion is necessary of art in the earlier period, especially the revolution begun by the Impressionists and taken over, diverted perhaps, by the Post-Impressionists.

In addition, during the course of the 19th century a number of artistic developments took place which had little direct impact on the actual forms of art of the 20th century but acted as a sort of forcing compost. The Arts and Crafts movement and the style known as Art Nouveau are the best-known examples. Others are Nabism and Symbolism, both of which included artists working well into the present century, and 'Secession' art, which had a profound importance for the development of German Expressionism, itself a recurrent influence during this century.

One material difference between 19th- and 20th-century society has had a significant effect on artists. In the 19th century society was organized in a generally accepted hierarchy which ranged from the privileged aristocracy to the poor and ignorant masses, and in few countries was it possible to move easily from one social class to another (though it was not impossible). Only the upper classes were the proper users of art. The lower classes knew their place, and it did not include art. However, even in the 19th century it was possible for the successful practitioner, through his work, to gain entry to upper-class society. To this extent the arts offered a rare way out of the constrictions and deprivations of the lower class. It was only the upper levels of society that bought paintings or looked at them – and a successful artist therefore became part of the privileged world of culture.

Marx and the social reformers of the later 19th century hastened the great change that led towards what, throughout most of Western society, is thought of as a 'classless' society. Not, of course, that privilege has been done away with, but it is now more a matter of money than breeding. In the 20th century the arts are the proper concern of anyone who wishes to make them so. Indeed, at different times during the century, artists have insisted – or suggested – that art is for all. Not all artists, however, believed this, as Arnold Schoenberg's well-known remark typifies: 'If it is art it is not for all, and if it is for all it is not art.'

The fact remains that a consideration of the role of art in society in this century must emphasize its wider application.

The growth of printmaking, of both historical and modern works, was one incidental effect, which also contributed to the cause: greater familiarity in society generally with the forms of art. Since the development of high-quality colour printing, a veritable tidal wave of books on all aspects of the visual arts has poured forth. The trade of art critic and historian has flourished. There is no longer any excuse for anyone to be unable through ignorance to have an opinion on a particular piece of art or an individual artist. In fact, art has become an industry of huge, international proportions, in which vested interests play a large promotional role. The greater the popular interest in art, the more money is made by dealers, gallery owners, printmakers, publishers and, it should be said, writers. This is a new development. Now, the industry requires raw material, and the artists themselves are part of the industry. As Samuel Butler commented in the late 19th century, 'Most of those who call themselves artists are in reality picture dealers, only they make the pictures themselves'.

The growth of the art industry in this century is everywhere apparent, and nowhere more so than in the United States, which for some years past has dominated the art scene much as France once did. A whole language has been built up to accompany the growth in trade. The art ad. writers, whose role is to disguise vacuity rather than to expose it, have developed a jargon of impenetrable complexity and, frequently, calculated incomprehensibility. The explosion of galleries, private and public, the avid collectors, the assiduously promoted careers – and the incidental tragedies along the way – are witness to the continuing public curiosity. The importance of the galleries and dealers will be more fully considered later, but it may be noted here that this trade is actually independent of the art it feeds upon. Moreover, it may have been instrumental in disguising the marginal nature of the practice of art today.

While the jargon of the publicity men frequently causes confusion, the existence of a sensible art 'language' is valuable as a form of shorthand. It has become difficult if not impossible to write on art without recourse to more or less technical terms, and accordingly some terms used in this book should be considered.

'Abstract' art needs amplification. Many painters describe their work as 'abstract'. The term is used generally to indicate that the work is not representational. This is a help but it does not go far enough. Some works, for example a Malevitch from early in the century or an Ellsworth Kelly of recent date, are constructed of forms in which it is virtually impossible to identify any reference to anything outside itself. The work does not appear to have been inspired by any object, seen or imagined. Insofar as abstraction has any meaning, these are undoubtedly abstract works. However, there is a difficulty, emphasized by some recent works, when the painting or sculpture is not *purely* abstract. The word 'abstract' properly denotes a work of the Malevitch kind, but an 'abstract' painting by Picasso is very different; in fact, Picasso was not an abstract painter at all. He was, however, an 'abstractionist'. This indicates a work in which the forms are derived from some other natural form, however much distorted or changed. They are 'abstracted'. Most painting is of this kind when the original inspiration can be seen to have a natural origin. Despite the pervasive 'tendency to abstraction', most 20th-century painting is not strictly abstract but 'abstractionist'.

Avant-garde is another term, superficially obvious enough, which requires comment. The French statesman Clemençeau once remarked in respect of the Impressionists that the future is always with the *avant-garde*, and during this century, we have come to believe that the latest is the best, even if it is not immediately clear why, and that therefore our judgement should be cautious, especially if our response is initially antipathetic. A process of indoctrination seems to be going on in which the incomprehension or distaste of an observer is rapidly converted into an indication of his or her inadequacy. Of course it may be so, but not inevitably, and in any event it is of no real significance to the observer either way. The cult of *avant-gardism*, which demands immediate acceptance for the new, is dangerous.

There is a corresponding tendency, encouraged by the pace of 20th-century change, that only the latest style, school, product or whatever is in question, that the recent past has already achieved 'old-master' status. Far from it. Even the earliest modern movements, even Cubism, have not yet acquired general critical consensus. The name of Cézanne indeed may be universally revered, but it is improbable that his work is fully comprehended.

We should also remember that the appreciation, understanding and evaluation of a work of art are essentially the result of a personal response, a response subject to change just as the individual making that response must change. All responses are filtered through the individual temperament, and are coloured by his or her sensitivity, education, intelligence and so on. They are relative, not absolute. It is as well to bear in mind, particularly when commencing a survey of this kind, that equal enthusiasm for everything is no enthusiasm at all.

The Historical Background. The 20th century opened with an event of considerable historical symbolism. Queen Victoria, on whose empire the sun was said never to set, died in 1901, in the first weeks of the new century. She represented, more than any other single individual, the spirit of the 19th century. During her reign the great empire of which she was the head reached its apogee of power and world culture became Eurocentric. While the securities of religious faith were shaken and the confidence of power was challenged, the basis of scientific knowledge was extended. When Victoria died the 19th century may be said to have died with her. It was a time for regret but also for opportunity; for the old it meant nostalgia and decline, for the young adventure and revolution. Although there is no real significance in the beginning of a new century, it always suggests a new start – just as a new year does but, new centuries being rare, more momentously. With this new century and the death of Queen Victoria, the end of an epoch was clearly signalled.

Already, political events were moving Europe towards the great internecine conflict that engulfed and almost destroyed the intellectual youth of the continent, reaching out to inflict damage on North America too. In the gathering cultural gloom before the First World War, young creative spirits became aware that the long-secure social order was preparing for its own immolation, that the accepted artistic standards of Greece and Rome and the Renaissance had become anachronistic and that the Christian Church was no longer the central prop to moral conduct that it had been for centuries. A piercing wind of insecurity blew into the first decade of the century.

The sources of that insecurity were many and varied. Among them stood the influential figures of Karl Marx, upsetting confidence in the social and economic order, Charles Darwin, whose disruptive theories seemed to threaten the whole fabric of Christian belief, Sigmund Freud, whose revelations of the functions of the subconscious mind and particularly its sexual nature threatened even the sanctity of family life, and Albert Einstein, whose conception of the universe undermined the whole structure of Newtonian physics. Nothing was sacrosanct. The arts were also under notice of change.

Budding young artists, perhaps unaware of the significance of the changes going on, could not be expected to react artistically to those changes specifically. But it is a characteristic of the creative spirit to respond to or anticipate circumstances of which it may not be consciously aware. It is perhaps possible to go further and say that the creative spirit expresses a sensitivity which appears to be in advance of its time; meaning really that it is the plodding majority who are behind the times. It is for this reason that, looked at in retrospect, the significant art of any time is that created by truly creative spirits whom time identifies.

The mounting intellectual enquiry of the 19th century was accompanied by a rapid growth in scientific knowledge. A number of developments had special importance for the world of art, photography being the most obvious example. Technology made possible new investigations of the manufacture of colours and new colours, both permanent and inexpensive, became available. Physicists investigated the nature of colour while painters such as Seurat attempted to codify its emotional content. Around the turn of the century the new, selfconscious use of science in aid of art was one of the many elements that promoted the belief that art itself should be new and different.

The changing status of the artist in society is an important element in the background to modern art. Throughout history, the artist has had many roles. In the medieval period he was simply a respected, often anonymous craftsman, like a mason or carpenter. During the Renaissance he became an accepted member of cultured society, admired and often revered, like Michelangelo, to a point not far short of divinity. The cult of the 'artistic personality' began at this time and has vigorously survived through the succeeding centuries. Most artists aspired to personal fame through official channels, through patronage and commissions. In the 17th century, the influence of the academies of art, originally just training schools, became dominant. In Louis XIV's France, for instance, the Académie Royale, as a great state institution, virtually monopolized art and decoration.

During the 19th century the restrictive professional practices of the academies became inhibiting to young creative spirits and encouraged the birth of a new image of the artist – independent, bohemian, hostile to the establishment. The artist in this persona was popularly seen as an antisocial creature, working only to satisfy his own creative needs and, probably quite rightly, condemned to starve! For the academicians, art was a career; their work was a saleable commodity; for the independent, art was not merely a living, it was life itself. This conception of the independent, solitary and radical role of the creative artist has continued into this century. However, whilst the importance of the academician has clearly declined, that of the radical has, since the eventual general acceptance of Impressionism towards the end of the 19th century, dramatically increased. The artist of the 20th century is expected to be a nonconformist. His other activities often arouse as much interest as his art. He is a personality, and his art is a 'personality object'.

This was the situation created by the new art movements of the early 20th century. Although strenuous efforts have been made by some later artists to 'depersonalize' art, they have usually been frustrated by the demands of the commercial commodity market, in the shape of the art dealer.

Much of what has happened in the history of art in this century is the result of the artist trying to reach a decision about the precise nature of his role. It cannot be said that this matter has yet been resolved, but such recent developments as Performance and Environmental art have a great deal to do with the artist's concern with his identity.

In abandoning his traditional role, the modern artist has also very often abandoned traditional materials and traditional methods. For many artists the familiar oil painting on canvas or the carved figure in stone has seemed for some time an uncomfortable anachronism, and to explore new materials is a natural consequence of the attempt to extend the artist's role. That in turn has led to new art forms.

The forms themselves, being different objects, become – or imply that they become – a different art. Thus it has apparently become important to find materials and/or methods that are unknown to or at any rate unexploited by other artists on the assumption, often supported commercially, that the resulting work is both new and valuable simply because it is different.

However, the creation of art is a human activity undertaken by members of a society and culture of which they inevitably form a small representative part. The work is observed by others, members of the same or perhaps another culture, who are also a small representative part. The social value of art lies in the unknowable communication that may privately take place between the two. As Man Ray, one of the founders of Surrealism, put it, 'A creator needs only one enthusiast to justify him.'

Paths Through the Jungle. Before embarking on a survey of the essential precursors of what we call modern art, i.e. art from about 1900 to the present, a preliminary sketch of the main changes in the attitude of artists to their work during that time may help to prevent the sense of bewilderment which is easily induced by the profusion of movements, schools and 'isms' making up the art of our period. That the last 80 years have seen dramatic developments will be obvious; they will be examined in the main part of this book.

The general direction can be indicated fairly simply. Although it is convenient to set out what appears to be a sequence of specific developments each following the other, art, like life, is actually less straightforward, and the true course of events is considerably less tidy. Artists change direction, absorb new influences and make new statements; groups of artists plan unified programmes on the assumption that they have similar intentions, but later discover that their aims and interests are different, perhaps incompatible. Observers see influences, similarities and conjunctions which the artists themselves are unaware of and angrily deny. The work of some artists seems at first part of one movement but turns out to be more closely associated with another; some artists, who seem quite unrelated to a particular group, are subsequently seen to be critically placed in the centre of it.

For these and other reasons which will emerge later, our simple sequence – starting at 1900 or thereabouts, identifying what is new and following the trail forward – soon disintegrates.

The legacy of the past must be incorporated and the work of earlier, seemingly irrelevant artists taken into account. It is worth recalling that while Monet is thought of as an Impressionist, indeed the arch-Impressionist, many critics today regard his later work, done after 1900, as his most significant. In fact Monet lived until 1926, when the early modern movements – Fauvism, Cubism, Futurism, German Expressionism – were already in the history books. Between 1905 and the 1920s a number of groups of artists appeared whose members certainly had some aims in common if not total identity of purpose. These groups, or movements, directed attention to traditional values in art, and called most of those values into question. Cubism was the most significant of these movements, but others, such as Futurism, Surrealism, De Stijl, Suprematism, Constructivism and Expressionism, all had startling, disturbing statements to make about what art should be or could be about.

Nevertheless, these movements were mainly concerned with art as an activity within the social structure in the established sense. The innovations were visual, intellectual and intuitive but, with rare exceptions, artists still regarded themselves as producers of art objects of a physically traditional kind. In other words, they produced paintings on flat surfaces and free-standing sculptures which were meant to be looked at and appreciated personally by the individual observer. The difference between – say – a Picasso Cubist painting and a Rembrandt lay not in the object itself, nor in the physical approach to it (they were both pieces of canvas covered with oil paint and hung on walls to be looked at), nor in the mental attitude which was brought to them. Neither was the nature of the response expected from the observer significantly different. So what was all the fuss about?

It is easier to see in the perspective of over fifty years that the great visual revolution that has marked the course of this century's art was initiated with no great change in the actual activity of artists. Art was created in studios, taken to a place of execution, as it were, and pronounced dead or alive as the case might be, just as it had in previous centuries. The fact that most observers gave most of it the thumbs down obscured the strong elements of continuity in its creation.

It is important to recognize this because as the century has progressed, artists and critics have seen an innate conservatism in art which has led them to question not only the role of art and the individual work of art but the whole nature of creative activity.

One result of this is that the observer has become a figure of interest to the artist. Since the Second World War, and particularly in the last twenty years, the activity of artists has produced an essentially new attempt at visual language which directly involves the observer – as participant and actor.

The observer's take-it-or-leave-it role, which survived up to the 1950s, began to change, perhaps surprisingly, with the development of what is known as Pop art (a simple term for a diverse and complex scene), when the work was not something to be examined externally for qualities inherent in it but was in itself a kind of situation, which was only completed by the participation of the observer.

Since the 1960s, much as happened in the earlier days of Dada, the activities and spoken or written statements of the artists have become an element in the completion of the work. The restrictive, elitist nature of this development exacerbated a 'them' and 'us' division, between people who continued to suppose that art was something to go and look at in a gallery or elsewhere, and those who knew it was not there, because it was something quite different which of its nature could not have been put there.

Although the warning of Dada's later years may suggest a similar fate for much recent art activity, it should not be supposed that these recent developments are either uninteresting or inaccessible. What must be understood is that they cannot be approached with the same expectations as the early modern movements of the century or even more recent kinds of art, such as Abstract Expressionism.

Since the beginnings of Pop art in the late 1950s an increasing number of artists – we must continue to use the word although they do not perform the traditional artistic activity – have attempted to produce an anti-elitist, anti-'masterpiece' art dependent only on the observer's sensibilities. Its debt to Surrealism is apparent, but Marcel Duchamp's 'It is art if I say it is' (1917) becomes, in the words of Donald Judd, a modern Conceptualist, 'It is art if *someone* says it is.'

The effect of the earlier movements in breaking the traditional mould and the recent abandoning of the historical activity itself by the most dedicated of the *avant-garde* should not be seen merely as something to regret or deplore. The vitality of art lies in its creative response to the circumstance from which it arises.

It would therefore be wiser and more fruitful to consider the reasons for this rejection of every facet of what 'art' traditionally meant, reasons which must be sought in society at large.

Our century has experienced horrors and disasters on an unprecedented scale: moreover, modern communications have brought them vividly into our homes and minds. Consequently, human insecurity and moral doubt exist on a scale only comparable with that of medieval man contemplating an imminent Day of Judgement. It is surely not surprising that creative people in society, sensing subconsciously or reflecting consciously, seek to express their understanding in ways that are entirely new.

Academy and Salon

During the Renaissance the role of the artist was upgraded from the position of artisan/craftsman which it had held throughout the Middle Ages. At the cultured courts of Renaissance princes, such artists as Raphael, Michelangelo and Titian achieved an extraordinary eminence and initiated the notion that the 'artist' had a special – and privileged – role in society which demands a certain respect.

The relationship between the patron and the artist also changed. The Church, still the principal patron through the 16th and 17th centuries, was gradually superseded by the state and the private patron or institution. By the 18th century the role of the artist had become that of an independent, creative figure whose work was bought for its individual qualities, no longer for general, craftsmanlike abilities. Thus of course the personality of the artist himself became an important factor.

To give artists a shop window where they could display their wares, in hope of selling them or of attracting commissions for new ones, was the main function in the 19th century of the academies, such as the Royal Academy in England and what became known as the Salon in France. Their seasonal exhibitions were great social occasions and, as a kind of trade union for the best artists, they achieved great influence, becoming in fact virtually the sole arbiters of taste and fashion. This was very convenient for customers: they did not have to risk forming personal judgements, the academies would tell them what was good and bad.

The dominance of the academies had important results for art in several ways. Firstly, painting and sculpture became, like books, part of the cultured man's life. Secondly, the varied interests of the artists began to break down the vital hierarchy of 'categories' which had been accepted dogma since Classical times. Animal subjects, still-lifes, etc. became acceptable. Landscape, which had always occupied a somewhat ambivalent role in painting, became during the 18th and early 19th centuries increasingly attractive to collectors who in previous generations would only have been interested in 'subject' paintings. Thus the subject matter of art was enlarged. Thirdly, the masters of Academy and Salon, the 'great artists' of their day, generally ran their own *ateliers*, in which apprentices and students learned their methods.

The Royal Academy and the French Salon, with other, similar, professional bodies throughout Europe, were, as is the nature of such institutions, conservative, self-interested, and restrictive. By the middle of the 19th century an institutionalized art hierarchy existed which had no interest in change and was in a position to inhibit efforts towards more liberal attitudes. The academies controlled the art scene in a way that would seem impossible today, and that is why so much later 19th-century 'official' art is characterized by sterile repetition and moribund pomposity. This is of course not to say that there was no talent in the academies. There was brilliant technical command, fine seriousness of purpose and imposing self-confidence. As teachers the academic artists performed a great service; for art schools as we know them lay in the future. Their studios were the centres in which young and eager minds came together. They provided a focus for discontent and a forum for discussion. It was here that the young painters who were to become the Impressionists and Post-Impressionists first cut their artistic teeth.

No one paid much attention to these young men. A far worse threat to the masters of the academies in the mid-19th century, as it seemed to them, came from the camera. For they were tonal painters. They used colour merely to identify the colour of the object being painted; for them, the form itself existed only in the light and dark aspects of the subject. This was the Classical tradition, followed since the Renaissance. The camera directly threatened this method of making a picture and thus appeared to threaten art itself.

The Impact of Photography

The invention of the photograph has had, and continues to have, an important effect upon art. This may seem blindingly obvious, but the vital point is that the impact of photography is a continuing feature of the study of modern art, not just an element in its history during the 19th century.

By 1839 Daguerre and Fox Talbot had developed a means of fixing a photographic image constructed of a pattern of the tones supplied by the subject. The sensitivity of the process available from the beginning enabled the tonal arrangement to be more closely accurate than any painter could achieve. In the early photographs the exposure time was long, necessitating static subjects, but as the process was refined it became possible to photograph figures and faces with absolute clarity. By the time of the Crimean War and the American Civil War it was possible to photograph combat, and the photographs of Roger Fenton and Matthew Brady (who, with colleagues, produced over 7,000 images of war) made the photograph, as a means of recording events as they happened, a permanent feature of communication.

In the early years it was supposed that photographic images could not be made in colour, and they were frequently coloured by hand. This was felt to be one powerful advantage that artists would have over photographers. Paul Delaroche, an early 19th-century painter, remarked on first seeing a photograph that 'from today painting is dead', but his despair would have been sharper had he known that in 1861, less than a decade after his death, the first true colour photograph was to be produced by the physicist James Clerk Maxwell – though it was another thirty years before colour photography became a practical proposition.

In the 150 years since the first photograph there has been endless consideration of the photograph as an art form. Delaroche was not alone in feeling that the photograph threatened art, but was it an alternative art? Was it art? Could it be art? And if photography *is* art, how does it affect the theories and practices of accepted art? It might be supposed that by this time there is a general consensus of opinion on these questions, but that is by no means true. Although the photograph has become a ubiquitous form of visual communication, as widely used as words, it has clearly not replaced painting and drawing as a means of expression.

At the same time it has evidently had a dramatic effect on the forms that painting and sculpture adopt. From the beginning, those academic painters whose concern was with the representation of appearance – with an attempt to produce a pictorial equivalent of reality – saw a threat that they could not meet. Even the (short-lived) inability of the camera to reproduce colour was small consolation, since tone, not colour, was their main preoccupation.

Other painters from the beginning regarded photography as a tool they could use. Indeed, Daguerre himself was a painter and saw his invention as an aid to painting. Such artists as Delacroix and Ingres, representing the opposite poles of Romanticism and Classicism, both used photography for their portraits, even making sketches from photographs. To set against Delaroche is Delacroix's comment, 'I can only say how much I regret that such an admirable discovery should have come so late!' Degas was an enthusiastic amateur photographer who used photography not only as a source of visual information but as a direct aid to composition. In fact it can be said that the most creative painters were not frightened but attracted by its possibilities.

The French Realist painter, Gustave Courbet, as early as 1848 took the lighting effects for his painting *The Burial at Ornans* from daguerreotypes, while Corot's misty, soft, light effects were probably influenced by a group of enthusiastic photographers who were working at Arras while he was there after

1852. Toulouse-Lautrec, later in the century, frequently had his model photographed as he worked so that he could continue in her absence. There are many such examples to set against the fear of the academicians.

Photography also solved a number of visual problems. It was able to capture and 'freeze' movements too fast for the eye. As is well known, the motions of a running horse were first clearly shown in a series of photographs made by Eadweard Muybridge, which put an end to paintings of racehorses proceeding in dramatic bounds.

From the beginning, however, photography did pose a serious, fundamental question. What was the painter doing that the photographer was not? Photographers themselves in the process of creating a fast-growing business had little time to reflect at great length upon the matter, but they, too, speculated on whether photography was or could be art, and a number of photographers, somewhat naively, composed groups of figures in historical costume in the manner of the academic history painters of the day. The effect was generally unhappy and, in the case of posed 'Classical' nudes, often ludicrous. But it still made a point. All artists at that time believed that the representation of natural form was the basis of their art, and the majority found this task difficult enough, consuming all their effort and justly earning general admiration when they were successful. But for others, for most serious artists in fact, representation was only part of the making of a work of art. Intellectual exercises in the service of an idea, philosophy or political belief engaged the interest of some; others sought to incorporate their responses to a theme, heroic or mundane; yet others sought to express their feelings by an emotional treatment of their subject. But whatever their artistic aim, before the development of photography, no artist questioned the basic presumption of representation.

Photography changed all this. It focused attention on the artistic purposes of representing natural form and the ability of the painter to accomplish it accurately. Realism had become a powerful mode in the 19th century and it was increasingly evident that painting could not achieve the effect of natural light falling on objects with total accuracy. It could only achieve a partial representation of the range of tone and colour as illuminated by sunlight and daylight.

The importance of this point for the development of 20th-century art can hardly be overemphasized. The range of tones in colour pigments, from black through the colours to white, does not equate to the range of light (daylight and sunlight) to pitch black (absence of any light). The painter is compelled to adopt a convention of tones from light to dark, or to choose, as Turner did, to paint in a high key – that is adopting only the top range of colours to represent the effect of sunlight on objects, which meant abandoning the lower ranges of colour. Some of the Impressionist work that appeared in the 1870s reflects these considerations.

Equally important was the effect on the treatment of subject matter. The early photographers were interested in precisely those subjects that had been the prerogative of the artist. Landscape, still-life, figure composition, and above all portraiture became popular with the public. To have one's photograph taken, though something of an effort in the early years when it was ncessary to preserve perfect stillness for minutes on end, was still much less time-consuming than sitting for a portrait painter. And in most instances much more visually accurate. It also cost a lot less.

The painter was obliged to reconsider his position. At this point the possibility of turning away from representation came into consideration. The first response was connected with the question of colour. This became a prime concern of the Impressionists. It was not until the end of the century that colour photography achieved commercial potential, and even at that time not altogether convincingly. At that stage too, moving pictures were being pioneered, and a new aspect of actuality was introduced – nature viewed in time. However, the experiments of the Impressionists and Post-Impressionists, which were the first effective response to photography, were over before moving pictures became commercially available.

Later responses led further towards abstraction, or the distortion of natural images. Gradually, the artist's position in relation to representation shifted.

Instead of feeling merely dispossessed, he began to feel liberated, even inspired. The great variety of imagery that the camera made available could be inspiring. Simultaneously, moreover, there was growing interest in the visual arts of other lands and other cultures, particularly those of primitive peoples who were seen to have a refreshing disregard for actual appearance and, notwithstanding, a striking ability to convey their message in direct and simple forms.

The exploration of movement which photography stimulated led specifically to the experiments of the Futurists. The photograph became a natural part of the artist's equipment. Some residual sense of 'cheating' was felt by some artists, but generally the photograph became incorporated in artistic activity, first as an aid, later as a physical part of the work of art – for instance in early Cubist collages and Surrealist photomontages. In more recent times this practice has become common. Literally hundreds of artists have employed photographs directly – De Kooning pasting cut-out photos on canvas, Warhol with his silkscreen images, Hockney and his multiple-image constructions, etc.

Since this book is concerned with modern art, it is important to establish why photography does not form a constant theme. That photography is a visual form of expression of considerable importance in 20th-century sensibility is clear; that it is, in all its moving forms, the most accessible means of communicating visual information is equally obvious. Most people would also accept that it is a form of art. Nevertheless we have not yet reached the stage when artist and photographer stand side by side, figures of equal stature in an identical enterprise. Moreover, even if it is considered desirable to treat the work of artists and photographers as part of the same subject, pressure of space alone would prevent justice being done to either.

Were it possible to include photography in this book, a further question would arise. If photography, and more recent laser and holographic effects, have the visual importance as communication that most people accept, what is the position of the painter and the sculptor, relative to the situation BC (Before Cameras)? It has been argued that art has ben relegated to the margin of culture. It is a measure of the significance of photography on the graphic arts that this question can be asked.

The Arts and Crafts Movement

The development of photography, in the context of society as a whole, was just one small aspect of the unprecedented advance of science and technology in the 19th century. Before the Industrial Revolution, which began in Britain towards the end of the 18th century, large factories and large machines were rare; practically everything was made by hand and, in a sense, all manufacturing workers (a much smaller proportion then) were craftsmen.

By the middle of the 19th century, that society was fast vanishing. The new industrial state had risen, vast new cities were spawned where the workers lived in regimented housing under a constant pall of smoke, working in factories which were organized on the principle of the division of labour. One individual performed the same small, monotonous task hour after hour, six days a week.

Whatever joy they may have found in life, it was impossible for factory workers to experience what we would call 'job satisfaction'. He or she worked for one reason – wages.

There was from an early stage no shortage of critics of the new industrial society, though they were not at all united in what should be done about it. The practical school of reformers advocated trade training and moral improvement. Others took a more idealistic view. Their prophet was the famous aesthetician, John Ruskin, the greatest art critic of his day.

Ruskin could see practically nothing to admire in industrialism, and he helped to crystallize the feelings of a younger generation of artists and others who were dissatisfied with Victorian standards. Ruskin taught that 'art is the expression of man's pleasure in labour.' Men, he wrote, 'were not intended to work with the accuracy of tools ... If you will have that precision out of them you unhumanize them ...' He loathed the capitalist system, and protested that money had become the only source of enjoyment.

Among the younger men influenced by Ruskin was William Morris, one of those Victorian superheroes whose abilities and energies would have sufficed a dozen ordinary mortals. In a way, Morris *was* the Arts and Crafts movement; at least, it is hard to imagine it without him, and there were few of its activities with which he was not concerned. He may be best remembered for his designs for fabrics and wallpapers, but he was also the founder of the Kelmscott Press, the first and most successful of private presses, and played a major part in the revival of many other handicrafts. In design, there was a link with Art Nouveau (see page 41). There were of course many others involved – painters, potters, weavers, cabinetmakers, potters. All these trades, languishing in the wake of mass-production methods, were revived and, in a small but significant way, flourishing by the end of the century.

The Arts and Crafts movement took as its inspiration a romantic conception of the medieval craftsman, dignified and self-sufficient. A romantic notion of medieval society lay behind the 'picturesque' and intellectual recreation of medieval forms, notably in architecture. But it also expressed a real belief in honest labour. In some ways it was a futile attempt to turn back an unstoppable clock. But it highlighted the dehumanizing effect of modern industrial society, and served to reinforce the value of individual, creative effort.

Impressionism

When the Impressionists first exhibited in a group show in 1874 their work was ridiculed, compared to the scribbles of a child, called wretched and insulting. Since then the art of the Impressionists has given immeasurable pleasure to countless millions for whom the whole history of art is a matter of general indifference. Their appeal lies in the immediate attraction exercised by the freshness and directness of the treatment, the comprehensible ordinariness of the subject matter, and the clear difference from the common idea of 'old master' paintings. It is now difficult to see why these works should have occasioned such dismay in critics and public alike. It certainly surprised the Impressionists.

To any student of the history of art, however, the achievement of the Impressionists was nothing short of revolutionary: a 'bourgeois' revolution perhaps, but nonetheless a dramatic attack on the accepted standards and conventions of the art of the mid-19th century. Its importance in providing the basis for the subsequent 20th-century revolution can hardly be overrated. Without the Impressionists and the Post-Impressionists, it is hard to see how the movements of the first decade of the 20th century could have taken place.

The precise nature of the Impressionists' revolution is not so immediately apparent. Much of what they did now seems so obviously necessary and unexceptionable that it passes unnoticed.

Their work appeared when the academic art establishment's control of public taste was most rigid. The prevalence of intellectually based subject matter – historical, religious or mythological – meant that art was reserved for the educated, i.e. the privileged and the rich. It also meant that paintings were 'read' for their content rather than enjoyed for their felicity in the handling of colour or technique. They were documents rather than visual delights. But the concentration of the academics on tone rather than colour as the means of form building placed them in a vulnerable position, as they themselves thought, with the arrival of the photographic image.

In the Paris studios of the academic masters the young student painters of the day learnt their trade. Most of them entered the academic world and became in their turn the fashionable masters of the Salon, but there were a few for whom the teaching they received seemed outmoded, irrelevant and restrictive. Among these were the future Impressionists.

It was hardly to be expected that they would continue to paint as their masters recommended, and in fact they rejected almost all that the academicians held dear.

As they developed their characteristic style, the Impressionists abandoned grand Classical, historical and intellectual subject matter in favour of the commonplace and familiar: everyday scenes and objects. They rejected histrionic gesture and conscious posturing and turned to the labour and leisure of ordinary people. They made no intellectual comment nor philosophical analysis; they merely observed – acutely – the scene they had chosen. They did not consciously make a compositional analysis of their subject as the academicians did, preferring to take a slice of real life as it was presented to their eyes – or at least they seemed so to do. In reality they naturally adjusted their vision to make arrangements that pleased them.

Most importantly, they abandoned the tonal approach to form in favour of construction achieved by colour, and they forsook the defined forms of academic painting in order to capture the evanescent effects of light in nature, where all is movement. They arrived at these effects by a painting technique involving distinct and separate, nervous and 'living' brush strokes. This was a vital and fruitful new step in painting.

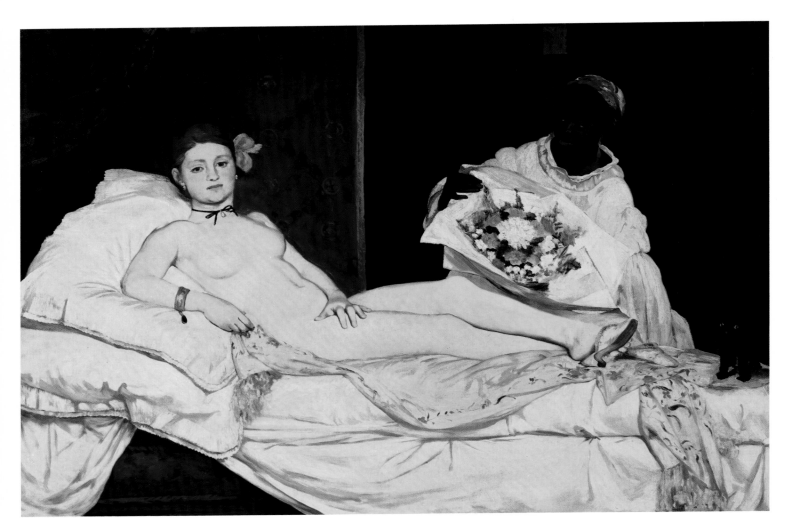

Olympia, *1863. Edouard Manet*
(Musée du Louvre, Paris).
A modern version of a traditional theme,
this reclining female nude was first
exhibited in the 1865 Salon, where it
was much abused for its 'vulgar' realism.
Muted erotic fantasy in Classical style
was expected of such a subject. Accepted
by the Louvre in 1907, it was still
reviled by some.

Its contribution to the foundation of
modern aesthetic attitudes is highly
important. A traditional subject given a
modern sense of actuality, the frank
appraisal of the observer by the model told
a different kind of story from the remote
romantic associations in the paintings of
earlier masters.

The academic painters defined form in a clear and constructed space, where everything was properly and clearly related. They created a space 'box' which suggested an exact recession into the space provided by the breaking of the picture plane. Although the Impressionists also suggested a spatial box, their technique of identifiable and insistent brush strokes left an awareness of the flat surface they were painting upon. With this one effect, the story of modern art really begins. It was probably this more than any of the more obvious anti-academic aspects of their work that so offended critics and public. The looseness of their paint application seemed to many to be mere incompetence; their mundane subject matter indicated a lack of seriousness and a deficient education; their failure to construct compositions correctly, according to Classical rules, was seen as wilfulness, and their refusal to render forms tonally as juvenile rebellion. But aside from all that, the way their paintings failed to recede happily from their frames on the walls but boldly advanced to meet the observer's eye – that was probably the crucial objection.

Needless to say the Impressionists also had their friends and allies. But it was not until the late 1880s that they gained general acceptance, and by then the public was confronted with their still more problematical successors, the Post-Impressionists.

It has been said that it is difficult to identify the true Impressionists, and that no satisfactory definition which includes all Impressionist artists has been offered. Any definition that excludes such artists as, for example, Manet and Degas could be regarded as inadequate, yet their work is clearly not Impressionist in many respects. It is also difficult now to realize that the work of artists outside their group was throughout the whole Impressionist period so different as to seem to come from an earlier age. In this connection one example may be helpful: Edouard Manet (1832–83) was actually 18 months older than Sir Edward Burne-Jones (1833–98), a leading member of the Pre-Raphaelite Brotherhood and a specialist in meticulous pictures of medieval myth.

The Bridge at Argenteuil, *1874.*
Claude Monet (Musée du Louvre, Paris).
After the Franco-Prussian War, some of
the putative Impressionists moved to a
small town on the Seine near Paris and
painted their first Impressionist works
there. They were attracted by the effect of
light on water and trees, and here the two
were readily available in a pleasant
small-town context. This painting, very
similar to one painted by Renoir at the
same spot, shows Monet's early
experiments in breaking down form in
pursuit of the effect of sunlight in
dissolving the solidity of perceived objects.

Perhaps the most 'typical' and incontrovertible Impressionist was Claude Monet (*1840–1926*); indeed, the name Impressionism comes from the title of a painting he exhibited in *1874*. But, as mentioned earlier, Monet's interesting late work is far from the Impressionism of the 1870s.

However, Monet was certainly typical in sharing the primary concern of the Impressionists with the effect of light, its play over surfaces, its constantly changing quality, its illumination and effect on shadows, its colour and its form-defining character. The Impressionists were little concerned with emotional responses to their subject matter; nor were they interested in making statements not inherent in vision itself. It was said of Monet, 'Only an eye – but what an eye!'

The importance of Impressionism in releasing painting from its academic chains and in producing fresh and immediately attractive work is clear enough. Their greatest significance, however, lies in their introduction, as an important element in picture-making, of the surface of the painting and thus of its separate identity from its subject. The individuality of the painting as an object is a basic tenet of much 20th-century work, and although the Impressionists themselves never clearly identified this important element, it was assuredly there, and rose to full consciousness in the work of the Post-Impressionists.

Above:
After the Bath, c.1895. Edgar Degas
(Phillips Collection, Washington, D.C.).
Degas's place in Impressionism is difficult
to assess. A complex and dedicated
painter, interested in composition and art
history, he does not fit into the movement
easily but must be included for his concern
with movement and optical effects. The
distinction of his draughtmanship and his
brilliant control of colour place him among
the great figures in the history of painting.
His special achievement in pastels, of
which this is a good example, make him
perhaps the greatest practitioner in that
medium.

The female nude before, during or after
bathing was a favourite subject. He seems
to observe them in unguarded moments,
when they suppose themselves to be
unobserved.

Right:
The Côte des Boeufs at L'Hermitage,
near Pontoise, 1877. Camille Pissarro
(National Gallery, London).
Pissarro's importance in the history of
modern painting is considerable. Not only
was he a most accomplished technician
but through his influence on the Post-
Impressionists, particularly Cézanne and
Seurat – whose technique for a time he
used – he formed a link between
Impressionist visual exploration and Post-
Impressionist structure.

This view through the trees is more
defined in form than the Renoir (page 24)
but in its concern for the evanescent effect
of light it is characteristically
Impressionist. Pissarro was, despite a
tendency to pursue a variety of ideas, the
most consistently Impressionist of all the
painters in the movement.

23

Post-Impressionism

This familiar name is both informative and misleading. What we call Post-Impressionism certainly came after Impressionism and had some relationship to it, but, in the way that Impressionism identifies a certain development in 19th-century French (and later European) art, Post-Impressionism does not. It was not a 'movement' or a style and the most important Post-Impressionist artists had no common aim or programme. The name identifies a period rather than an aesthetic and it was not devised by or known to any of the artists now associated with it. The name arose mostly by chance, some years later, when most of the principal figures associated with it were already dead and others had acquired different preoccupations.

According to tradition, in 1911 the art critic and painter Roger Fry was arranging a London exhibition of 'modern' French art in something of a hurry, and after much discussion of possible titles he said in some impatience, 'Oh, let's just call them Post-Impressionists; at any rate they came after the Impressionists'. His intention was to show all the most recent developments in French art since Manet, and the exhibition included the work of Matisse and Picasso, works which were Impressionist, Symbolist, Cloisonnist, Fauvist and even Cubist, as well as the painters whom we now know as the Post-Impressionists – Cézanne, Seurat, Van Gogh and Gauguin. Fry's exhibition demonstrated how effective the Impressionist revolution had been in releasing such diversity.

It is important not to look at Post-Impressionism as a coherent and purposive successor to Impressionism, but to recognize that a new spirit was abroad and the restrictive intellectualism of the long-established academic tradition had been largely blown away.

For the leading figures among the Post-Impressionists, it was partly the deficiencies they discerned in Impressionism that governed their development. The gravest of these deficiencies, in their eyes, was the absence of any emotional statement to match their visual discovery – a 'bourgeois' lack of commitment. Like sons reacting to the values of their fathers, they rejected their revolutionary aesthetic parenthood – no longer so revolutionary to them. The Impressionists, initially at least, had spurned the academic world of exhibitions, galleries and collections, but the Post-Impressionists, in the often-quoted words of Cézanne, wanted to make something 'solid and durable like the art of the museums'. They looked for structure and content, for emotional involvement and even intellectual distinction.

Here they enjoyed one practical advantage which, again, was an outcome of the Impressionists' independence. A new type of dealer/collector/gallery-owner had appeared who organized exhibitions to show the work of the many groups proliferating in the liberated climate of the time. In addition, a number of professional bodies and societies unconnected with the Salon arranged exhibitions of new work. During the 1880s new paths were opening in all directions, some leading nowhere, others making small but significant innovations. In Paris at least, groups or individuals who wanted to show something different seldom encountered any difficulty in catching the public eye. The dealers were often both commercially alert and artistically sensitive, frequently providing support in the face of critical antagonism, for the critics were far less receptive.

There were of course some critics of sensitivity and discernment, but generally it was a difficult time for them. By 1880 Impressionism was in dissolution as a movement almost before it had gained public acceptance. It required not only courage but great confidence to adopt an independent aesthetic stance. Most critics remained basically traditional, applying the old critical criteria which, not surprisingly, they found unworkable, unhelpful or unrelated to the

Opposite:
The Lily Pond, *1899. Claude Monet (National Gallery, London).*
In 1890, at the age of 50, Monet bought the house and garden at Giverny that he had known and loved since the early 1880s. He devoted time and money to stocking the garden and restoring the house. In the garden was a lily pool which he painted many times in the years before his death at Giverny in 1926. The pool was spanned by a Japanese bridge which he had built.

Monet's concern for light, movement and colour are beautifully reflected in this delicate but strong work. His late, large panels of water and lilies in a floating space of colour are not only his finest works but among the great paintings of the century.

works confronting them. Their commonest response was denigration or condemnation. It is not difficult to understand, and even to sympathize, but in retrospect the overall effect of critical inadequacy was to assist in a blurring process in which little new work was given any significance at all. The particular role of the four principal Post-Impressionists in the 1880s was singularly misunderstood.

It is usual to distinguish two main strands of Post-Impressionist developments, Cézanne and Seurat representing one and Van Gogh and Gauguin the other. In identifying the deficiencies of Impressionism, Cézanne and Seurat in their different ways emphasized its unstructured, unorganized quality, while Van Gogh and Gauguin were more concerned with an emotional or spiritual response to subject matter.

But, most importantly, all of them clearly laid out what had been only implied by the Impressionists with regard to the painting itself. As we have seen, the Impressionist technique, *en plein air* painting, and the influence of photography and other factors combined to produce a picture image which had a strong surface quality: it looked like colour on a surface besides being a particular scene. As a later artist, Maurice Denis, was to say, 'Remember that a picture – before being a horse, a nude or some sort of anecdote – is essentially a flat surface covered with colours assembled in a certain order.' The Post-Impressionists translated their predecessors' awareness of surface into an insistence on surface. The painting did not attempt to represent a scene as it was observed but as it was responded to. In this respect at least it obeyed the traditions of art, and the aptness of Cézanne's comment is apparent.

Van Gogh's cypress tree struggles in a resistant sky, but on an evidently flat plane. Cézanne's rocks are tautly structured and related both to each other and to the picture area and surface. Seurat's pictorial organization is even more methodically and programmatically carried through in both composition and colour, while the intensity of Gauguin's spiritual response to his Tahitian subjects expresses itself in colour, line and form, thrusting itself from the surface. In none of their paintings is there a casual line, an inconsidered or unfelt brush stroke; the intensity of emotional and intellectual creativity infuses all their work.

This Post-Impressionist contribution is of vital importance since it is the one stream from which so much – one is tempted to say all – 20th-century art flows. The significance of Cézanne's work lies in the inspiration that his researches have given to so many apparently differently directed artists throughout the century that has elapsed since he was at work.

Paul Cézanne (1839–1906). Cézanne's overwhelming importance was not apparent to most of his contemporaries. Since his death it has been widely acknowledged, yet it has remained difficult to convey the nature of his achievement to people generally. His name often evokes an uncomprehending awe. Since he has proved to be an inspiration to so many artists – indeed still is – there are evidently many aspects to his genius. That they are not always immediately apparent is due in some measure to his sensitive and reserved technique. His is a reflective art, not given to bold, eye-catching gestures. His life was equally quiet and private. Whilst not a recluse, he did not court publicity, and he presented no arresting public image as did Van Gogh and Gauguin.

An analysis of Cézanne's work and influence demands extra sensitivity and no small degree of caution.

Cézanne was a contemporary of Monet and was one of the group, including Renoir and Pissarro, who used to meet at the Café Guerbois in the days before Impressionism gained its name. He worked with them and painted on the spot (*en plein air*) with them. (He once sat next to Renoir painting the same dovecote.) Although sharing some aspects of the Impressionist approach in those days, he never really belonged to Impressionism and always showed a care for structure that they did not. However, his relationship with Pissarro was crucial, especially in convincing him of the importance of pure colour and confronting him with the study of nature. When they were working together in Pontoise in 1877 it was early Impressionist days but already Cézanne was adopting one of his important

Le Château Noir, *1902–05. Paul Cézanne (Private Collection).*
The Château Noir was a property near Aix-en-Provence which Cézanne wished to buy in 1897. Although the owner refused to sell, he did rent a small room to Cézanne who worked there in the last years of his life although obliged to return to Aix to sleep in a rented apartment.

He made a number of paintings of the Château Noir of which this is one of the finest, revealing the discipline of struggle in his mature work. Nothing is casual: all is related to a surface structure and a flat space. The surface of the painting and the tautness of the relationships are almost painfully evident. It is not easy, perhaps, at first sight to appreciate the qualities of such a painting as Château Noir *but it assuredly repays the effort, for this is an example of the work that makes Cézanne the inspiration – not to say desperation – of so many 20th-century artists.*

procedures, what he described as the 'constructive stroke'. Still painting in the open air and with the Impressionists' sketchy, thin paint, broadly applied, Cézanne was already massing and directing his image by unifying the brush strokes to produce a pictorial order. These brush strokes were not following and building form but were, in juxtaposition, building themselves individually into a coherence which, while representing the subject, also existed as marks on a surface. In Cézanne's later painting, the directional and organized strokes became part of his means of expressing his conviction of the inherent order in nature and the essential relationship between all observed things.

This belief was largely responsible for Cézanne's superficial lack of adventurousness. Believing that order existed in his subject matter wherever it might be found, he had no need to travel in search of inspiration nor to strive after extreme effects. His work largely consisted of landscapes, still-lifes, portraits and, in his later years, a series of nude bathing subjects – all conventional enough. He did not pursue variety but painted and repainted what he called his 'motif', each time penetrating slowly, cautiously but with certainty to an image of organized paint which has balance, order, harmony and structure. The finished work has an appearance of immutability and the same 'Classical' organization that is found in the subject paintings of the great 17th-century Classicist, Nicolas Poussin – and perhaps nowhere else. Cézanne's example appears crucial in the changing nature of the 20th-century painted image, which is generally a surface before, or instead of, being a spatial subject.

There is, in his last paintings, a further element. His concern with his 'motif' becomes dominant. When Cézanne referred to his motif, he did not mean simply his subject. In a well-known explanation he says, 'There must not be a single link too loose, not a crevice through which the emotion, the light, the truth may escape'; it is his search for the total integration of all the elements of the painting that constitutes the successful achievement of the 'motif'. The 'motif' is therefore an unemotional, intellectual and practical unity. It has a lot to do with appearance but it is not appearance; it has a lot to do with intellectual geometry but it is not pictorial composition. The 'motif' comprises total sensitivity.

In the last analysis it is probably that unique dedication to the totality of the 'motif' that accounts for Cézanne's pervasive influence. The painting as an experience in itself, calling for all the sensitivity and responsiveness of the observer, was a new aesthetic base and it is that which has secured the respect of almost all painting practitioners with any claim to distinction.

Georges Seurat (1859–91). None of the other Post-Impressionist giants had quite the same commanding influence as Cézanne, but all made important contributions to the future development of painting. All of them also displayed in their lives utter devotion to their art, to the exclusion of almost everything else.

Georges Seurat died at 31, having already suffered severe physical damage as a result of his devotion to his theories. All his major canvases were painted during the last seven years of his life.

Twenty years younger than Cézanne, Seurat had some sympathy with Cézanne's response to Impressionism, which had a strong influence on the development of his own unique and demanding style, known as *pointillisme* or Divisionism.

The frozen stillness of Seurat's paintings suggest that he was engaged in a search similar to that of Cézanne. Their interests, however, were as different as their lives. The reserved and retiring existence of Cézanne was not for Seurat. His short life was packed with emotional experience, which became manifest in the ascendancy of feeling over his intellectual intent. The patterned monumentality that Seurat gives his subject matter is quite different in kind from Cézanne's effects.

Seurat, together with his friend Paul Signac (1863–1935), became interested in the theories of colour propounded by various scientists, especially Eugène Chevreul and Charles Henry. From these he arrived at his own theoretical structure of colour which became his controlling compositional method and makes him one of the outstanding creative artists of the period.

Seurat's method, *pointillisme*, employs small dots of colour – recalling the short strokes and dabs of the Impressionists but actually quite different – which, when placed in juxtaposition and viewed from the correct distance, fuse optically and create the colour that would have resulted from mixing them – but with greater purity and intensity.

The technique is theoretically sound, and to an extent works equally well in practice, but the distance between eye and canvas and the size of the dots are critical. In most actual examples there is considerable inconsistency. However, the construction of the painting entirely in dots certainly is consistent and gives it unity, which is reinforced by Seurat's ordered geometric scheme of composition. The drawback is that the method is extremely demanding on the artist and it seems certain that it was responsible for damage to Seurat's eyesight.

Seurat was a conscientious and extraordinarily hard worker who made many studies for all his major works; his tonal and linear drawings and his small colour sketches show extreme sensitivity. In such paintings as *Le Cirque* and *Le Chahut* he applies his control to a highly transient scene and the effect is to remove it entirely from reality, turning the painting in the process into an independent object with significant arrangement of colour and line. In some measure Seurat echoes the picture-identity of Cézanne's motif, but the effect really springs from a structural theory softened by emotion.

Seurat had a number of followers whose theorizing was not accompanied by

Right:
The Bridge at Courbevoie, *1886.*
Georges Seurat (Courtauld Institute Galleries, London).
The demands of Seurat's technique, developed as a result of his theorizing on colour, composition and content in painting, ensured that his production would be slow, his completed works few and his health seriously affected. His method is sometimes called Neo-Impressionism, Divisionism, or pointillisme, *all inadequate, though the latter does give some indication of his way of applying his colour in dots (points) with the avowed if not always realized intention of creating an 'optical mixture' of colour. The term* pointillisme *does not indicate Seurat's concern for pictorial structure, which makes him the significant figure he is in the development of modern aesthetics. This painting is a strong example of his ability to produce compositional balance and emotional atmosphere of calm and anticipation through the use of verticals, horizontals and a slight imbalance in the right-angle of the tree in the foreground.*

so technically rigorous a method, the 'points' being replaced by larger spots which did not mix optically and resulted in colourful images of what has come to be called a 'chocolate-box' hue. The most talented of these was undoubtedly Signac, whose association with Matisse had a great effect on the Fauvist movement, linking it with Seurat and his colour theories.

Signac wrote *From Delacroix to Neo-Impressionism* (the latter name having been bestowed on Seurat's work by his friend, Felix Fénéon), which is an accomplished presentation of the theory of *pointillisme* and Seurat's art.

In the work of the Divisionists the combination of structure and emotional involvement is often unbalanced. Yet they provide a link with the more overtly emotional Post-Impressionists, Van Gogh and Gauguin.

Vincent van Gogh (1853–90). With Van Gogh we encounter one of the most admired and most easily recognized of all painters of the fairly recent past. People who have little acquaintance with painting generally know of and can recall individual paintings by Van Gogh. His popular fame is due in some degree at least to his image as the tortured Bohemian artist *par excellence*. Stories about him and his extraordinary life are the stuff of legend, and it is perfectly true that his life, regardless of his art, is strange and fascinating. But the popularizing of his life has had unfortunate effects. It has become difficult to see and understand his art because his life gets in the way.

That is a fate not unique to Van Gogh, but it is something which should make us wary. The artist's life, however intriguing, is not his work, and Van Gogh's paintings would be exactly the same if we knew nothing whatever of his life. There is a danger that we may search for characteristics in his art which are suggested by our knowledge of his life, and though these characteristics may indeed be present, it is also possible that we impose them on his work.

Nevertheless, a passionate nature is likely to produce passionate art. That is certainly true of Van Gogh.

The passion of his nature eventually destroyed his intellectual control. His inability to realize what he felt in terms of his painting, and his deep need to create a reality – everything indeed that had meaning for him – placed an insupportable pressure on him. His suicide was, it seems in retrospect, an inevitable outcome.

The calm statements of Cézanne and Seurat seem far from the wild tensions of Van Gogh's struggling trees and rocks, but the distance is shorter than it looks. Cézanne's rocks are closer in Classical structure to Van Gogh's than they are for instance, to Gauguin's symbolism.

Van Gogh was searching for a pictorial reality, as were Cézanne, Seurat and Gauguin, though his search was of a different order. For him reality lay not in the *motif* and its construction; it was in the captured paint of the new actuality of the painting itself. The painting was not of, for instance, a chair, or the church at Auvers, it was a new reality of that chair or that church. It was not a representation of the subject, it *was* the subject. The tortured, expressive line, seemingly carrying the emotion dripping from the brush, is in fact a controlled statement of the actuality he sought. This point must be emphasized as, despite the immediate impact of Van Gogh's paintings, they are difficult and demanding, especially those done in the last few months of his life.

There is another aspect of Van Gogh's work that is not always appreciated. It is sometimes thought that he was untutored and technically deficient, that he was unconcerned with aesthetics and the history of art. This is not so. His painterly technique was a marvellously efficient tool of his imagination, and his debts to the great masters of painting were great, and acknowledged; but he was conscious of creating a new art for which the traditional observational rendering was not adequate.

His linear and patterned style derived from such disparate sources as Japanese prints, the Symbolist Puvis de Chavannes, the landscape painter Corot, the Romantic Delacroix, and even from the pre-Renaissance Florentine master, Giotto. The early influence of the Impressionists and of the great master of peasant life, Millet, can be seen in his paintings of miners from the Borinage area of Belgium.

The insistence on the reality separate from the painting links him with the other Post-Impressionists, particularly Cézanne and Seurat. His links with Gauguin, which at first seem closer, are both more complex and less artistically direct.

Paul Gauguin (1848–1903). At a time when the popular view of the artist was of a romantic figure living *la vie bohème* in the cafés and brothels of Paris, painters like Cézanne and Gauguin hardly fitted the image. Gauguin first showed his dedication to work in Pont-Aven in Brittany in the late 1880s; later, after he had gone to live in the South Seas, he sent back to Paris his powerful and richly painted works, and became a legend almost in his own lifetime. His restless spirit, his desire to travel (he had been a merchant sailor in his youth) and his strong personality made him, once he had gained confidence in his work, a natural leader. He came to believe what time has confirmed, that he was a great artist. To achieve that greatness he sacrificed his family, his friends, and his comfortable living as a stockbroker, dying in poverty in the Marquesas Islands in 1903.

After his death his reputation was quickly established by a major exhibition of over two hundred of his works – paintings, prints, sculptures and drawings – at the Autumn Salon of 1906. His influence in Paris during the period immediately prior to the First World War was considerable and, with the other Post-

Right:
The Church at Auvers-sur-Oise, *1890. Vincent Van Gogh (Musée du Louvre).*
Van Gogh sold only one painting during his lifetime and it is a measure of his dedication that he devoted all his energies and eventually his life to a creative struggle that has identified him as the epitome of the tortured genius destroyed by the force of his own creativity. The church at Auvers was painted the month before his death, when he was losing the struggle with reason: a mind divided as the paths divide around the church. His work represents the emotional, subjective aspect of Post-Impressionism, as distinct from the control and structure of Cézanne and Seurat.

Impressionists, he forms the bridge between the art of the past and the modern period.

Unlike Cézanne, Gauguin was never an Impressionist, although as he himself says his first mentor, like Cézanne's, was Camille Pissarro. He quickly mastered Impressionist methods and discovered, as the other Post-Impressionists had done, what he thought was their artistic inadequacy or what at least did not suit his temperament. The apparent lack of commitment to the subject itself in Impressionist work was objectionable to his passionate nature, which demanded emotional involvement.

His mature style evolved in the early years at Pont-Aven. The control and power of these paintings of familiar subjects are in some ways a more profound indication of his quality than the more exotic and symbolic work from the South Seas. For Europeans the romantic strangeness and eroticism of his paintings of the islanders, the festivities with their unknown symbolism, are inherently attractive, and this has tended to obscure Gauguin's real contribution. The quality of his art does not reside in revelations of another culture but in the aesthetic position he arrived at in the more familiar Breton landscape.

Pont-Aven was the haunt of artists before Gauguin's arrival but he attracted a number of young painters, most importantly Paul Sérusier (1863–1927), who painted under Gauguin's direction *The Talisman*, the foundation painting of Nabism (see page 37), and Emile Bernard (1868–1941). These three were the founders of Synthetism, a word in use by 1876 to distinguish the artistic from the scientific aspects of Impressionist painting though it later became specifically anti-Impressionist. With Gauguin it represented a synthesis of 'a single form and a single colour'. The Symbolist critic Albert Aurier used the term to describe this reduction or confinement of the form and colour within a single element. Colour is used in a non-naturalistic way and the line borders flat, decorative, patterned forms in a way that suggests *cloisonné*, a technique in which fired enamel panels are contained within wire inlays. Synthetism thus received the alternative name, Cloisonnism.

In Gauguin's art the strength and simplicity of colour, line and form served an important artistic purpose – to heighten the power of the idea contained within the subject to suggest the symbolism of nature. He uses strong colour to express the effect of the natural subtleties of natural colour in magnified form. In the *Yellow Christ* from the Pont-Aven period, the trees are bright red, a blood-red in contrast with Christ's yellow, blood-drained body: here the symbolism is insistent.

The Importance of Post-Impressionism. The four major Post-Impressionists are central to the development of 20th-century art. They suggested a new pictorial language based on the identity of the painted surface as the object to be looked at, reacted to and appreciated *for itself*, and not as a nostalgic mnemonic of some other visual experience or idea. The vague, suggestive, atmospheric, rectangular hole that the Impressionists created was replaced by the Post-Impressionists with a flat, resistant surface. Modern art follows from that. Cézanne, Seurat, Van Gogh and Gauguin are not only the great founding fathers of modern art but also represent the culmination of the whole history of art since the Renaissance aesthetic, its last creative expression in fact. The artists who followed them and understood their message – not so clear at the time as later – were to create an art that was wholly divorced from the standards that had inspired the art of the previous five centuries.

Nave Nave Mahana (Days of Delight), 1896. Paul Gauguin (Musée des Beaux-Arts, Lyon).

This lyrical, almost idyllic painting, completed after his return to the South Pacific for the last time, reveals a life close to nature, unhurried and dignified. It may be seen as an emotional protest against the increasing Europeanization of the islands, although Gauguin, already syphilitic, was an outcast and a pauper. The supposed romance of his life at this time is at variance with the reality of his degraded and desperate condition. Nevertheless, he still contrived to paint such works as Nave Nave.

Although his genius was only recognized at the retrospective exhibition in Paris after his death, Gauguin's contribution to the modern movement parallels that of the other Post-Impressionists in laying emphasis on the surface structure and emotional content of the painting.

Symbolism

Symbolism was a literary and artistic movement which arose in France towards the end of the 19th century. It made considerable impact on Parisian intellectual circles and contributed to the 20th-century aesthetic. Essentially French, it nevertheless had disciples in other cultural centres, in Germany and Belgium particularly.

The poet Jean Moréas first defined 'Symbolism' as 'the only term able adequately to describe the modern tendency toward the creative spirit in art'. Supported by a number of publications which appeared after 1886, the movement included a number of well-known French literary figures, among them Paul Verlaine, Stephane Mallarmé, Arthur Rimbaud and the critic Albert Aurier, who wrote extensively in support of the new aesthetic attitude. Maurice Maeterlinck and Henri Bergson were also associated with the Symbolists, as was the 'Decadent' writer J.-K. Huysmans; his *A Rebours* includes an expression of admiration for the Symbolist artist, Odilon Redon (1840–1916).

The principal Symbolist artists, besides Redon, are Gustave Moreau (1826–98) and P.-C. Puvis de Chavannes (1824–98), although Puvis's delicate Romanticism is now recognized as being little in sympathy with the more robust, strange aesthetic of Symbolism. A more important influence than any of these was Gauguin, who was never purely a Symbolist although, largely through the influence of Bernard, his work took on Symbolist overtones in the late 1880s. A painting of 1888, *Vision after the Sermon*, is thoroughly Symbolist in character.

The essential ordinariness of the Impressionists' vision, the realism of Courbet's earthy art ('Painting is an essentially physical language made up of what is visible'), a rising Romanticism in literature and the revival of the Gothic, of which the medievalism of William Morris and his friends was a powerful example – all these helped to inspire Symbolism. The Symbolists emphasized the role of the mind, the imagination and the spirit. In painting this meant treating nature with imagination, but not abandoning it. They showed an interest in science and intellectual speculation generally; it was, after all, a literary movement first. For the Symbolists the physical world was real; but equally real were the mind and spirit and, through them, new aspects of the physical world were revealed.

For Moreau this meant a new examination of myth and religion from which his visionary idealism drew strange and obscure images. For Redon, a Surrealist *avant la lettre*, it meant the imaginative exploration of the imagery of dreams, with a poetic density that has provoked constant fascination. The work of Puvis is less significant for the development of modern art than in the effect he had upon Gauguin to whom he introduced the Symbolist attitude. What is sometimes known as Pont-Aven symbolism (Cloissonism by Bernard) had a direct effect upon the Fauves later. A fourth painter, Eugène Carrière (1849–1906), had a more direct, realist style, but he was close to the Symbolists in spirit: 'the eye is dependent on the mind', he said.

So far as subsequent developments are concerned, Moreau had the most direct influence. In his remarkable *atelier* this strangely effective teacher directed an extraordinary group of young, eager and gifted students. Among them were some of the leading painters of the early 20th century: Matisse, Marquet, Manguin, Dufy, Friesz and Braque, a group including many of the leading Fauves. Georges Rouault (1871–1958), a mystical Expressionist sometimes linked with the Fauves, was another of Moreau's pupils.

As Symbolist ideas spread among writers and painters throughout Europe, it was embraced with more or less vigour by such different artists as the Swiss Ferdinand Hodler (1853–1918), who incorporated Wagnerian Teutonic symbolism in his later paintings, and the Dutchman, Jan Toorop (1858–1928)

Right:
Jupiter and Sémélé (detail), 1894–95. Gustave Moreau (Musée Gustave Moreau, Paris).
In Greek myth Zeus (father of the gods) seduced Semele, mortal daughter of King Cadmus of Thebes, and she conceived Dionysos. Semele repudiated Zeus who in anger destroyed her by lightning, but not before the unborn child had been saved. Moreau's painting shows Zeus in majesty with Semele as an awed but compliant lover. The trappings of the painting reveal a world of imaginative imagery, of unreal forms and exotic landscape. The pale figure of Semele contrasts with the Olympian figure of Zeus, framed by a vivid red aura. Such a painting was far removed from the usual academic treatment of the subject.

Moreau, a strange and independent artist, became a teacher, through his atelier, of great influence on the Fauves, several of whom were his pupils.

Overleaf:
The Cyclops, c.1894. Odilon Redon (Rijksmuseum Kröller-Müller, Otterlo). The mystical Symbolism of Redon is evident in this important late work. The Cyclops were a tribe of giants who fed on human flesh and had one eye in the centre of the forehead. Here, the Cyclops Polyphemus gazes with a simpering leer at Galatea, a sea nymph with whom he has fallen in love. The idyllic landscape and the Classical reclining nude are dominated by the gross and savage figure: an uneasy disquiet prevails. The theme of the Cyclops fascinated Redon and Moreau, who also painted this subject.

who produced curious, decorative, coloured panels, Symbolist in style. Even the Viennese artist Gustav Klimt displayed Symbolist characteristics in his decorative murals. In Germany Max Klinger (1857–1920) and in Italy Giovanni Segantini (1858–99) were among others who adopted Symbolism.

36

The Nabis

This short-lived movement of mainly French painters and sculptors takes its name from a Hebrew word for prophets. It began in 1888 as the result of a meeting between Gauguin and Sérusier, and was associated with the *Revue Blanche*, which printed articles by the Nabis and gave editorial support. By 1900 it was all over: all the artists involved were pursuing their individual interests.

Whilst of considerable theoretical interest, and responsible for introducing an important element into developing modernism, Nabism gave birth to only a few works of major importance. Most of the figures associated with it produced work of greater significance after their Nabi period. Nevertheless, in Maurice Denis (1870–1943), the movement possessed a major theorist whose writings have been of undoubted value to 20th-century artists.

The basis of the Nabis' creed is expressed by Denis as the theory of two distortions, 'the objective distortion that is based upon a purely aesthetic and decorative concept as well as technical principles of colour and composition, and the subjective distortion that brings the artist's individual perception into play . . .'

Nabi work was in opposition to contemporary Symbolism with its literary and historical base and its concentration on colour. The Nabis adopted an essentially bourgeois, observational art based on colour but without the gleaming, varnished look of traditional painting. To this effect they abandoned hard outlines and used absorbent surfaces such as cardboard, instead of canvas, to soften the colour effects and sometimes tempera instead of oils. The result was domestic paintings in soft, vibrant colour.

Besides Sérusier and Denis, one of the most important Nabi painters was Pierre Bonnard (1867–1947) who is chiefly remembered for his later work, exploring the possibilities of colour in a private world of figures in interiors – often a bathing nude.

In the work of Edouard Vuillard (1868–1940), the intimate images of his family, wearing patterned clothes in patterned interiors against patterned wallpaper, without the use of form-defining lines, are essentially Nabist in spirit. But the painting that Sérusier painted after his meeting with Gauguin, *The Talisman*, identifies the Nabi spirit most closely. It is a landscape painted in pure strokes of crimson, violet, blue and green, without tone or line. Not only is it, as it was named, the 'talisman' for the group, it is also a clear presage of Fauvism.

Overleaf:
Women with a Dog, 1891. Pierre Bonnard (Sterling and Francine Clark Art Institute, Williamstown).
Most of the characteristics of Nabi painting are to be found in this work. There is a concentration on pattern rather than form, and form is not modelled but only bounded by line or, more precisely, by the nondelineated boundary where one pattern, indicating a form, is succeeded by another. Thus, the check dress mixes with the shapes defining the dog.
The strong decorative elements of Nabism are derived from Japanese as well as European sources.
The flat patterning of familiar subject matter goes further in the work of the Nabis than in any of their contemporaries, and this characteristic is part of the background to the predilection for abstraction which is a feature of so much 20th-century art.

Left:
Interior with Madame Vuillard, c.1897. Edouard Vuillard (by courtesy of Christie's, London).
Vuillard studied at the Academie Julien after a short period at Ecole des Beaux Arts where the teaching methods were restrictive and depressing. At Julien's he met Bonnard and Serusier. He was attracted by the Japanese print and, for a time, by Gauguin. With Bonnard he is the best known of the Nabis and the intimacy of his interiors of patterned materials and the clutter of private objects together with the Japanese pattern influence formed the basis of his work.

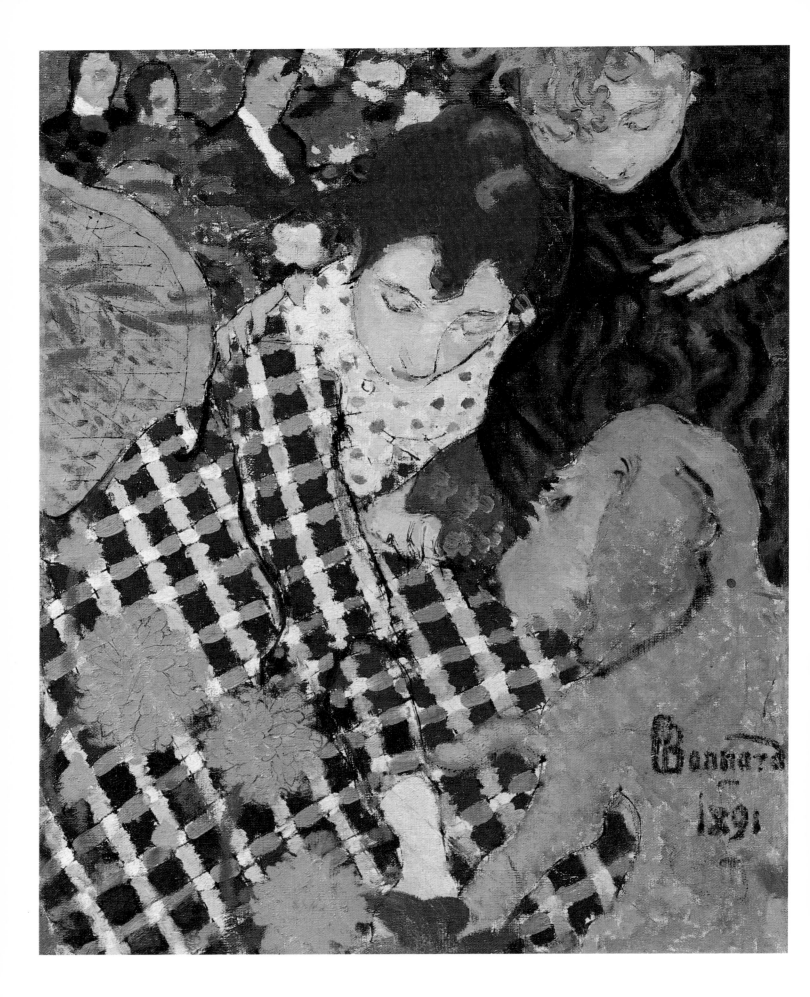

The Vienna Secession

The term 'Secession' was given to a number of *avant-garde* groups that started in Germany and Austria in the 1890s. Contemporary with Art Nouveau, they were also part of it, but they were more consciously forward-looking.

The most important Secessionist groups were in Munich, the earliest, founded by Franz von Stück in 1892; Berlin, formed in 1899 at the instigation of Max Liebermann and arising from a dispute caused by the refusal of the Berlin Artists Association to exhibit the works of Edvard Munch; the New Secession, a breakaway group from the Berlin Secession led by Max Pechstein, later a member of the earliest Expressionist movement, Die Brücke; and most memorable of all, the Vienna Secession founded by Gustav Klimt (1862–1918) in 1897.

The decorative character of Art Nouveau and its strong architectural connections are discussed below. Art Nouveau is sometimes called 'the decorative style' and it was this that made it important to the artists of the Vienna Secession, especially to Klimt. The decorative quality of Klimt's work is so obvious that it often seems to be the main concern, outweighing all others.

There is a widely held belief that to describe a work as 'decorative' is to relegate it to an inferior position in the hierarchy of art. The word suggests something designed merely for pleasure, probably commercially orientated, and therefore not fine art. In that case, what of Klimt? The precise observation and subtle drawing of the human figure in his paintings, occupying more often than not a small area of the surface, often seems to be swamped by the rich, patterned, flat decoration of the rest of the area. The richly ornamental effect is strengthened by his frequent use of gold and by the near abstraction of the patterning, which is related, though rather casually, to the forms of the figures.

But these works require more consideration. They make some important points about the nature of decoration and its independence of 'commercial' taint. Apart from the extremely rich quality of the decorative elements in themselves, they are integral to the purpose of the work. The isolation of head, hands or body in that decorative splendour serves to emphasize the emotions and relationships they represent with extra poignancy. The decoration is an essential element of the content, not a meretricious device; Klimt's paintings remain powerfully evocative.

Mother with Two Children, *1917.*
Egon Schiele (Österreichische Galerie, Vienna).
Most of Schiele's work expresses a controlled anguish manifest in disgust, despair, and ultimate resignation. More decorative and – if such a word may ever be applied to Schiele – lighthearted than most of his works, these puppet-like babies, one reserved and introspective, one extrovert, are held by their mother whose preoccupied, reflective stare separates them, as does the grey/white central falling shape. This deeply emotional work derives its power not so much from a realist presentation of the subject but from Schiele's ability to construct a potent image – much out of key with his contemporaries but influential upon his successors.

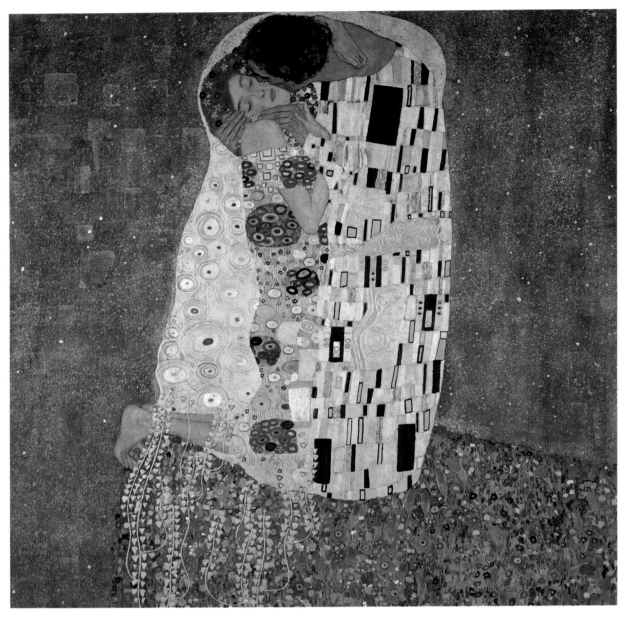

As leader of the Vienna Secession and a regular contributor to the movement's periodical, *Ver Sacrum*, Klimt was an influential figure. His inspiration was important in the formation of the style of Schiele and Kokoschka, the former especially.

In his drastically curtailed life, Egon Schiele (1890–1918) developed into one of the most powerful – if isolated – figures in the art of the early 20th century. Recognition of his difficult, harsh talent is steadily extending. His determination to proceed with a self-analysis stripped of all conventional restraints makes his art a raw document of human pathos.

His father was a syphilitic who refused treatment and died insane in 1904 after fathering seven children on a young wife. The first three were stillborn; only one daughter lived to old age. Klimt was Schiele's early inspiration and his work was first regarded as an inferior pastiche of the older man's. Although there is an evident relationship, this notion makes one wonder if the Viennese critics were totally blind. In some respects two artists could scarcely be more different. Klimt, through the use of decorative Art Nouveau elements, examined the isolation of the spirit, but he did not probe into the dark recesses of the psyche which lie behind that isolation (even in the most luxurious surroundings), as Schiele relentlessly did. For Schiele, the image is centralized and undecorated, awkward and vulnerable but uncompromising and usually uncomplaining. His superb draughtsmanship – few artists have ever drawn a more powerful line – adds to the pathos of his treatment. His work is acidly erotic, coarse yet subtle and tender, in a world where actions are brutal but feelings are most easily bruised.

The Kiss, *1907–08. Gustav Klimt (Österreichische Galerie, Vienna). The decorative quality evident in Schiele's painting is more pervasive in the work of Klimt. This canvas is square and gold covers most of its area, which also bears small patches of silver. The highly decorated patterning of the foreground leaves the lovers almost submerged in pattern while the great, womb-like, encompassing shape emphasizes the symbolic nature of the composition. A man of great physical presence, admired and fêted in Vienna, Klimt was one of the great emotive decorators of the age.*

Art Nouveau

The style known as Art Nouveau – also by other names in different countries – emerged about 1890, became for a time universally pervasive, and lingered on until the First World War. Arguably it had no real connection with so-called fine art, but it had an important influence on the formation of the modern aesthetic, established during the first two decades of the century.

During the 19th century in the whole field of architecture and design a rampant eclecticism reigned. The Arts and Crafts movement inspired a revival of medieval values – as people like Ruskin and Morris conceived them. The pre-Raphaelite painters had encouraged notions of medieval chivalry and romance. The leading architect of the Gothic Revival, Augustus Pugin, had compared the honest and sympathetic nature of medieval architecture with the harsh formality of the Classical styles predominant since the Renaissance. In France, Delacroix and the Romantics had awakened interest in the exotic styles of North Africa and the Arab world. The palazzo style of early Renaissance architecture in Italy proved remarkably attractive to the new mercantile barons who wanted to establish their own high cultural standing. Some Oriental styles were also in favour.

From these and other influences came a plethora of often incongruous buildings, furniture and domestic artefacts in a bewildering mixture of styles deriving from past societies. In retrospect it seems inevitable that a nonhistorical style would emerge from this derivative morass.

Hence Art Noveau, which appears to have no direct connection with preceding fashions and, with the exception of its 1930s corollary known as Art Deco, with nothing subsequently. Of course it had certain origins and inspirations of its own. They need not be traced here, but the character of Art Nouveau should be briefly established.

The style is characterized by a sinuous line which may convey both an elegant langour and taut, whiplash tension; a combination which suggests struggling natural growth, particularly of plants.

Art Nouveau is essentially a style in design rather than art. It is associated with architects and designers such as Henri van der Velde, Victor Horta, Hector Guimard (the designer of the Paris Métro entrances), August Perret, Antoni Gaudi (an extraordinary Spaniard whose work in Barcelona is the most extreme expression of the style), and Charles Rennie Mackintosh (a Scot whose designs for tea rooms and an art school in Glasgow had considerable impact on the continent, particularly in Vienna). In the United States the architect Louis Sullivan, working mainly in Chicago, developed his own influential version of Art Nouveau, while the firm of Tiffany gave its name to the style.

So pervasive a style, current during the heyday of the Post-Impressionists, was not entirely without effect on fine art. Painters such as Henri de Toulouse-Lautrec (1864–1901), Pierre Bonnard (1867–1947) and even Van Gogh show its influence. In England, Aubrey Beardsley's graphic art exploited Art Nouveau's erotic curves.

Art Nouveau acted as a postscript to the 19th century; in Paris it was known as the 'modern' style. While it was not a continuation of any 19th-century style, it was not the start of anything else, and it seems as irrelevant to the modern art movements that appeared while it was still current as it was to the 19th century. Perhaps its most significant effect (apart from causing the creation of beautiful objects) was to put a full stop to tradition, thus providing a new climate in which new aesthetic ideas could grow. Its own limited potential and its idiosyncratic nature helped to stimulate an aesthetic rethink. Nevertheless it was an original style owing little to historical influences.

The Twentieth Century

Above:
Luxe, Calme et Volupté, *1904–05.*
Henri Matisse (Musée du Louvre, Paris).

Left:
Still-life with Guitar, *1922. Pablo*
Picasso (Rosengart Collection, Lucerne).

Right:
Kastura *(oil and epoxy on aluminium,*
wire mesh), 1979. Frank Stella
(Museum of Modern Art, New York.
Acquired through the Mr and Mrs Victor
Ganz, Mr and Mrs Donal H. Peters and
Mr and Mrs Charles Zadok Funds).

Fauvism

As the earliest of the movements of modern art to appear in the first decade of this century, Fauvism has a position of special significance. It is important as a sign of what was to come and also as evidence towards resolving an old question. Was there a total revolution in artistic values at the beginning of this century? Did an old and irrelevant art die, to be replaced by a new art appropriate to our own age? These questions may seem redundant to students and scholars, but they are still asked by ordinary people – those, at least, who are interested in the matter.

There is no doubt that with the appearance of the Fauves, a consciously modern attitude is evident. The name Fauvism is itself indicative of change. Earlier movements such as Impressionism or Symbolism, or the current decorative style of Art Nouveau, had all related to artistic themes, attitudes or approaches, however outrageously *avant-garde*. Fauvism does not relate to art but to personality. *Fauve* means wild beast in French; the name was first applied in print by the critic Louis Vauxcelles in his review of the Autumn Salon of 1905. In one room, through the accident of a decision by the exhibition director, paintings by Matisse, Derain, Vlaminck, Marquet, Manguin, Valtat and Puy were hung together while the centre was occupied by a number of traditional sculptures including a head by a sculptor named Marque in Classical style. Possibly the intention was to ameliorate the effect of the violent colours on the walls. Vauxcelles, a sensitive and by no means reactionary critic, repeated in print his reported exclamation on spotting Marque's sculpture, *Donatello parmi les fauves* ('Donatello among wild beasts'). The painters themselves rather liked the name and were thereafter tagged as 'wild beasts'.

Other critics were equally hostile and less witty. 'The effect is deplorable ... and a serious loss of prestige for the Salon. It has landed us with parasites who will be difficult to dislodge ... What have the daubs of Mm. Matisse, Vlaminck and Derain to do with art?' asked one. Another complained of 'Formless streaks of blue, red, yellow and green all mixed up ... the naive and brutal effects of a child playing with its paintbox'. The child-and-paintbox sneer has become very familiar, and the Fauves were not the first to incur it. 'They provoke laughter and are altogether lamentable. They show the most profound ignorance of design, composition and colour. Children amusing themselves with paint and paper can do better': that was written in 1877, about the works of Monet and Cézanne. Naturally, as the critics found the work of the Fauves incomprehensible or reprehensible, the public was correspondingly hostile or bewildered. But some critics responded differently. A young critic, new to his role, André Gide, used curious words: 'This is the result of theory ... This painting is entirely reasonable. It is even pedantic'.

At any rate the Fauves thoroughly outraged sensibilities which had only just learned to accept the work of Cézanne and Van Gogh. And this is strange. For the Fauves were more the last expression of essentially 19th-century attitudes than prophets of the new.

The origins of Fauvism are to be found in the early artistic development of Henri Matisee (1869–1954). After a brief unhappy stay in the studio of

Landscape at Collioure, *1905. Henri Matisse (Statens Museum for Kunst, Copenhagen).*
Not yet a Fauve work, Luxe *initiated a freedom of colour handling in Matisse which the study made at Collioure, in preparation for his large* Joie de Vivre *painting, shows clearly. Essentially Fauvist, this landscape sketch has a vivid directness and freshness rarely attained by minor Fauves such as Marquet, Manguin or Puy.*

Bougereau, a successful academician who specialized in large voluptuous nymphs, Matisse studied with the Symbolist, Gustave Moreau, who perhaps suprisingly was an inspiring teacher. Through Moreau, he met Albert Marquet (1875–1947), Henri-Charles Manguin (1874–1949), Charles Camoin (1879–1965) and Jean Puy (1876–1960). When Moreau died in 1898 the group dispersed, but Matisse's dominant personality inspired them to emulation when he returned from a trip to Corsica and the south of France with a number of strongly coloured canvases, which incidentally exhibited some Divisionist characteristics. By 1901 André Derain (1880–1954) and Maurice Vlaminck (1876–1958) were also members of the group. Until the Autumn Salon of 1905 they continued to paint strongly, even violently coloured canvases in-

fluenced by the Divisionist work of Signac, Seurat's disciple, and – Vlaminck especially – by Van Gogh.

Other influences were also at work during these years. Several exhibitions of interest to the Fauves took place in Paris in 1904: a memorial exhibition to Gauguin, an exhibition of French Primitives, a first show of Islamic art (greatly admired by Matisse), and a large retrospective of Manet, who was seen as one of the first to unite perception with subjective expression and technical originality. Gauguin was of special significance to them, not only for his work but for his independent character. Their increasing conviction that colour was the one essential expressive element led them to treat their traditional subject matter with scant regard for its normal characteristics. Tonal values, perspective, proportion – all were subordinated, although not

The Houses of Parliament, 1906. André Derain (Private Collection). Derain met Matisse in the studio of the academic painter Carrière and introduced him to Vlaminck, whom he knew from his birthplace, Chatou. These three, with Manguin and Rouault, exhibited the first Fauve paintings at the Autumn Salon of 1905. Derain was an enthusiastic Fauve until, like Braque, he was attracted to Cubism as a result of his devotion to Cézanne. He visited London in 1906 and completed a series of paintings based on the River Thames of which this is one.

entirely ignored, in their pursuit of colour. Colour, of course, not for its natural equivalent but for its emotional possibilities, as in Gauguin or Van Gogh. Since the Fauves were not a coherent, mutually compatible group (Matisse and Vlaminck rarely agreed about anything), their researches soon led them in different directions. During the brief Fauvist period Vlaminck was the most typical exemplar of the style.

Despite the difficulties that most people apparently had when confronted by the Fauves, for us Fauvism is the most accessible of all the movements. Its relationship to both Gauguin and Van Gogh is clear. So are the affinities with German Expressionism (Jawlensky and Kandinsky both exhibited in the Autumn Salon of 1905 and knew Matisse and Vlaminck), though the Fauves lack the sense of anguish always evident in their German contemporaries. They pre-

serve an attractive, French *joie de vivre*, a vital optimistic zest which is entirely absent from German Expressionism.

There is one aspect of Fauvism not yet mentioned, which arises more centrally in Cubism a few years later and plays a part in the whole revolution of the early 20th century. From Impressionism forward, consciousness of the picture as a surface had been growing. As distortion of forms became increasingly insistent, the possibility of viewing the work as a spatial reflection of visual experience was diminished. At the same time the surface treatment also became steadily more insistent. In the work of the Fauves, the use of colour as an independent, emotional part of a painting removed one more barrier to the acceptance of painting outside the traditional pattern.

Fauvism lasted for about two years, 1905–07; thereafter the individual

The Bridge at Chatou, *1906. Maurice Vlaminck (Musée de l'Annonciade, Saint-Tropez).*
Through his friendship with Derain, Vlaminck became an enthusiastic painter. His strong, abrasive personality responded to Van Gogh's linear technique and his first paintings at Chatou show this influence. The link between Van Gogh and Fauvism is clear in the early work of Vlaminck, who participated in the Autumn Salon of 1905.

The strong colour and linear build-up of his paintings during his Fauvist period gave way, as with Braque and Derain, to the influence of Cubism in 1908. His work became almost monochromatic and more structured. Later landscapes show Expressionist qualities, with an almost theatrical rendering of stormy skies, deep shadow and striking light effects.

La Rue Pavoisée (Street Decorated with Flags), 1906. Raoul Dufy (Private Collection).
An early convert to Fauvism through a visit to the Salon of 1905, Dufy recalled, 'I understood the new raison d'etre of painting and impressionist realism lost all its charm for me as I looked at this miracle of creative imagination at work in colour and line'. He had his first show in 1906 and exhibited seven works in the Salon of 1906 including the street scene with flags illustrated, which represents the celebrations of the 14th July. In 1908, working in close association with Braque, he abandoned Fauvism for a Cézannesque Cubism and a much reduced colour range.

48

painters pursued their separate careers. Most of them had exhausted their creative capabilities, but Braque and Derain turned to Cubism and their contribution to that movement was no less vital than their Fauvist work. Vlaminck in his later work turned towards a more violent and less colourful form of Expressionism. Raoul Dufy (1877–1953) temporarily adopted an elegant and decorative 'society' style.

It was mainly in the later work of Matisse that the possibilities inherent in Fauvism were pursued and the greatest creative achievements made. Matisse's subtle colour became a language parallel in importance to the different work of Picasso. He continued to enlarge his pictorial language long after the brief sensation of Fauvism had turned into history.

L'Estaque, 1906. Georges Braque (Musée de l'Annonciade, Saint-Tropez). Braque, Dufy and Othon Friesz came from Le Havre where they were friends from youth. All became Fauves. Like Dufy, Braque was excited by the Fauves in the Autumn Salon of 1905 and for a short time became an enthusiastic member of the group. Later he came to regard it as only a minor stage in his work. He was already interested in Cézanne, and after spending the early part of 1906 in Antwerp with Othon Friesz he went to the little port of L'Estaque in Provence where everything reminded him of the master. He painted a number of Fauvist works at L'Estaque, including this view. Already his work shows a structure and organization uncommon in Fauvist work, and although his colour is strong it is well balanced. It is, however, characteristic of Fauvism in that the use of colour serves to distract attention from the essentially traditional picture-box composition.

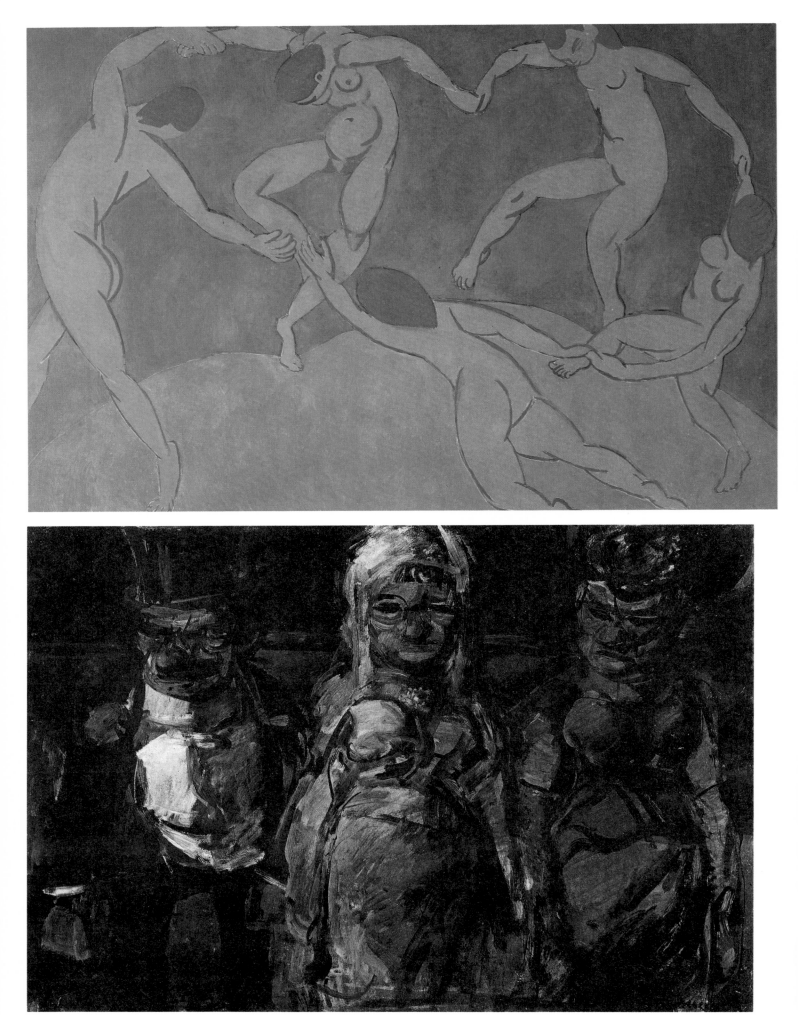

Opposite above:
The Dance, *1910. Henri Matisse
(State Hermitage Museum, Leningrad).
This was painted for the staircase of
Sergei Shchukin's house in Moscow.
Matisse explained that, 'entering the
house, the visitor sees the first flight of
stairs and the effort of climbing them
demands a feeling of release. The panel
therefore represents the dance, a ring
flung over a hilltop'. He had painted the
subject the previous year and in later
years was to return to it again. There is a
lyrical, abstract suggestion of movement
which illustrates Matisse's adoption of a
very different, more personal style than
that of the Cubists. From about this time
onward he remained separate from the
main movements in modern art, but his
total achievement was among the most
dedicated and uncompromising work of
this century.*

Opposite below:
The Bride (Aunt Sallys), *1907.
Georges Rouault (Tate Gallery, London).
Although he exhibited in the Autumn
Salon of 1905 with the Fauves,
Rouault's work can only be considered
Fauvist to the extent that it is highly
charged emotionally. In spirit and colour
he is closer to the German Expressionists.
His figures do not inhabit a happy world.
His coarse and heavy drawing is
nevertheless powerful and evocative, and
in his later work his thick black outlines
surrounding areas of strong colour show
his religious feeling and recall his training
as a stained-glass windowmaker.*

Above:
The Dessert, Harmony in Red, *1908.
Henri Matisse (State Hermitage
Museum, Leningrad).
This painting was exhibited in the
Autumn Salon of 1908 and bought by
Shchukin who, with Morosov, was one of
the great Russian collectors of modern art.
Their activities explain why so much
important early modern art is to be found
in Russia today (Shchukin owned 37
Matisses).*

The Dessert *indicates the direction
that Matisse took after the early stages of
Fauvism. The decorative control and
subtle colour became characteristic of his
painting, and his increasing command
over these elements is responsible for the
great authority of his later work. The
difference between this and the patterning
of the Nabis (for example) reveals Matisse
as more pointed, controlled, yet more
imaginative too.*

Les Demoiselles d'Avignon, 1907.
Pablo Picasso (The Museum of Modern Art, New York. Acquired through the Lillie P. Bliss Bequest).
So important has this painting been considered that it has sponsored a large and continuing volume of writing. It may justly be regarded as the work which, above all others, initiated the modern movements. Although Fauvism came earlier, it is through the innovations of the Demoiselles *that the modern aesthetic*

was launched.

The original sketches for the painting show that it began as a brothel scene involving a medical student, a sailor and five prostitutes. As the work progressed the student and sailor were removed and the women left in an undefined context of fractured forms. It has been noted that Picasso was here working out his own complex and contradictory emotional response to women, as well as incorporating new or existing aesthetic

enthusiasms such as medieval Catalan painting and African masks.

Although he hated the painting when he first saw it, Braque recognized that it broke new ground and his own interest in Cézannesque structure was quickly joined to Picasso's zest in establishing Cubism as the leading avant-garde movement.

Cubism

The main figures of Cubism are, firstly, Picasso and Braque, who were soon joined by Gris and Léger. The principal ideas, techniques and works belong to these four artists, although many others who were part of the Cubist movement for a time made individual contributions.

Between the years 1907, when Pablo Picasso (1881–1973) revealed his work *Les Demoiselles d'Avignon* to Georges Braque (1882–1963), and 1925, when the original inspiration had played itself out, Cubism, the central revolution of 20th-century art, dominated the creative thought of a generation of young painters, first in Paris and subsequently throughout Europe and America. Most art since then owes something to the extraordinary independence of mind shown initially by Picasso.

The tentacles of Cubism embraced other near-contemporary movements such as Futurism in Italy, Der Blaue Reiter Expressionism in Germany and the pre-Revolution artists in Russia. In England Vorticism, though influenced by Futurism, owed more to Cubism. In North America the Armory Show of 1913 introduced Cubism to a stunned public and resentful art community.

As we have observed, the art of the 20th century shows an apparent disdain for the history of art from the beginnings of the Renaissance in Italy to the academic art of the late 19th century. But even Fauvism had not abandoned the idea of the single-point image – the subject viewed from one place and one point in time. The revolutionary paintings of Picasso and Braque between 1908 and the beginning of the First World War had, to most viewers, no antecedents in art. They were seen, as innovations frequently are seen, as ludicrous and dangerous.

Undoubtedly they were revolutionary, but they were not without antecedents – in the work of Cézanne on the one hand and of African sculpture on the other.

A large selection of African sculptures had recently been exhibited in Paris (mainly from the French colonies). Their simplification of forms and the obvious lack of concern for actual appearance were attractive to a number of young artists in Paris, Picasso among them.

Cézanne was also the object of growing interest in Paris at this time. A retrospective exhibition of his work had stressed his simplification of form and his lack of ultimate concern for the actual appearance of nature. Cézanne and the African carvers combined to offer a release to the young artists from the tyranny of the whole tradition of painting in the West, which had increasingly concentrated upon the intellectual use of appearance as the foundation of art.

The origins of the Cubist revolution perhaps lie deeper even than this. Far-reaching propositions had recently been advanced concerning the nature of the universe and Man's place in it. Einstein had upset the established laws of physics; other scientists were exploring the structure of matter and were soon to split the atom. Darwin had seriously unsettled Man's view of his own uniqueness; Freud had posed disturbing questions about the mind; Marx's revolutionary political ideas had become a disruptive force in society and a threat to the security of property.

In these unsettled times, young artists, apart from any specifically artistic experience, were seeing the world with new eyes. A new century suggested a new start. If the accepted ideas concerning the most fundamental aspects of life were being proved inaccurate, it is not surprising that young artists wondered whether the fundamentals of painting and sculpture were not wrong too. Retrospectively, therefore, we can say that the revolution in art occurred just when it might have been expected.

The effects of the Cubist revolution were so far-reaching that its nature must be considered more fully than is necessary for any other 20th-century development. Without a grasp of its motives and of the reasons for its success, most of what has happened subsequently is incomprehensible.

Of course it must be said that the impact of Cubism, tremendous as it was, is not necessarily a justification of the path it took. The influence of Cubism has permeated the art of the 20th century but it has also inspired antagonism and rejection. As we shall see, hostility to Cubism was also a factor in subsequent aesthetic developments.

The Nature of Cubism. What then is the nature of this revolution? The word 'Cubism' is only vaguely descriptive of the art it identifies. Cubist painters do not paint in cubes. Nor is an often-quoted Cézanne letter as important in Cubist thought as is sometimes supposed. In 1904 Cézanne wrote to Emile Bernard, 'May I repeat what I told you here: treat nature by the cylinder, the sphere, the cone, everything in proper perspective so that each side of an object or plane is directed towards a central point'. Apart from the fact that Cézanne does not mention cubes, there is no suggestion that nature should be simplified in simple geometric shapes. More importantly, Cézanne was looking for the underlying structure of nature, as it could be translated on the plane of his picture. The important influence that Cézanne exerted was to suggest that the structure of the subject could be presented without illusionist space – without destroying the picture plane as a part of the painting. To Picasso and others it became important not to create a painting which created an effect of space and in the process removed any sense of the surface as the object being looked at. From Cubism on, painters have felt free to cover their surfaces with paint or other materials regardless of their being an illusion of something else. Among other things this is directly connected with all forms of abstraction, not only those that appear more or less obviously related to Cubism: Kandinsky and Mondrian share that derivation.

In the decades that have passed since Cubism first appeared it has become an increasingly popular subject of art-historical study. No episode in art history has been more frequently examined for sources, style, influences, etc. The effect has been perhaps to falsify the picture of what was actually happening at the time. For those who created it, Cubism was not, of course, part of serious, conscious, progressive art-historical development. To Picasso and Braque, it sprang from their exciting sense of freedom.

Unlike Futurism and some other movements, Cubism has no manifesto expressing the intentions of the artists involved, but some comments have been preserved. For example, Picasso called Cubism an intellectual game, and it is this sense of free activity rather than consciously directed experiment that their work between about 1908 and 1912 best expresses. That they made a number of pictorial discoveries is unquestionable. The exact nature of their discoveries, however, is not easily identified or described.

The importance of Cubism as a creative force lies in the nature of Cubist enquiry. Once the idea that painting need not be representational, however much historical, philosophical, emotional, propagandist or other matter was included or added, had been aired – as it had been, at least embryonically, by the Fauves – then anything was possible. It took many years to explore the possibilities thus opened; indeed, it might be said that the whole of the 20th century has been preoccupied with the question of what the visual arts may be about and how expressed, an inquiry that has included many dead ends and false trials, all enthusiastically promoted for a time.

Cubism now seems tentative by comparison with some later developments, which has encouraged art historians to propose rather more and closer links between Cubism and earlier periods than seem warranted: make no mistake, it was a revolution!

At first Cubism continued the tradition of drawing in paint on canvas. The colour adopted from 1909 for the landscape-based subjects and still-lifes owed something to Cézanne, which again has been seen as reinforcing a historical connection through Post-Impressionism back to Impressionism – and earlier. The images that Picasso, Braque, Juan Gris (1887–1927) and Fernand Léger (1881–1955) made were all paintings on canvas of traditional subject matter, for instance still-life or landscape – again continuing historical tradition – but the treatment was assuredly quite new.

The painting which by general consent initiates Cubism and has in consequence become one of the most important paintings in modern art is Picasso's *Les Demoiselles d'Avignon*. Started in 1906 and often altered before Picasso stopped work on it in 1907, it depicts a group of nude female figures in an indeterminate location. In the foreground is a roughly drawn still-life cameo consisting of a slice of melon, an apple, a pear and some grapes: this is the most consistently representational part of the painting. The human figures are distorted in the physical relationship of parts, in proportion and in spatial relationship. The background and the figures seem to have no proper spatial relationship either. The background advances as an object in relation to the figures. The treatment of the heads is also different. The two central figures, it has been noted, owe a lot to early medieval Catalan wall paintings (Picasso came from Catalonia) while the other three derive from African masks. These, particularly the pair on the right, were painted at a late stage. The origin of the subject and its title can be seen in a number of preliminary studies made by Picasso. The title comes from a notorious street of brothels in Barcelona, Avignon Street, although it was bestowed by Picasso's friend, André Salmon – in 1916 – and is said to have been disliked by Picasso. In any event it is only an identifying label. In earlier, traditional works the title frequently contributed to the understanding and importance of the work, but increasingly in modern art the identifying title is deliberately intended to give no guidance to content. In the case of the *Demoiselles* it is certainly no help.

Indeed, it is misleading. The critic and historian Leo Steinberg has used a term 'devenusation' to express a central point in the painting and its revolutionary character. By this he indicates the abandoning of the ideal of beauty which characterized the whole tradition of painting since the Renaissance. Picasso's young ladies threw the ideal, Classical tradition out of the window.

Picasso's famous painting treats a subject of traditional interest – the female nude – but in a brutal and disturbing manner. It is reasonable to ask to what purpose and to what end? Initially, at least, to no special end and with no clear purpose. Here we have a youthful, exuberant exploration of painting possibilities in a newly discovered jungle of ideas. It introduces the 'What if . . .?' approach which has been a common ingredient of art ever since.

The discoveries of Cubism following the *Desmoiselles* are based on undirected, intellectual exploration of treatment, with more or less traditional subject matter. Cubist paintings after 1908 are still-lifes, portraits, landscapes; all are in some degree figurative.

In the stage known as Analytical Cubism, which followed the *Desmoiselles*, natural forms were broken down into simpler angular elements which seemed to disturb the picture surface rather than to construct consistent forms in a pictorial space. The connection with Cézanne's spatial construction was frequently emphasized by the use of Cézannesque colour.

It was during this period that Picasso and Braque worked most closely together and Braque's *The Portuguese* is an example of their affinity. The effect is of an image made on paper that has been crumpled then flattened out again, emphasizing the surface of the paper. This emphasis on surface – on the painting as a painting – is the chief characteristic of Analytical Cubism.

It was Braque, the son of a house-painting contractor, familiar with the materials of his father's trade, who introduced the next stage. The rendering of surface textures with manufactured materials led, about 1911, to the application of the actual materials, wallpapers, veneerwoods, newsprint, etc. to the painting surface. This technique, known as collage, marks a new aspect of picture-making. In applying textured surface areas in juxtaposition, Picasso and Braque were making texture/pattern decorations in which spatial qualities derived from the shapes,

Seated Woman (Nude), *1909–10.*
Pablo Picasso (Tate Gallery, London).
The earlier, Analytical phase of Cubism is
represented in this work. The form,
although treated inconsistently in blocked
forms on a fractured background, can
easily be distinguished as a female nude in
an armchair by a window. The subject is
clearly less significant for the painter than
his treatment of it and the surface of the
canvas itself. The subject becomes part of
a structural rearrangement of the surface
into a closely knit organization. The
colour emphasizes the Cubist debt to
Cézanne, which is a distinguishing
feature of Analytical Cubism in the hands
of both Picasso and Braque.

The Portuguese, *1911. Georges Braque (Kunstmuseum, Basle).*
This painting represents the stage in Cubism which followed the Analytical phase (see previous illustration). Here, facets are manipulated over the surface of the canvas so that the subject – *a figure playing a mandolin – is submerged in a pattern of tilted and interlocked planes. In this painting, unlike Picasso's* Seated Nude, *the form is difficult to distinguish, only small elements emerging. The surface* design is closer to abstraction, and this form of Cubism has been described as Hermetic (sealed, enclosed). Painted at Ceret in a room near Picasso's, The Portuguese *is similar in style, content and colour to Picasso's 'Ma Jolie'.*

'Ma Jolie' (Woman with a Zither *or* Woman with a Guitar), *1911–12.* Pablo Picasso (Museum of Modern Art, New York. Acquired through the Lillie P. Bliss Bequest).

Like Braque's The Portuguese, *the subject of this work is a figure with a guitar (or zither). The elements are difficult to read but the song title 'Ma Jolie' and the treble clef identify its nature as musical and there are other small items that may be discerned. The composition is an example of the stage of Analytical Cubism sometimes called Hermetic.*

Still Life Before an Open Window,
1915. Juan Gris (Philadelphia Museum
of Art. Louise and Walter Arensberg
Collection).
Of all the early Cubists Gris is the most
careful constructor of integrated,
balanced, geometrical work. A controlled

if not inspirational colourist he puts
together a counterpoint of pattern on a
geometric base which makes his work
more easily accessible and more
'comfortable' than that of the other
Cubists. Even when highly complicated,
his work seems to follow an intellectual

course. The elements of the composition —
balcony, utensils, newspaper, etc. — are
clearly distinguishable.
His early death deprived Cubism of the
one painter who had the discipline and
dedication to explore its pictorial
possibilities with clarity.

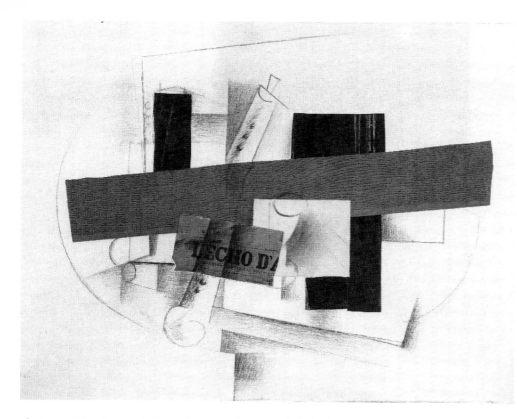

Clarinet, *1913. Georges Braque
(Museum of Modern Art, New York.
Nelson A. Rockefeller Bequest).
This elegant collage shows how far
towards a decorative use of shapes and
patterning Braque had gone by 1913.
The combination of chalk and charcoal
with pasted paper and newsprint (which
has yellowed in time to alter somewhat the
tonal balance of the composition) is
handled with assurance and a command
of spatial relationships that is surprising
in a new method. At this time Braque's
collages were more controlled than
Picasso's but less aggressively exploratory.*

their positioning and the colour, and not (as traditionally) from the observation of tonal relationships, perspective, etc. The effect of this was again to increase the emphasis on the surface as subject.

In 1911 the first combined display of Cubist work was shown at the Salon des Indépendants. In Room 41, which has come to identify the whole show, appeared most of those who had produced Cubist work, other than Picasso and Braque. They included Gris, Léger, Jean Metzinger (1883–1957), Albert Gleizes (1881–1953) and Robert Delaunay (1885–1941). Predictably they were fiercely attacked in the press. The criticism generated intense interest and the show was crowded. Cubism became the *avant-garde* fashion.

Cubism changed the idea of what a work of art could be more than any other of the early modern movements. The latter suggested various new directions, but the destruction of the philosophy of representation as the necessary precondition of picture-making was the work of the Cubists. As the real driving force, Picasso was the extrovert proselytizer, Braque the careful, creative constructor of images. The reputation of Picasso in popular imagination as the premier representative of modern art is therefore not unjustified. His present somewhat reduced status is temporary.

After 1911 Cubism spread beyond France, and its influence became apparent in already established movements while helping to inspire or direct new ones. Cubism made an appearance in German Expressionism (in the Blaue Reiter exhibition in Munich), in the first real Futurist work, in English Vorticism, in studios in Berlin, Zurich, London and Moscow, as well as its city of origin, Paris.

The influence of Cubism was seen in the United States in the work of Stanton Macdonald Wright and Morgan Russell, followers of Delaunay, in 1912. From 1913 to 1920 they developed their Synchromist movement, from which the only early American modern movement developed. 'In our painting colour becomes the generating function.'

The documentation and critical evaluation of the aims and achievements of the Cubist revolution are voluminous and pervasive in writing on art. Since Fauvism was still largely bound by picture-making of a traditional order, Cubism must be acknowledged as the decisive force which finally broke with the past and looked only forward.

Additionally, the universal acceptance of Cubism by *avant-garde* artists initiated the continuing schism which has been a feature of art theory throughout this century. Every critic, writer and indeed artist or sculptor has been analyzed for basic allegiances before his work is evaluated. This has caused difficulties for those who have not wished to take sides.

The Violin, 1914. Pablo Picasso
(Musée National d'Art Moderne, Centre
Georges Pompidou, Paris).
This painting represents an extension of
Picasso's work in collage. Here the shapes
of cutout textures are themselves
simulated in paint. The freedom of
Picasso's imagination suggested to him
that once the clear-cut pattern possibilities
of assembled collage are achieved there is
no reason why the effect should not be
realized in the traditional painting form,
without cutout shapes. The violin is only
schematically expressed but its general
shape is much more clearly identified than
that of the guitar in earlier Analytical
Cubist examples.

Bottle, Glass and Pipe, *1914. Georges*
Braque (Private Collection).
The close integration here between the
piece of simulated panelling, newsprint
and drawn objects again shows Braque's
mastery in handling abstract elements in
a composition. Braque's familiarity with
printed textures through his father's
decorating firm was important in the
development of Cubist collage.

The Wedding, 1912. Fernand Léger
(Musée National d'Art Moderne, Paris).

This painting is untypical of Léger's later
work but it represents a form of
Analytical Cubism that comes close to
Futurism in its repetition of forms. The
structure and content of the painting can
be more easily disentangled than most
Analytical Cubist work and there are
suggestions of spatial representation as
well as of simplification of form that echo
qualities in Léger's later, 'tubular'
paintings.

Dancer in a Café, 1912. Jean
Metzinger (1883–1956) (Albright-
Knox Art Gallery, Buffalo, New York.
General Purchase Funds, 1957).
In this painting Metzinger shows the
influence of Futurist ideas. With Albert
Gleizes he had published the first attempt
by painters to analyze the nature of
Cubism and he had been excited by the
first Futurist manifesto when it appeared
in 1909. He knew Severini, and his
work was for a time highly regarded by
Boccioni, the most perceptive of the
Futurists. His Dancer in a Café has
many similarities with Severini's dancer
in Dynamic Hieroglyphic of the Bal
Tabarin, although the sequential
movement of the figure in Severini's
painting is not seen here. Metzinger's
qualities as a decorative Cubist and his
acute sense of colour are evident here.

Above:
Little Girl at the Piano, *1912. Jacques
Villon (Museum of Modern Art, New
York).*

Right:
Woman at the Piano, *1914. Albert
Gleizes (Philadelphia Museum of Art.
Louise and Walter Arensberg Collection).*

These two paintings of similar subjects adopt very different Cubist solutions. The charming lyricism of line and delicacy of colour in Villon has a truly muscial quality, even suggesting in its points of strong colour emphatic notes of music. Apart from the somewhat coarse treatment of the head, the integration of line with form in a vertical, flowing pattern makes this painting one of the most appealing of all Cubist works.

Gleizes's painting, on the other hand, is unresolved and the forms are unintegrated to the extent that an awkward struggle seems to be taking place between natural space and a formal idea of pictorial structure. In the same way that Villon was unsuccessful in resolving the Cubist problems of the head, Gleizes has avoided a solution with the hand resting on the keyboard.

Orphism. By 1913 new tendencies and directions were appearing. The Analytical phase of Cubism had given way to the Synthetic phase, though there is no clear division and Picasso often combined both varieties in the same work. The difference was aptly explained by Gris; Cubism is 'synthetic' when the artist progresses from bottle to cylinder. Synthetic Cubism was more colourful (the earlier works were mostly in monotone), and even more two-dimensional.

Among the new developments was Orphism, the creation of Robert Delaunay, which owed its name to the writer, Guillaume Apollinaire. It was, broadly, an abstract version of Analytical Cubism – the first significant pure abstraction stemming from the Cubist revolution. Delaunay was convinced that the Cubist colour range was too limited, and depended unreasonably on identification of subject matter. This led him to his own theory of

'Simultaneous Contrasts'.

Delaunay propounded his belief in an art founded on the concept of light as the simultaneous contrast of colour. The impact of the colour itself, particularly in his series of disc paintings, was sufficient for him. He and his wife Sonia Terk Delaunay were, however, the sole members of the Orphist 'group', though the Czech painter, František Kupka (1871–1957) was linked with Delaunay. Kupka's geometric abstractions of 1910 are among the first examples of pure abstraction. Moody, with carefully orchestrated colour, they are some of the most attractive of early abstract works.

Above:
Ranging Verticals, *1912–13.*
František Kupka (Musée National d'Art Moderne, Paris).
A Czech painter whose early training was in Bohemia, he moved to Paris at the age of 25 and remained there for the rest of

his life, participating in the development of the modern aesthetic and becoming one of the pioneers of nonfigurative (abstract) painting. Pursuing his own vision of an independent geometric abstraction, much as Mondrian did but with different results, he became an isolated figure who eventually arrived at a serene abstraction of balance and lyrical harmony.

Right:
Circular Forms, *1912–13. Robert Delaunay (Musée National d'Art Moderne, Paris).*
Influenced first by Gauguin and later by Seurat, whose interest in colour theories led Delaunay to Chevreul's examination of simultaneous contrast in colour, his own method of abstract colour composition, known as Orphism, is really an extension of Cubism. Delaunay had adopted Cubism as a result of his enthusiasm as for Cézanne. He explored the possibility of nonfigurative painting at the same time as Kupka, Mondrian, Kandinsky and Malevich.

66

Cubist Sculpture. Although Cubism was initially a movement in painting, during its Synthetic stage a number of sculptors contributed to its development. Picasso and Braque themselves produced Cubist sculptures and Picasso's *Head of a Woman* (1909) is a carefully worked-out early example. The major work of Raymond Duchamp-Villon (1876–1918), *The Horse*, displays both Cubist and Futurist ideas. Altogether, the sculptors who explored Cubist possibilities, although few in number, made a considerable contribution.

Picasso's work was always very closely integrated in the pattern of his life. It is, more than any other artist, the day-to-day expression of his emotions and responses. The historical, traditional artistic practice demanded an ordered and steady development of style which usually makes it possible to identify a work chronologically in an artist's development. Even with such modern masters as Matisse and Braque such development can be observed. With Picasso it is not possible.

The sculpture and ceramics that he produced from about 1905 to the end of his life are as closely connected with his moods and needs of expression as are his paintings. Given his unbounded energy, it is not surprising that he left a large number of sculptural works, yet it is difficult to relate them directly to parallel trends in his painting. His sculpture on any one day was not necessarily an extension of his painting on that day, or vice-versa. His sculpture is best examined as a separate activity.

Firstly, it should be noted that there is a playfulness about much of his sculptural work that gives it charm at a time when his painting is more demanding. From his early Cubist sculptures, he moved to Surrealist images and a form of biomorphic rearrangement of human parts. In such sculptures as *Bull's Head*, a bicycle seat and handlebars ('I would like to think that a future generation would find this and decide that the sculpture could be used to provide a bicycle seat and handlebars'), and the *Monkey with Young*, the head made from a model car part, the work springs from the constant curiosity of his visual sense. There is no direct precedent for these evocative works. His use of colour and raw

Head of a Woman (Fernande), *1909. Bronze. Pablo Picasso (Museum of Modern Art, New York).*
During 1908 Picasso painted a number of Cubist portraits of Fernande Olivier, his mistress, and in the autumn of that year he made this Cubist sculpture, constructed from the portraits. The work,

16¼ in (413 mm) high is a three-dimensional translation of the Analytical Cubism with which he was currently preoccupied. It is a relatively restrained work which does not show the great plastic inventiveness characteristic of some of Picasso's later sculpture.

materials, iron sheeting, cardboard, clay, plastics, etc., again has no sculptural precedent. As in painting, his approach is uniquely his. It is partly for this reason that his place in 20th-century art is impossible to categorize. His fame in his lifetime was greater than that of any other artist in history, for in sculpture as in painting and drawing his work frequently makes his contemporaries seem pedestrian and plodding. It is difficult to envisage anyone achieving in his or her own lifetime the degree of supremacy Picasso disarmingly commanded.

The Spaniard Julio Gonzalez (1876–1942), although one of the oldest, came late to Cubism. He had known Picasso in Barcelona and met him again when he moved to Paris in 1900. At this time Gonzalez was a painter, like his brother Jean, whose death in 1908 so disturbed him that he became a recluse. Eventually he

adopted sculpture, with strong Cubist characteristics, working with hammered metal.

Henri Laurens (1885–1954), Ossip Zadkine (1890–1967), Alexander Archipenko (1887–1964) and Jacques Lipchitz (1891–1973) are the principal first-generation Cubist sculptors. Laurens achieved a mature Cubist style in which his great craftsmanship and love of materials (he had trained as an ornamental stone-carver) helped to give his work an authority often missing from more adventurous experiments.

Of both the Russian Archipenko and the Lithuanian Lipchitz, it could be said that their work does not so much explore Cubist possibilities as construct careful pastiches of pictorial elements. Their most important contribution is made in their later work.

Zadkine, also born in Russia, studied in England before settling in Paris in

The Horse, 1914. Bronze. Raymond Duchamp-Villon (Museum of Modern Art, New York. Van Gogh Purchase Fund).

The brothers Marcel Duchamp, Jacques Villon and Raymond Duchamp-Villon all contributed importantly to the development of the modern aesthetic. Duchamp-Villon was primarily a sculptor. A victim of the First World War, he died before his talent had fully matured, but in The Horse *he produced one of the seminal Cubo-Futurist works. Like Epstein's* Rock Drill, *this represents mechanized society in a dynamic abstraction of natural animal energy.*

1909. Whilst his work retained Cubist elements throughout his career, there were strong Expressionist overtones after 1920. The sense of strength in the relationship of forms makes Zadkine perhaps the most interesting of the Cubist sculptors.

Expressionism

Expressionism was predominantly a German movement and included virtually an entire generation of artists. There were two schools of German Expressionism, Die Brücke ('the Bridge'), centred in Dresden, and Der Blaue Reiter ('the Blue Rider'), in Munich. Additionally there were a number of artists unattached to either group whose work can nevertheless be described as Expressionist. (The term 'expressionist' can also of course be applied to many kinds of art having little in common with the specific movement we are considering here.)

There are clear affinities between Expressionism in Germany and Fauvism in France, and both followed from the dissatisfaction of leading Post-Impressionists with the lack of emotional commitment shown by their predecessors, the Impressionists. The differences, no less obvious than the affinities, are partly, it is often suggested, a matter of differing national characteristics. There is perhaps inherent in German history and art a spirit of universal anxiety or *angst*, to use the German word for it, which, artistically, is manifest in an uncomfortable mistrust of elegance. A strong and puritanical conscience, a sense of life as a struggle, a foreboding awareness of mortality – these appear to be particularly German characteristics. At any rate they are not noticeably French ones.

One can see this characteristic in German art from Dürer in the Renaissance up to 19th-century artists such as the fantasist Arnold Böcklin (1827–1901). In the work of painters like Christian Rohlfs (1849–1938) and Lovis Corinth (1858–1925), contemporaries of the Expressionists, we see the same high emotional charge evident in Expressionist work (Rohlfs, indeed, eventually became a kind of Expressionist himself). More influential than any German precursor, however, was the extraordinary and tragic Norwegian painter, Edvard Munch (1863–1944).

Munch's relationship with modern German painting has been likened to Cézanne's in respect of French painting: he both indicates the path and travels on it. Munch spent the last years of the 19th and the first years of the 20th century in melancholy wandering around Germany. From his earlier experience of Parisian Symbolism and his own tragic Norwegian background he developed an art of neurotic and morbid emotionalism, preoccupied with death and isolation. Influenced by the philosophy of Nietzsche and Kierkegaard, his analyses of modern man's plight suggest all the doubt and anxiety of a sensitive spiritual soul in a hostile, materialistic world.

Munch's powerful influence on the young German painters, particularly the Bridge group (though they imbibed more of his spirit than his style), inclined them towards that agonized view which reflects the doubt and foreboding of the new century rather than its opportunist enthusiasm. Most of them knew Munch personally, but their uneasy, taut and forceful style owed much to the German tradition. The graphic art of the woodcut, of which Dürer was the first great master, gave the inspiration for harsh images. The general situation in prewar Germany also suggested plenty of reasons for disquiet.

In the words of Carl Schmidt-Rottluff (1884–1976), the name 'the Bridge' suggests the means 'to draw all revolutionary and fermenting elements to itself', a path to the young artists of the future. It is a feature of all the early modern movements that their members believed themselves to represent the future. In the case of the Bridge, this view was not unreasonable, for not only were they the first 20th-century German revolutionaries, but their inspiration permeated the future art of Germany and had an extensive influence throughout Europe.

Besides Schmidt-Rottluff, the original members of the group in 1905 were Ernst Ludwig Kirchner (1880–1938), Erich Heckel (1883–1970) and Fritz Bleyl. They were all architectural students with an interest in painting which soon became dominant; only Bleyl became a professional architect. They were joined by Max Pechstein (1881–1955), Otto Mueller (1874–1930) and Emil Nolde (1867–1956). Although more closely associated with the Blue Rider group in Munich, Alexei von Jawlensky (1864–1941) painted works very close to the Bridge in character.

The Bridge maintained an interest in traditional subject matter and, in close affinity with Fauvism, retained clear figuration. The strong line of the woodcut, which was seen as a separate and powerful art form, influenced the paintings of the group – and thereby distinguished them from the Fauves.

Bridge colour moreover was usually more strident than Fauvist, often concentrating on the use of complementaries. At that time the label 'Expressionist' marked both schools, suggesting an opposition to Impressionism; only later did the name become identified as the specifically German emotional language of the Bridge group.

The later Blue Rider (Der Blaue Reiter) group is distinguished from the Bridge by their exploration of the subjective potential of Cubism. Centred in Munich in 1911, the Blue Rider was led by Wassily Kandinsky (1866–1944) and Franz Marc (1880–1916). Other important members were Paul Klee (1879–1940), August Macke (1887–1914) and Gabriele Munter (1877–1962). A less unified group than the Bridge, its members were more open to international influences, and both Cubism and Futurism had an evident effect on their work. The name Blue Rider appears to have been concocted by Kandinsky and Marc since, as Kandinsky put it, 'We both loved blue; Marc loved horses and I riders; thus the name arose by itself'. There was a mystical, spiritual aspect

of the art of the Blue Rider group
which gave their use of Cubism and
Futurism a sense of internal purpose
not evident in Fauvist work and entirely different from the movements it
derived from. Kandinsky was the
dominant spirit; in his essay *Concerning
the Spiritual in Art*, written in 1910
and published in French in 1912 (first
English publication 1914), he issued
one of the most important and intellectually influential documents of the
modern movements. Like Jawlensky,
Kandinsky came from Russia and
brought with him something of the
deep sense of mysticism which is often
identified with that great nation and
seen in other Russians, such as Marc
Chagall (1887–1985).

Between this and Marc's sympathy
with the natural world was great
affinity, while the sensitive and acute
temperament of Gabriele Munter,
Kandinksy's mistress, and the enormous
vitality of Jawlensky provided the basis
for the group's eager exploration of the
possibilites of abstraction as a means of
identifying and capturing their spiritual
response to the natural world.

The Dance of Life, 1899–1900.
Edvard Munch (Nasjonalgalleriet, Oslo).
*Munch's influence on the course of
German Expressionism was profound, and
although he was not a member of either
Expressionist group he exhibits many of
their characteristics. His tragic life made
him a pessimistic and introspective figure
with a Nordic seriousness which accorded
well with the strong emotional content of
all Expressionist work.*

*The Dance of Life, infused with
symbolism, is built up with heavy,
contained forms and strident, clashing
colours. The fresh young enthusiasm of the
girl in white (already stained with blood?)
is contrasted with her worldly-wise self on
the right, in distressful black,
contemplating with despair or disgust the
merging figures of the central dancers. A
disturbing work of great power, it heralds
the cultural angst of Germany before the
First World War.*

The Artist and Model, 1907. Ernst Ludwig Kirchner (Kunsthalle, Hamburg). Kirchner was the leader of the Bridge group by sheer force of personality. His uncompromising view of the realities of life can be seen even in his less intense works. In this painting Kirchner, the artist, looks at a mirror with the canvas arranged off left. What he sees of the unwilling and anxious model does not give him pleasure and the strident oppositions of colour in primaries and complementaries make for a composition of emotional complexity.

Professor Will Grohmann has described the vivid experience in which Kandinsky first saw the emotional possibilities of abstraction. 'One day at twilight, he came into his studio and suddenly saw an "indescribably beautiful painting, permeated by an inner glow." He saw in it nothing but forms, no subject matter at all. It was a picture he seemed to have made. The next day the spell was gone and he recognized the objects represented in it with painful distinctness. "Now I know for certain that the object harms my paintings." He had regarded the object as indispensable but now he realised the "ends (and hence also the means) of nature and art differ essentially, organically and by virtue of a universal law",' as he described it.

Landscape, Lofthus, Norway, *1911. Karl Schmidt-Rottluff (Kunsthalle, Hamburg).*
This landscape, almost Fauvist in its colour and simplification of form, nevertheless – because of its strong opposition of colour and heavy formal shapes – carries a strong emotional content which places it in the German Expressionist school. Schmidt-Rottluff was an original member of the Bridge and gave the group its name. He remained throughout his long life essentially an Expressionist, though in his later work there are elements of Symbolism and mysticism, particularly in a well-known series of religious woodcuts.

The Harbour, *1922. Max Pechstein (Stedelijk Museum, Amsterdam).*
A violent emotionalism invests this painting, in which the strong colour contrasts and the crude representational drawing work together to produce an image of brooding power. Although at first sight it has many Fauvist characteristics, there is nothing of the lightness and sophistication of Fauvism in this work. Pechstein was accepted by the public, unlike other members of the Bridge group, since the naturalism of his drawing was more accessible. This led to a certain spurious facility in his later work.

Henceforward for Kandinsky the question was not 'What does it mean?' in visually logical or intellectually coherent terms but, 'What does it do in perceptual experience to my physiological and psychological makeup – what aspect of the spirit does it touch?'

Marc did not aspire to the degree of complete abstraction that became characteristic of Kandinsky. In a painting such as *Fighting Forms* he came very near it, but there is still a sense of large if scarcely identifiable animals in mighty combat.

The Blue Rider carried the Cubist revolution into a new dimension. The protean imagination of Picasso was neither reflective nor spiritual: Cubism for him was a powerful intellectual exercise. For Braque, more reflective, it was an opportunity to discover a new and subtle world of colour. For neither man did it suggest the opportunity for a spiritual expression. Much has been made of Kandinsky's idea of the 'inner

necessity to create' as part of the essential artistic element; it is clear that for him that inner necessity was spiritual in origin.

The painting of Jawlensky shows something of the same spiritual nature, but his joy in colour and his absorption with the human form, and the human head, constrained him to more figurative work, closer to the Fauves.

As observed above, neither the Bridge nor the Blue Rider members thought of themselves as 'German Expressionists', the term 'Expressionist' first being applied to the Fauves and their associates. It was only when an essentially German emotional character was ascribed to them that they acquired the name.

The various breakaway groups in Germany known as the Secessionists (see page 39) contributed towards this emergence of a thoroughly German school by creating, on the eve of the formation of the Bridge group, an

The Windmill, *1924. Emil Nolde (Stiftung Seebüll Ada und Emil Nolde, Neukirchen).*
Nolde's subtle and sensitive compositions have a psychological sense of rightness for the subject, his colour is balanced and inventive, his draughtsmanship is strong and keenly observational. Of all the Expressionists he seems most able to express his emotions in a controlled pictorial form without over-theatrical treatment.

Peonies, *1909. Alexei von Jawlensky (Von der Heydt-Museum der Stadt, Wuppertal).*
Jawlensky was Russian and studied first in Moscow, but by 1903 he was in Paris and in 1905 painted in Brittany, showing a number of his Breton paintings in the Autumn Salon of 1905 which inaugurated Fauvism. He was essentially a colourist, with a strong decorative sense, and many of his works are close to Fauvism. Peonies is one of his most popular works. Although employing the complementaries of red and green as the *main elements of the painting, he has combined them without the strident opposition that characterizes much Expressionist painting. His great admiration for Nolde links him with the Bridge group.*

Black Lines, *1913. Wassily Kandinsky (Solomon R. Guggenheim Museum, New York).*
One of the central figures in the development of 20th-century abstraction, Kandinsky's importance is not confined to his contribution as a member of the Blue Rider group. Founded by him in collaboration with Franz Marc, it was nevertheless the most important development in Germany, the bedrock of modern German art.

It is important to note that Kandinsky represents one attitude to abstraction – its availability as a subjective, free expression of an emotional state or sequence. His progress towards this freedom took him through many disparate experiments, some in combinations of forms defined and derived from natural sources, others, like Black Lines, *composed of floating forms crossed by aimless lines, bursting with some undisciplined energy but capturing a real if amorphous feeling. It was in this*

form of abstract construction that Kandinsky first expressed himself; later, the forms took on a more geometric structure seemingly placed on a flat ground.

Fighting Forms, 1914. Franz Marc (Staatsgalerie moderner Kunst, Munich). Marc was influenced by Cubism and his earlier Blue Rider works often depict animals in a simple, blocked, Cubist form. He was fascinated by animals and the forces of nature, and his work attempts to express through the unifying Cubist method the unity and force of nature. In the example illustrated the animal forms are abstracted so that they convey only a sense of antagonism and struggle, while the colour carries conscious emotional overtones derived from theories of colour worked out by Macke and Marc.

Marc explained his progress to abstraction: 'I felt human form to be ugly from an early stage, animals seemed to be more beautiful, purer; but I came to discover in them so much that was repulsive and ugly that my depiction of them. . .became more schematic, more abstract.'

Landscape with Cows and Camel (detail), 1914. August Macke (Kunsthaus, Zurich).
Marc and Macke were close friends who shared ideas on the nature of painting. Marc's romantic Expressionism, however, was not intellectually controlled enough for Macke's taste. An almost rigid structural grid and an adherence to theory distinguish his work from Marc's. Both were killed in the First World War, Macke a month after the war began, Marc in 1916. Macke would surely have made a very significant contribution to German painting had he lived.

The Cows and Camel is based on a clear, diamond-form grid, with strict organization of colour and structure in contrast to the strong emotional content of Expressionist work generally.

Overleaf:
Yellow, Red, Blue, 1925. Wassily Kandinsky (Musée National d'Art Moderne, Paris).
This painting, one of the most important works of its period, is a synthesis of Kandinsky's ideas of colour, shape and line at that time. The three centres located in the primary colours are different in character, the red and blue in joined conflict, the earthy yellow serene. Characteristic of the form of abstraction that his beliefs inspired, it makes an

interesting comparison with a painting by Mondrian with a similar title. In Mondrian's work the title explains the colours used. Apart from black lines and white areas it is a red, yellow and blue painting. In the Kandinsky a full range of colour appears. He is dealing only in preponderances, tendencies and influences, to produce an emotional free-association pattern; not for him the rigours and austerities of Mondrian's aesthetic.

A Young Lady's Adventure, 1922. Watercolour. Paul Klee (Tate Gallery, London).
In this painting, which includes elements of Surrealism, the abstraction is of a different order from that found in Kandinsky. Klee, one of the great masters of modern art, is concerned to reincarnate experience in a visible form. This results in the widening of the division between his own being and nature, which gives him a conviction of 'under-existence', and the idea of 'creation as a genesis beneath the surface of the work'. His paintings generally use recognizable forms but with what has sometimes been wrongly considered a childish disregard for real relationships.

Portrait of the Artist's Parents, *1924.*
Otto Dix (Sprengel Museum, Hanover).
Dix was aware of all the modern
developments both in Germany and in
Paris and at different times used elements
from most of them. Cubism formed a
constant aspect of his later work. He was,
however, essentially a German
Expressionist disturbed by the war and its
aftermath, and there is a strong element
of protest in much of his work. In this
portrait of his parents the harsh reality of
the presentation accords with his
uncompromising vision.

Metropolis, *1917. George Grosz*
(Museum of Modern Art, New York).
Grosz's Expressionism was both
stylistically and emotionally different from
either of the main German groups and
from others working in Germany in the
war and postwar period. A deeply
disillusioned man, he saw humanity as
essentially bestial and the city of Berlin as
a sink of depravity and deprivation, its
streets crowded with unprincipled
profiteers, prostitutes, war-crippled dregs
and a variety of perverts. A Communist,
his feeling of social outrage stimulated him
to produce the most biting and
disillusioned drawings and paintings to
emerge from the First World War – and
perhaps any war. His work is loaded with
symbols of social class and economic
status: the bowler hat, the stocking and
garter, the medal, the duelling scar are all
telling points in the reading of the work.

atmosphere in which new beginnings were possible. The inclusion of all kinds of artists – architects, graphic artists, workers in decorative arts, as well as painters and sculptors, and contact with other Europeans such as Charles Rennie Mackintosh in Glasgow, Henri van der Velde in Belgium and the Paris Maison Moderne group created an open, international climate which later helped to give a number of German painters independent of the main Expressionist groups a European voice.

Of these the most significant are Max Beckmann (1884–1950), Oskar Kokoschka (1886–1980), George Grosz (1893–1959), Otto Dix (1891–1969) and the sculptor Ernst Barlach (1870–1938).

Beckmann achieved his most important work after his release from the army in 1915, following a nervous breakdown. Like most Expressionists he wanted to 'penetrate as deeply as possible into the fundamentals of nature, into the soul of things'. The horrifying visions of war in which people are puppets, casually ignored and jettisoned, is reflected in his distorted images of marionette-like figures who can, it seems, only register one emotion at a time – and the dominant

emotion is fear. Beckmann's art is tortured and joyless, but direct and powerful; his treatment is basically traditional.

Grosz and Dix shared Beckmann's disgust with war and its aftermath: with surgical precision they exposed grafters, exploiters, prostitutes and profiteers of the Weimar Republic during the gross inflationary years following the war. Appropriately known as the New Objectivity, their work is perhaps the most ferocious dissection of human weakness in the whole of 20th-century art. The inherent and ingrained German *angst*, together with the characteristic harshness and angularity of much German art, painting, sculpture and print-making, from the time of Dürer and Grunewald is allied here with passionate and dedicated protest.

Kokoschka by comparison seems almost lyrical, although his emotional nature is expressed in a nervous brush stroke that has an Expressionist lack of confidence in the future. It is the pervading feeling of anguish approaching despair, so characteristic of the German Expressionists, that gives them an earnestness and strength and makes much of the abstract work of their European contemporaries seem merely elegant and superficial.

The Tempest, *1914. Oskar Kokoschka (Kunstmuseum, Basle). Kokoschka's position in German Expressionism is isolated and unique. An artist of great power and energy, he commanded a fine technical ability with a nervous sensibility of line to produce some of the most powerful works in pre- and postwar Germany.*

The Tempest (also called The Bride of the Wind) *celebrates a famous love affair with an extraordinary lady, the great femme fatale of prewar Germany, Alma Schindler, who married Mahler, had affairs with a number of artists including Klimt and Kokoschka, later married Gropius and indirectly had a lasting effect on art education through her introduction to Gropius of Johannes Itten. The painting, Kokoschka's last important work before the war, is a summation of his total output to that stage. After a terrible war in which he was nearly killed, his work continued to show the same nervous energy but perhaps not quite the intensity of insight of his prewar painting.*

Self-Portrait, 1914. Max Beckmann (Bayerische Staatsgemäldesammlungen, Munich).

Like George Grosz, Beckmann felt depressed resentment at the nature of man as revealed by his traumatic war experiences. Brutality, self-interest, amorality presented themselves to him as the essentials of human nature, and in this searching self-portrait he expressed his sense of alienation with uncompromising directness.

Futurism

Futurism, as its name suggests, is dedicated to the idea of an art for the future and as such might be supposed to refer to all *avant-garde* art. In fact it is the name for a specifically Italian movement.

Futurism starts with the activities of an extraordinary, extrovert, literary figure, Emilio Filippo Tommaso Marinetti (1877–1944), an Italian poet, born in Egypt, educated in Paris; wealthy by birth and aggressive by nature. In the February 1909 issue of the journal *Le Figaro* he published the founding manifesto of Futurism, a document of violent polemics and aggressive language. He extolled the beauty of speed, the virility of the new machine-based society, the possibilities inherent in the nascent scientific age of a new dynamic humanism. Following a violently descriptive introduction in which Marinetti romanticizes a headlong drive in the most powerful Fiat then made across the night countryside (which ends with the car upside down in a muddy ditch and Marinetti and his friends 'torn, filthy and stinking'), the article outlines what the poetry of the future should contain: 'We shall chant the love of danger . . . Courage, audacity and revolt will be the essential elements in our poetry. . . life at the double, with somersaults, slaps and punches . . . The magnificence of the world has been enriched by the new beauty, the beauty of speed . . . A racing car is . . . more beautiful than the Winged Victory of Samothrace . . . We will glorify war . . . We will destroy museums, libraries and academies, and will combat moralism, feminism and all vile opportunist utilitarianism.'

This uncomprising condemnation of the past and lurid embrace of the future did not fail to find a response in many young men. A wild irresponsibility in action and public gesture soon attached itself to Marinetti, who became the enthusiastic propagandist for a new, as yet unrealized, art.

The first manifesto of the Futurist painters appeared under his influence in 1910. It was signed by Umberto Boccioni (1882–1916), Carlo Carra (1881–1966), Luigi Russolo (1885–1947), Giacomo Balla (1871–1958) and Gino Severini (1883–1966). They became the leading Futurist artists, and in the same year they published a 'technical manifesto' of Futurist paintings. Marinetti was a ringmaster with international ambitions and during the next four years, until the outbreak of the First World War, he took his Futurist circus around Europe, including Russia where his message was received with more enthusiasm than most other places. On the whole the circus met with the ridicule that its activities deliberately invited. Throughout these years the group and their sympathizers published manifestoes on many subjects offering a Futurist view on such subjects as food, women, clothes, photography, sculpture, the cinema, music, theatre and, in 1914, perhaps the most interesting, on architecture – an imaginative piece by Antonio Sant' Elia.

There is no difficulty in identifying the intentions of the Futurists, nor in approving of at least some of them. It is not as easy to admire the art that they produced, with the exception of a few extraordinary works mostly from Boccioni.

The difficulty, of course, was how to fulfil the laudable desire to provide art appropriate to the future when, according to the Futurists, the foundations of all art lay in a totally irrelevant concern for the past, as represented above all by the ludicrous Italian reverence for the art of the Renaissance. For them Venice, Florence and Rome were the most depressing cities in Italy; their hearts lay in Turin and Milan, where mighty factories hummed. Another minor problem: how was their art to be seen if the galleries and museums were to be destroyed?

Worst of all, of course, there was, they supposed, no form of art available to them that could reflect their ideas. The closest approach to it was a late form of Divisionism, in which they first worked. But during their visit to Paris in 1910 Severini, who worked in Paris and knew the artistic *avant-garde*, introduced them to Picasso, Braque and Cubism – a revelation. They intended to exhibit in Paris themselves in 1911 but were dissuaded from doing so until they had achieved some genuinely Futurist work. Their first exhibition took place the following year and it included some of the most significant early Futurist works.

The nature of early Futurism can be identified in the main preoccupations of the Futurists; speed and movement, and the modern machine. Like the Cubists, however, their pictorial answers often seemed closer to the traditional than they would have liked. However strong their desire to incinerate the past and leap into a glorious stainless-steel future, they had been brought up in a traditional manner and they were not really all that young: most were around 30 in 1912, Balla over 40. They retained an interest in subject paintings while treating their material in a new way that owed a good deal to the Cubists.

One of the group, Anton Giulio Bragaglia (1890–1960), was a photographer and his experiments moving the camera to get broken-action images were one influence. In a series of drawings and sculptures Boccioni examined the human figure in successive stages of motion and from this came one of the undeniably great works of the movement: the bronze sculpture usually known as *Unique Forms of Continuity in Space*. This work, interlocking stages in the movement of a running figure in one dynamic form, bears comparison with the famous *Winged Victory* deprecated by Marinetti in his original manifesto. Both are expressions of speed and energy, the delicate yet powerful treatment of figure and drapery in the *Winged Victory* is translated by Boccioni into a modern mechanistic image of similar authority.

Nude Descending a Staircase, No. 2, 1912. Marcel Duchamp (Philadelphia Museum of Art. Louise and Walter Arensberg Collection).

At the time Duchamp painted this, the Futurists had not produced any of their own characteristic work. The Nude is nevertheless an independent example of one of the chief features of Futurist interest throughout the short history of the movement. Duchamp himself described the sequential movement it represents. 'It is an organization of kinetic elements, an expression of time and space through the abstract expression of motion. . . . When we consider the motion of form through space in a given time, we enter the realm of geometry and mathematics, just as we do when we build a machine for that purpose.'

84

Elasticity, *1912. Umberto Boccioni (Dr Riccardo Jucker Collection, Milan).*

The horse frequently appears in early 20th-century art as a device for physical energy or natural force. In this colourful, flowing Cubist exercise, Boccioni expresses a sense of taut, controlled and contained energy in the form of horse and rider. Although not carried through with the consistency of Duchamp's Nude Descending. . . there are interlocked suggestions of different positions of the horse's feet and head. This is an early, decorative example of Boccioni's search for a new dynamism in pictorial expression which is better and more fully expressed in his sculpture.

In searching for an art as up-to-date as the latest technology the Futurists nevertheless employed traditional picture-making methods; they painted in oils on canvas and in common with the members of all the other movements of the period continued initially to use traditional subject matter – to 'sweep the whole field of art clean of all themes and subjects which have been used in the past' was not so easily done, they found. However, they did make considerable changes of emphasis which led them quite quickly to a translation of the picture image into something that approached abstraction. They attempted to express what in their first technical manifesto of painting they called the 'dynamic sensation itself'. Severini's *Dancer* is designed to express energetic movement, not a girl dancing. The result was the fractured image we see and the attempt to present sequential movement – to introduce a time element. In Balla's

Dynamism of a Dog on a Leash (1912) this is given charming expression, and suggests the later cinema technique, familiar from Westerns, in which the camera concentrates on the striding horse and sets the ground in motion. References to motion pictures show how forward-looking the Futurists genuinely were and how attached, despite themselves, to the traditional notions of art. Perhaps the greatest 'mechanized gesture' came from Russolo, with his noise machines that anticipated *musique concrète*.

The attempt to involve Futurism with all aspects of life, from politics to food, characterized the early activities of Marinetti, but in general proved too idealistic. However, Marinetti was a singularly effective propagandist for Cubism as well as Futurism, and a form of Cubo-Futurism gained dominance in Russia in pre-Revolutionary times.

Among the most brilliant feats of

Development of a Bottle in Space, 1912. Silvered bronze. Umberto Boccioni (Museum of Modern Art, New York. Aristide Maillol Fund).
In this famous sculpture Boccioni is concerned with another preoccupation of the Futurists – the inner life or 'universal dynamism' attributed to all objects, including machines. In the ordinary subject of a bottle on a table Boccioni discerned a living relationship which allowed the bottle, its internal nature laid bare, to grow in a natural spiral movement from the tilted and involved table top. This notion of mechanistic life in the essentially inanimate has inspired many to see their surroundings, and their own relationship thereto, in a different way.

Unique Forms of Continuity in Space
*1912. Bronze. Umberto Boccioni
(Museum of Modern Art, New York).
This sculpture is not only Boccioni's
masterpiece but also one of the great
works of the century. It is Boccioni's
monument to Futurism and the modern
world, and in this striding figure, energy
and motion are expressed in sculptural
form in a way that John Golding has*
*described as 'blindingly simple and totally
successful'. The integration of the forms of
the lower part of the figure is not difficult;
regarding the upper part it is worth
noting that in early studies for this work
and in other sculptures and paintings (e.g.
those of the artist's mother) the figure and
its background interpenetrate. The latter
is usually of buildings, and here the
armless upper part bears rectilinear*
*shapes and a visor-like grille that suggest
buildings and window shapes. The
absence of arms consciously recalls the
Hellenistic* Winged Victory, *a sculpture
which held much fascination for the
Futurists.*

Futurist imagination are the drawings
of Antonio Sant' Elia who, with the
help of Marinetti, produced the manifesto of Futurist architecture in 1914.
In the same year he made a drawing for
an airport and railway station on a
multi-level scheme which, when one
recalls that it was barely ten years since
the Wright brothers first flew at Kitty
Hawk, shows remarkable prescience.

Although it cannot be said that the
Futurists effectively carried through the
aims and programme that they set
themselves, the emphasis on the idea of
an art reflecting the age of the machine
gave them great inspirational importance in the long run.

Until relatively recently that importance was obscured by the activities of
the Futurists themselves, particularly
Marinetti. True to the Futurist manifesto, Marinetti worked hard to get
Italy into the First World War (he
became a recruiting sergeant for a
while) and most of the Futurists joined

the army. Marinetti was seriously
wounded; Sant' Elia and Boccioni, the
most talented, were killed. Most
damaging of all to the future reputation
of the Futurists was Marinetti's
association with Mussolini. The identification of Futurism with Fascism,
although inaccurate, has delayed full
recognition of its achievements.

*Funeral of the Anarchist Galli, 1911.
Carlo Carra (Museum of Modern Art,
New York. Acquired through the Lillie P.
Bliss Bequest).*
*This painting represents the funeral
which Carra witnessed in 1904 of an
anarchist killed in a demonstration, which
itself provoked another riot. Carra's
passionate reaction eventually expressed
itself in this painting. It is one of
comparatively few to illustrate a specific
contemporary event, which is surprising in
view of Futurist convictions. The
emotional colour, particularly the
dominant red of the flag, and the
repeating forms of the crowds make this a
compelling work despite its somewhat,
rudimentary understanding of Cubism.*

*Carra abandoned Futurist ideals
when he met Giorgio de' Chirico, whose
'metaphysical' painting attracted him, in
1916. Although never in sympathy
with all of Chirico's ideas, he painted
semi-Surrealist metaphysical works for
the rest of his life.*

Above:
Dynamic Hieroglyphic of the Bal Tabarin, *1912. Gino Severini (Museum of Modern Art, New York. Acquired through the Lillie P. Bliss Bequest).*
Before he signed the first Futurist painting manifesto Severini was already a successful painter in Paris, influenced by Seurat. His intention to capture 'dynamic sensation itself' resulted in such paintings

as this, which presents a dancer in different stages of movement integrated in a single all-over pattern. In this early work he was already introducing fractured images of heads, arms and figures and evocative words. There are also echoes of Gris's Cubist analysis (e.g. bottom left) in this work. Like other Futurists, Severini later abandoned the fractured image and returned to a more representational and conventional style.

Overleaf:
Flight of Swallows (*more correctly,* Flight of Swifts; *also called* Birds in Flight), *1913. Giacomo Balla (Rijksmuseum Kröller-Müller, Otterlo). In this painting, completed less than a year after* Dog on a Leash, *Balla moved to another level in his pursuit of the pictorial expression of motion. He made a number of studies of swifts in flight.*

Above:
Dynamism of a Dog on a Leash,
*1912. Giacomo Balla (Albright-Knox
Art Gallery, Buffalo, New York. Bequest
of A. Conger Goodyear to George F.
Goodyear, life interest, and Albright-
Knox Art Gallery, 1964).*
*Balla was of an older generation than
most of the Futurists (he was Severini's
teacher), but his early experiments with
abstraction identify him as the most
inventive of all the Futurists. He not only
exceeded the limits of Futurist ideas but
produced a few of the most advanced
abstractions of the period up to the
1920s. He was concerned with the
expression of sequential motion and in
some of his earlier work such as this,
which is also known as* Leash in Motion, *
the solution seems somewhat naive,
although charming and endearing.*

Right:
Zang-Tumb-Tuum (*page from the
book*), 1914. Filippo Tommaso
Marinetti.
*Always searching for a modern means of
expression, the poet Marinetti was
concerned with new possibilities in the use
of words and sounds. From this came
'words in their freedom', used not only for
the abstract combination of sounds when
they were read aloud, which Marinetti
did, but also for the decorative effect they
might produce in creating a sort of
dynamic of words not used for logical
meaning. The masterpiece of this form is
the novel Marinetti published in 1914
called* Zang-Tumb-Tuum, *a story of the
Balkan War that he had witnessed as a
war correspondent.*

Right:
Design for Station and Airport, *1913–14. Drawing. Antonio Sant' Elia (Villa Communale dell' Olmo, Como).*
One of the great prophetic drawings of the century, this illustrates the imaginative and inventive mind of the architect of Futurism. Drawn only a decade into the flying age, it shows an airport landing deck on a multilevel road/rail/pedestrian supply link-up, in considerable detail and with unhesitating assurance. Sant' Elia's early death in the First World War removed a figure of great creative potential. None of his architectural projects were realized in his lifetime.

Bottom right:
Noise Intoner (Intonarumori). *Photograph. Luigi Russolo.*
Although Russolo was a painter, his main interest lay in music. He invented, and made concert tours with, a 'noise intoner' which emitted a long catalogue of sounds, including rumbles, roars, bangs, crashes, snorts, whispers, grumbles, gurgles, groans and shrieks. Russolo was an extreme eccentric who said, 'I am not a musician, I have therefore no acoustical predilections nor any works to defend ... and so ... I have been able to initiate the great renewal of music by means of the Art of Noises.' The photograph shows Russolo (on the left) and his assistant Piatti with a group of noise intoners. Their first performance was to a distinguished private audience which included Stravinsky (he leapt from his divan like an exploding bedspring on hearing the first crack), Diaghilev (he went Ah! Ah! like a startled quail) and Massine, who simply swung his legs.

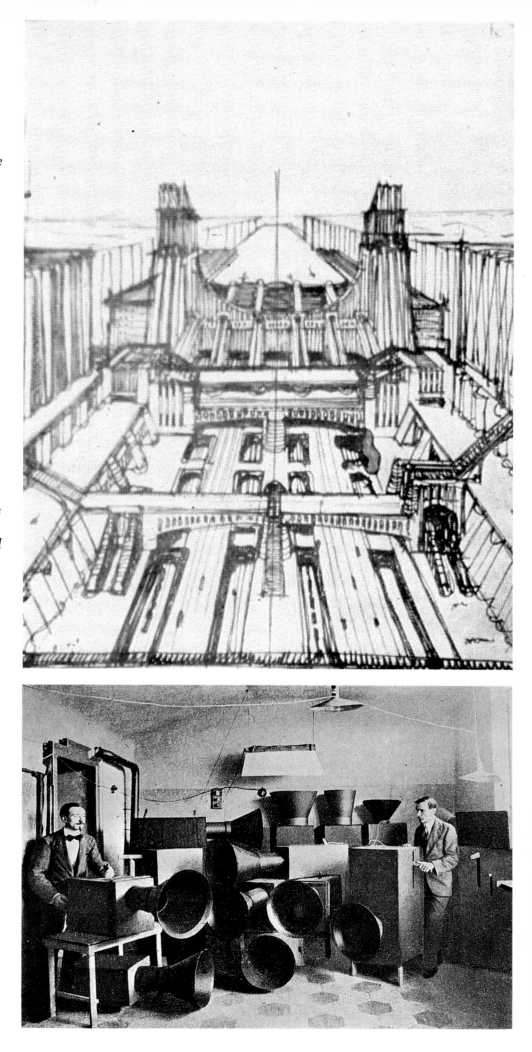

Vorticism

During the first decade of the century artists in England paid little attention to the dramatic developments in Paris and the rest of Europe. The 'art for art's sake' of James Whistler (1834–1903) and some response to Impressionism was England's nearest approach to the *avant-garde*. The Royal Academy still represented traditional artistic values, and it was not until Roger Fry, a sensitive, perceptive critic if heavy-handed painter, arranged the Post-Impressionist exhibition in London at the Grafton Galleries in 1910 that the work of Cézanne, Van Gogh and Gauguin burst rather late upon the astonished English. This important exhibition also included works by Picasso, Matisse and Derain. With a second, similar exhibition two years later, English artists were alerted to Cubist and Futurist experiments. The 1912 exhibition ranged wider and included some recent Russian work.

Meanwhile, the Italian Futurists had made their obtrusive appearance. The Marinetti bandwagon could not be ignored even by the English. Press coverage was extensive and uniformly antagonistic, but only served to augment the intended effect upon the young, who recognized a brash new spirit abroad. It was not only artists who were affected; by 1915 Futurism had become widely fashionable and attractive to the generation of youth unsettled by approaching war.

Vorticism was the expression of this *avant-garde* spirit, and during the movement's short span it was no less creative than its alternatives on the continent.

Vorticism was the outcome of the driving energy and inconsiderate aggression of Percy Wyndham Lewis, much as Futurism was the artistic child of Filippo Marinetti. Wyndham Lewis later characteristically defined Vorticism as 'what I did and said', though the name came from the poet Ezra Pound. Lewis insisted he was antagonistic to Futurism, and attended Marinetti's lectures in London in 1914 with the primary objective of pelting him with eggs. His antipathy may have been partly based on envy, since Vorticist art was all too obviously similar to the Futurists'. More so, indeed, than to Cubism, the other, more significant source of influence, though the Vorticists were certainly not attracted to the continued use in Cubist painting of still-life bric-a-brac like violins. Their interest in the machine was more significant and more profound. In the words of T.E. Hulme, the philosopher largely responsible for the anti-Romantic stance of Vorticism, 'the new *tendency towards abstraction* will culminate not so much in the simple geometric forms found in archaic art [so much for African sculpture and Picasso] but in the more complicated ones associated in our minds with the idea of machinery'.

But Vorticism had other aims. Recognizing that the English had not yet woken up to modern art, Lewis, himself only just awakened, assumed the mantle as prophet of the new art and ridiculed the vapid, nostalgic, *laissez-faire* spirit of English culture. In 1914 he founded the Rebel Art Centre and in July published a new magazine, *Blast*, containing the Vorticist manifesto. British feebleness was pilloried in an assertive and original typestyle; Lewis proclaimed that to find any life or vigour you had to go to the ports and dockyards. A second issue of *Blast* appeared in 1915, when preoccupations with war had redirected the interests of the intellectual world; the second issue was also the last.

However, the war itself, with its great machines of destruction, was susceptible to the methods of the Vorticists as of the Futurists. The enthusiastic machine images of prewar Vorticist paintings were turned into searing comments on the destruction of the human form by guns and bombs. One of the Vorticists, C.W.R. Nevinson (1889–1946), the only avowed

Right:
Composition, *1913. Wyndham Lewis (Tate Gallery, London).*
Much as Marinetti regarded himself as Futurism, Lewis considered himself as Vorticism, and possibly with more justice. A cantankerous and aggressively opinionated man, he was at once painter, critic, novelist and editor. He studied at the Slade School, London, before travelling in Europe for several years. On his return, a convinced modernist, he threw himself into battle for the cause: the magazine Blast *and Vorticism were the result. Both Futurist and Cubist elements make up the iconoclastic Vorticist aesthetic, which presents itself artistically in aggressive, active images, often mechanistic, as in this example.*

The Cinema, *1920. William Roberts (Tate Gallery, London).*
This painting, although it postdates Vorticism, shows the characteristic mechanistic treatment of forms derived *from Cubism and Futurism and adopted by Wyndham Lewis and Roberts during the Vorticist period. Roberts's later work* consists largely of heavy, bulbous figures *treated in strong colour and decorative pattern. It somewhat suggests a geometricised form of Léger's work.*

Futurist among them, produced during the war some of the most moving of political art documents.

The chief importance of *Blast* was that it brought the possibilities of a new art before an important section of the British intelligentsia. Lewis was a difficult man, but the failure of Vorticism to achieve a broader artistic impact was largely due to the artistic restraints that the Vorticists voluntarily adopted. The revolutionary spirit, strong in them in literary terms, was not reflected in their images, which tended to drift from the earlier spiky, mechanistic abstractions towards a mere decorative pattern. All of them moved from abstraction to more representational work in their later paintings. The strength of Lewis's work and character so dominated the Vorticist style that for the two years 1914–15 the paintings of William Roberts (1895–1980), Edward Wadsworth (1889–1949), David Bomberg (1890–1957) and others were very close to his in style and treatment.

It is in the work of Henri Gaudier-Brzeska (1891–1915) that the most original talent appears. His early death deprived British art (he was in fact French, but settled in London) of a sculptor of real potential significance. The other main Vorticist sculptor, Jacob Epstein (1880–1959), less naturally gifted, nevertheless produced one of the most powerful and original works of the movement and one of the great sculptures of the century, *Rock Drill*. In this work he originally included an actual rock drill, supported by a mechanistic human form, blurring the separate identities of man and machine and raising the question – who is in charge? Epstein described the work in his autobiography '. . . It was in the experimental pre-war days of 1913 that I was fired to do the rock drill and my ardour for machinery (short-lived) expended itself upon the purchase of an actual drill, second-hand, and upon this I made and mounted a machine-like robot, visored, menacing and carrying within itself its progeny, protectively ensconced. Here is the armed, sinister figure of today and tomorrow'. This prophetic note is echoed in David Bomberg's comment that it was a 'tense figure operating the Drill as if it were a Machine Gun, a Prophetic Symbol'. Epstein's later

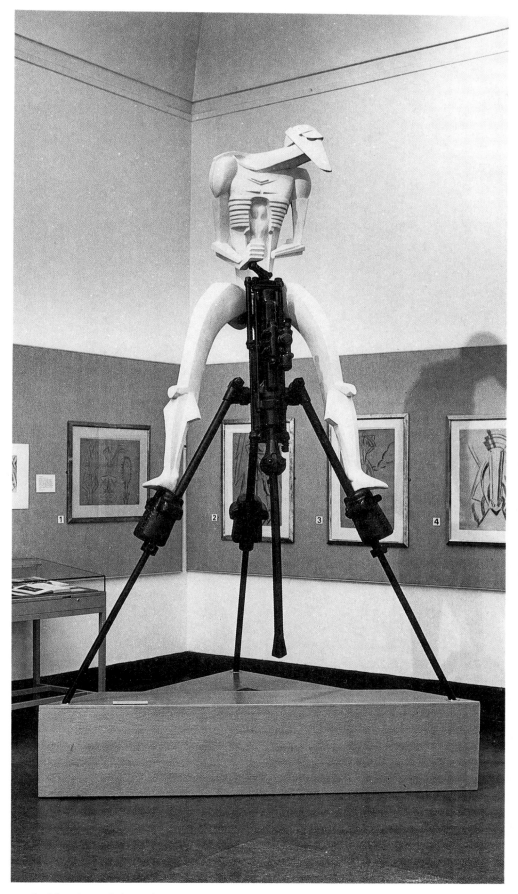

work, like that of the other Vorticists, returned to a heavy representational form lacking the inspiration of *Rock Drill*.

In the story of 20th-century art Vorticism does not occupy a place of the greatest significance; but in British art it is the one movement that made an original contribution to the new aesthetic.

Rock Drill, *reconstruction 1973–74. Jacob Epstein (City of Birmingham Museum and Art Gallery). Only the figure surmounting the drill remains from the original work. This reconstruction was made for a recent Vorticist exhibition.*

In the Hold, *c.1913–14. David Bomberg (Tate Gallery, London). Bomberg made a number of studies for this large painting, which is in effect a geometrically based abstract composition. The studies reveal that the original subject was a number of men handling freight in the hold of a ship. Through the use of a grid (used academically for enlarging a sketch), Bomberg constructed a strongly coloured, almost jazz-age abstraction which owes its basic inspiration to Cubism.*

Bird Swallowing a Fish, *c.1913–14.*
Henri Gaudier-Brzeska (Tate Gallery,
London).
Born Henri Gaudier (he added the
Brzeska to acknowledge a love affair with
Sophie Brzeska, twenty years his senior)
he showed enormous and precocious
talent, but after many heroic feats serving
in the French army he was killed at 24.
He said that he wished to 'derive my
emotions solely from the arrangement of
surfaces, the planes and the lines by which
they are defined'. In Bird Swallowing a
Fish *he has translated the event into a*
combination of mechanistic and natural
forms which seem to fulfil the Vorticist
creed as voiced in Blast.

Modern Art in Russia

In many ways a backward giant, Russia had been in close touch with cultural trends in Western Europe since the reign of Catherine the Great (1762–96). Her court attracted many European artists, and the latest European fashions were adopted in architecture and the arts generally. The outbreak of the Revolution in France may have delivered a sharp check to Catherine's liberal and reforming tendencies, but close cultural contacts continued between Russia and the rest of Europe, notably France, throughout the 19th century. At the same time, while the Russians looked West rather than East for artistic inspiration, the traditions of Russia herself were neither forgotten nor abandoned.

At the beginning of the 20th century, the latest ideas of Europe were appreciated no less thoroughly or speedily in intellectual Russian circles than they were in the cafés of Paris. Several wealthy individuals were avid collectors of modern art. The collection of Sergei Shchukin, for example, included Picasso and Matisse at a time when their works had scarcely been seen in many European countries. Fauvism, Cubism and Futurism were known, understood and appreciated in Moscow and St Petersburg as soon as they were in any other capital, perhaps not excepting Paris.

Of course, there had long been a good deal of traffic between Russia and her neighbours: we have already found Kandinsky and Jawlensky at work among the German Expressionists, and there is a very close resemblance between the portraits of Jawlensky and those of his contemporary, Ilya Mashkov (1884–1944), who never left Russia.

The social and political unrest following the accession of Tsar Nicholas II, the riots, strikes and revolts of the first few years of the century, the formation of the Bolshevik party and the dramatic ferment which eventually culminated in the October Revolution of 1917, was paralleled by the turbulent new developments in the arts, inspired partly by the Cubist revolution. Cubism made itself felt in Russian art almost as soon as it happened – and more publicly than in Paris. Futurism also made a considerable impact (Marinetti was in Russia in 1910 and 1914), resulting in a Russian 'Cubo-Futurism' of which the chief manifestations were in poetry, notably the poetry of Mayakovsky. The destructive attitude of the Futurists towards, as they saw it, the redundant culture of Europe was worked out in Russia more completely than elsewhere, and the pre-Revolutionary art of Russia is the most dismissive of the traditional past. In architecture, graphic design, theatre and cinema the extraordinary reforming energy of the artists between about 1910 and 1920 laid the intellectual grounding for some of the most dramatically explorative works of the 20th century. The great, icy, clamp-down on all manifestations of an independent human spirit by Stalin's cultural commissars was doubly unfortunate for, besides cutting short many brilliant careers (and of course obliterating an unknown number before they started), it has tended to obscure the important contributions, both social and artistic, made by gifted Russians to the early modern aesthetic.

In the rest of Europe, Russian culture was represented primarily not by painting, sculpture and architecture but by music and theatre – opera and ballet. Diaghilev and the Ballet Russe, whose first season in Paris (using exclusively Russian music and dancers) took place in 1909, represented modern Russian culture to most Western Europeans. Diaghilev's designers, especially Leon Bakst (1866–1924) and Mikhail Larionov (1881–1964) revealed a new imagination in stage setting. Russian film, too, soon offered further evidence of modern Russian arts and culture. Eisenstein's *Battleship Potemkin*, with its gripping Odessa steps sequence, using his new montage techniques, has become a classic of early cinema.

Glass, *1912. Mikhail Larionov*
(Solomon R. Guggenheim Museum, New
York).
Larionov's early career was characterized
by a number of stylistic changes, of which
Primitivism was the first. It was only in
1912, directly under the influence of
Cubo-Futurism, that he developed his
most recognizable form, of which Glass *is*
an example. After much disputation,
Larionov and his friend Goncharova, left
the 'Knave of Diamonds', an avant-garde
discussion and exhibition society, to
initiate their own little movement,
Rayonnism, and Glass *was the first*
exhibited Rayonnist work.

Cats, *1913. Natalia Goncharova*
(Solomon R. Guggenheim Museum, New
York).
Goncharova's Rayonnism is different in
many respects from Larionov's. Whilst he
uses muted colour in almost abstract
compositions, she uses strong and brilliant
colour for subjects that are usually
identifiable and seem closely related to
Futurist subject matter and treatment –
as in Cyclist, The Electrical Ornament
or Cats. *Rayonnism was short-lived and*
in 1914 Larionov and Goncharova left
Russia to join Diaghilev as designers.

In the decade 1910–20, Russia was decidedly a centre of the *avant-garde*.

Primitivism and Futurism. During the first decade of the century a movement derived from Russian folk art promoted a conscious primitivism whose principal exponents were Larionov and his pupil, Natalia Goncharova (1881–1962). Larionov and Goncharova imbibed Futurism and the other new developments almost as they appeared, so that they are the foundation figures of modern Russian art.

As the result of the influence of Cubism and Futurism and the primitivism of Goncharova and of the early work of Kasimir Malevich (1878–1935) a kind of Cubist form of peasant art developed. Meanwhile, Larionov was responsible for the evolution of a type of abstract painting which he called Rayonnism: 'the style of Rayon-

nist painting we are promoting is concerned with spatial forms which are obtained through the crossing of reflected rays from various objects . . . the ray is conventionally represented on the surface by a line of colour'. This short-lived phase lasted from 1911 to 1914 and was not adopted by other artists except Goncharova.

Malevich and Suprematism. Malevich's early Cubo-peasant art, in which the figures are simplified into bulky geometric forms, continued until 1912–13. He then initiated his own movement, Suprematism, which provoked considerable distaste and misunderstanding. Malevich, who was a charming person and brilliant speaker, described Suprematism as 'the new colour realism in the form of abstract creation'. Suprematism is firmly and entirely abstract. The images are

Head of a Peasant Woman, *1913 (above). Kasimir Malevich (Stedelijk Museum, Amsterdam).* Suprematist Composition, *c.1915 (right). Kasimir Malevich (Museum of Modern Art, New York).*
In his early work Malevich changed from a form of simplified Cubism applied to Primitivist peasant subjects towards a more complicated and abstracted form of Cubo-Futurism, of which Head of a Peasant Woman *is an example. He was moving steadily towards a complete form of abstraction, which he designated Suprematism, and his compositions became increasingly simplified. The process of simplification of, as Malevich described it, 'pure sensation' culminated in a series of white on white paintings (1917–18); the faintest indication of a simple white square was visible on a white ground. At this point Malevich virtually abandoned painting in favour of theory.*

simple. Malevich's first Suprematist work consisted of a black square on a white canvas; the last, painted in 1919, consisted of a white square on a white background. He then declared that Suprematism was dead. These paintings, which prefigure Minimalist abstraction of the period after the Second World War, are the most limited in means and serve rather as a determined statement against any degree of representation than as the statement of supreme spiritual values asserted by Malevich. However, Suprematism included a middle stage in which coloured shapes floated, as we might imagine debris of space technology now floats around the Earth, on white or creamy backgrounds.

Tatlin and Constructivism. Malevich had produced an abstract movement largely confined to painting, although he did undertake some sculptured reliefs. Sculpture and architecture, as we have noted, were an important part of Russian developments and, whilst architecture is outside the scope of this survey, the division between sculpture and architecture is blurred in the preliminary models usually made for architectural projects. The scale of the model, the ability to see it as an object in what is normally sculptural space, makes it necessary to consider, in the context of Constructivism, one significant architectural project which was never built – and probably could not have been built as it was conceived. Few of the daringly original projects of this period were realized and Tatlin's *Monument to the Third International* was, in vastness of scale and breadth of concept, the least likely.

Constructivism, of which the work of Vladimir Tatlin (1885–1953) is the

Above left:
Proun 99, c.1924. El Lissitzky (Yale University Art Gallery, New Haven, Connecticut: Gift of the Société Anonyme).
In 1921 the architect and painter El Lissitzky gave one of a series of lectures by practising painters examining the nature of art. His lecture was called 'Prouns – changing trains between painting and architecture' and advanced a theory amalgamating Suprematist and Constructivist ideas. He had been painting Proun works since 1919 which consisted, as in this work, of an arrangement of geometrically based shapes combined with line and colour. They partake of the same thesis which motivated De Stijl in Holland – that art is expressed as style. Lissitzky was a friend of Van Doesburg and was associated with De Stijl.

most important outcome, was essentially sculptural and architectural. The other originators were two brothers, Anton Pevsner (1886–1962) and Naum Gabo (1890–1977), both sculptors. The name – although not the intention – of Constructivism was established by them in their *Realist Manifesto*, issued in 1920. Constructivism was essentially a technical three-dimensional scheme in which materials and technology were to be brought together in a totally new, nonhistorical architecture. The subsequent elegant abstract constructions of Gabo and Pevsner followed from their early, strong, but technically crude reliefs.

It was Tatlin, however, who led the way, in a series of corner reliefs (now destroyed) which wandered across the angles of rooms in unrestrained and entirely untraditional sculptural form. The idea of the freedom of the sculpture from normal volume limits, which also was to surface again after the Second World War, started with Tatlin. His *Monument* is his greatest memorial. Designed to be twice the height of the Empire State Building, its materials were glass and iron. It was in the form of a spiral and was intended to rotate on its base once a year.

Another important Constructivist, Alexander Rodchenko (1891–1956) held (like Tatlin) that art should be useful. The role of the artist, he said, was also to be that of designer and

Left:
Composition, *1918. Alexander Rodchenko (Museum of Modern Art, New York. Gift of the artist).*
Russian art during the period immediately after the Revolution continued to pursue the ideas of the earlier movements, particularly Cubism and Futurism. Rodchenko was one of those who extended the modern aesthetic into design and he was one of the pioneers of modern typographical layout. His abstract compositions are frequently emblematic, and as a Constructivist his work usually has a bold, direct simplicity. The form of geometrically based abstraction seen in this drawing is characteristic of Russian abstraction.

Above:
Monument to the Third International, *1919–20. Vladimir Tatlin.*
In 1918, following the Russian Revolution, Lenin suggested that towns should erect monuments to the great heroic figures and to the Revolution itself. Great artistic figures were also to be commemorated including Moussorgsky, Courbet and, surprisingly, Cézanne. The results were mostly poor work in inferior materials, but in 1919 the Department of Fine Arts commissioned Tatlin to execute a monument for the centre of Moscow. Tatlin, with assistants, made models of an enormous structure which, although never built, remains the greatest legacy of Russian post-Revolutionary

imagination. 'A union of purely artistic forms (painting, sculpture and architecture) for a utilitarian purpose' was Tatlin's intention and unlike others his was to be a useful building, housing lecture and exhibition spaces, executive offices and, at the top, an information centre. It became in model form an inspiration and symbol for artists who saw the Revolution as an opportunity to build a modern art environment for the great new society then dawning.

architect. Rodchenko's principal contribution was the development of a poster graphic language of clarity and impact, much in demand after the Revolution.

Lazar El Lissitsky (1890–1941), a trained engineer, was a professional practitioner of Constructivist ideas. In his later years an important architect, he was also a designer and painter who produced (among other works) constructed, painted, relief abstractions which are close in feeling to the late work of Moholy-Nagy at the Bauhaus.

Constructivism declined in Russia in the early 1920s as it did not appeal to Bolshevik leaders, but it had a widespread influence in Europe. Its ideals were very close to those of the Bauhaus (see page 143).

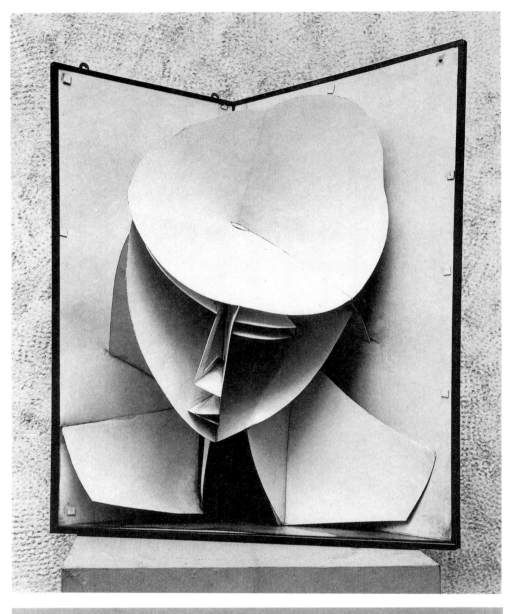

Top:
Head of a Woman, *c.1917–20, after a work of 1916. Naum Gabo (Museum of Modern Art, New York).*
The two representative sculptors of Russian modernism were the brothers Antoine Pevsner and Naum Gabo (the younger). Probably under Antoine's influence and the current impact of Cubism, Gabo, around 1916, began to construct a series of head and torso figures out of sheet metal and celluloid. Bearing some affinity with Tatlin's corner constructions they have a Cubist analytical base which is revealed clearly in a changing light pattern. This example is one of the earliest of these works. Gabo later made a number of elegant mobile geometric constructions which are close in feeling to those of his brother.

Right:
Maquette of a Monument Symbolizing the Liberation of the Spirit, *1952.*
Antoine Pevsner (Tate Gallery, London).
This work by Pevsner was an entry in an international competition to design a monument to the world's unknown political prisoners. It is representative of his involved wire and metal, three-dimensional constructions, which he first produced in post-Revolutionary Russia. (The monument was not erected and the prize was awarded to the English architect/sculptor Reg Butler.)

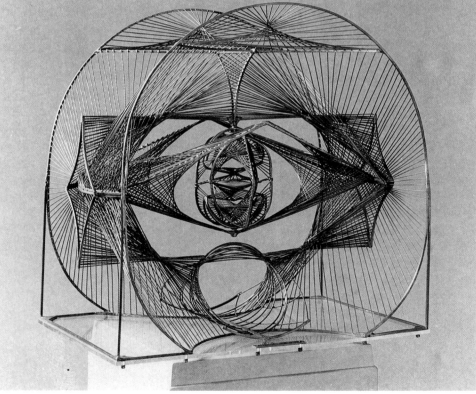

Modern Sculpture

Although clearly related to painting and the other graphic arts, sculpture has a somewhat different history and generally serves different needs. In this century especially, while paintings (except for some notably large-scale canvases) are bought and housed by ordinary (though rich) people, sculpture generally presents an accommodation problem, the more so as houses tend to get smaller. It is also confoundedly omnipresent. One may ignore paintings on walls but one has to walk around sculpture, or trip over it. Sculpture has therefore generally found itself in public places and museums.

Sculpture's traditional role was as an adjunct to architecture, enhancing the appearance of the building and in a sense part of it. Its value in this role is evident in Michelangelo's Medici Tombs in Florence or Bernini's work at St Peter's, Rome, to name two famous examples, but by the mid-19th century most public sculpture merely dripped from the building it adorned rather than supporting the architectural idea. It was nevertheless omnipresent. Theatres and town halls, public squares and parks, all carried the obligatory sculptural embellishment.

In modern times sculpture, more than painting, has depended on commissions. Until the late 19th century it scarcely existed otherwise. The only exceptions were studies for a major work or exhibition pieces designed expressly to attract commissions.

Sculptors, therefore, more than painters, are obliged to give the public, or rather the institutions that are their patrons, the kind of art they want. In the 19th century they wanted (as they still do very often) solid monuments and memorials in more or less Classical style. One would therefore expect sculpture to be a conservative art. It was hard enough for the Impressionists to go off and paint pictures in a revolutionary style which no one would buy. For sculptors, the difficulty was even greater. Nevertheless, in the late 19th century a revolution in sculpture

Balzac, 1892–97. Auguste Rodin (Kodak Factory, Hemel Hempstead). Although this work of Rodin's was made at the end of the 19th century, it may be taken as an important inaugural work in the history of 20th-century sculpture. In the same way as such figures as Cézanne and Gauguin are forerunners of modern pictorial language, Rodin is the dominant creative impetus preceding the modern sculptural aesthetic. Additionally, Balzac is perhaps the finest of Rodin's public sculptures. It has a plastic sensitivity comparable with, say, Cézanne's spatial innovations in painting. Its influence has been profound and lasting.

occurred which is no less significant than the Impressionist revolution in painting.

The mainspring of that revolution was one man, one of the greatest sculptors in the history of Western art after Donatello, Michelangelo and Bernini: Auguste Rodin (1840–1917).

It seems natural to regard Rodin as a sculptural equivalent to the Impressionists, but he was far from being an Impressionist in spirit. He did, however, share their poor opinion of the official art of the day, contemporary sculpture being a tired, repetitive, reworking of debased Renaissance ideas. In a letter to the mayor of Calais written while he was preparing for the commission of one of his best-known works, *The Burghers of Calais*, he wrote that it would be an improvement since 'all cities have ordinarily the same monument, give or take a few details'. While rejecting the vacuous works of his academic contemporaries he was nevertheless deeply influenced by the same sculptors in history that they claimed as their own mentors. His artistic roots are in Greek and Renaissance sculpture.

Although he failed admission to the Ecole des Beaux Arts and received his training in the craft school, the Petite Ecole, the basis of Rodin's art is his ability as a modeller.

There are, of course, two basic methods of traditional sculpture, carving and modelling. The carver reduces an existing volume of stone, wood or other material to arrive at his finished form by cutting away unwanted material. For him the subject exists within the material; he visualizes it, then releases it. He cannot afford serious errors and must have a clear conception of his finished form before he starts: an arm or leg cannot be moved later. With modelling the reverse is true. The sculptor builds the form from nothing with malleable materials, usually clay or wax, and at all stages the work is adjustable: any part can be reworked. For the modeller, therefore, the idea may be realized as the work actually proceeds; moreover, it is immediately responsive to his touch: his hands, his most sensitive tool, are directly used.

Rodin is certainly one of the greatest, many would say *the* greatest, modellers in the history of sculpture. For

Above:
The Bookmaker, *1894. Medardo Rosso (Galleria Nazionale d'Arte Moderna, Rome).*
An Italian, Rosso was a sensitive and popular modeller whose work, mainly (as here) in wax captures the flow of light over forms, revealing nuances without (as was then standard practice) defining the form in detail. This identifies him as more Impressionist than any other sculptor, including Rodin.

Opposite above:
La Source, *or* The Mediterranean, *1902–05. Aristide Maillol (Jardin du Luxembourg, Paris).*
After an early association with the Nabis, and while Art Nouveau was the dominant decorative style, Maillol began the series of Classically based nude studies which occupied him for the rest of his working life. La Source *is the earliest example of his mature style.*

Below:
Reclining Nude, *1907. Henri Matisse (Musée National d'Art Moderne, Paris). For Matisse sculpture was an extension of his pictorial language. From about 1904 he related his modelling to his painting and later included his sculpture in his painting. He had a more plastic sense than Picasso, for instance, and his* sculpture has a sensuous modernity which makes him an important innovator in this field as in painting. This early reclining figure relates closely to paintings and studies of the preceding period, including Joie de Vivre *of 1905. Matisse continued to sculpt throughout his working life, although his last works were not cast in his lifetime.*

him the clay was an extension of his perception; his touch was so sure that form with inherent life seemed to flow from his manipulation of the clay. Were it only for this unique facility, his achievement would be great, but his real contribution to the modern aesthetic was more significant.

Current sculpture was representational and illustrative. Town squares were filled with figures in dramatic but unvarying heroic poses. Rodin's great modelling ability enabled him to give his work convincing realism, and his first major work, *The Age of Bronze*, was so fluently modelled that he was accused of casting it from a living model. The importance of the work, however, is not that it was so realistic that critics thought he had been cheating but that this naturalistic figure was called *The Age of Bronze*. The title was clearly symbolic, suggesting the reawakening of humanity in the perfection of youth. But of course Rodin was not merely a realist. He endeavoured, like the Post-Impressionist painters, to express emotional content, exploiting the human form to express human hopes and fears. Again like the Post-Impressionists in painting, Rodin was as he put it, 'one of the last witnesses of a dying art', as well as the founder of the modern sculptural aesthetic. In his *Burghers of Calais* and *Balzac*, an extraordinary example of public-square sculpture and perhaps his greatest work, he set forth new ways of thinking about sculptural form.

His contemporary, Edgar Degas (1834–1917), is best known as an Impressionist painter, but he made a number of sculptures later in life, among them the *Young Dancer* of 1879 which demonstrates brilliantly modelled realism but is nevertheless much more than a piece of observation (though its realism caused offence when it was first shown). The psychological penetration evident in the expression of the insecure, gamine quality of a 14-year-old in the elegance of a ballet pose makes this a deeply affecting work. Degas's sculptured studies of his favourite subjects, dancers, women bathing and horses, all show his brilliant modelling enhanced by affection and understanding.

Another contemporary, Medardo Rosso (1858–1928), an Italian who worked in Paris in the 1880s, is more appropriately regarded as an Impressionist sculptor than Rodin (whom he knew – and quarrelled with). Working as a modeller, frequently in wax, his small images of everyday scenes suggest rather than create the forms, and the rough surface seems to model light itself. Important in suggesting the dematerialization of objects and a new and freer treatment of form, he is nevertheless essentially an observer.

Many sculptors were working within the new movements of modern art in the early years of the century. In some instances they were the most important and creative members, and they were often both painters and sculptors. For example, the most important creative figure in Futurism was Boccioni, two of whose works are not only the most significant works of the movement but also among the few really great sculptures of the century: *Unique Forms of Continuity in Space* and *Evolution of a Bottle in Space*. Both Picasso and Matisse made sculptures which are so important that they receive separate treatment.

Even sculptors who were not directly attached to a particular movement often show temperamental attachments, but here it is important to remember those major figures who were detached from all the contemporary 'isms' yet made their own contributions to the modern aesthetic.

There was and is a demand for sculpture to commemorate the notables of the day – politicians, soldiers, literary figures, etc. – in statuary. This kind of sculpture, although ubiquitously evident, hardly requires comment in a general history of modern art. It is a public activity which has little to do with the development of sculpture.

Rodin had one student and follower who seemed likely to carry his work further, Emile Antoine Bourdelle (1861–1929), but he succumbed to the attractions offered by academic commissions. His most famous work is the gigantic figure of the Virgin on a mountain in the Vosges.

Aristide Maillol (1861–1944) was another who started as a painter. He was associated with the Nabis and was a close friend of Maurice Denis. He turned to sculpture after an eye operation at the age of 40 and quickly settled

on a style and subject matter which varied little thereafter. Female nude figures in simple, restrained poses, well rounded like Renoir's models and given symbolic names with little variation in gesture: that describes almost all his *œuvre*. Influenced by the Greeks and affecting a sculpture that was different from the fluency and drama of Rodin, he suggests a new Classicism, self-contained and modern in feeling.

Raymond Duchamp-Villon (1876–1918), brother of Marcel Duchamp and the painter Jacques Villon (1875–1963), was precociously talented and quickly moved from academic work to simplified forms suggesting Cubist analysis. His major *Horse* series seems to incorporate the strength of both animal and machine; this work may reasonably be compared with Boccioni's *Unique Forms of Continuity in Space* and Epstein's *Rock Drill*, all produced within three years of each other.

The Kiss, c.1922–40 (above left). Constantin Brancusi (Musée National d'Art Moderne, Paris). Blond Negress, 1933 (left). Height 16 in (400 mm). Constantin Brancusi (Museum of Modern Art, New York. Philip L. Goodwin Collection). Bird in Space, 1928 (right). Constantin Brancusi (Museum of Modern Art, New York).
Brancusi was born in Rumania but spent his whole working life in Paris. Although a friend of many other artists in Paris he was an austere and dedicated man who disdained honours. His work developed slowly to a degree of refined abstraction which, for most observers, shows the keenest sensibility of all abstractionist work. Originally influenced by Rodin and Maillol, he had found his own style by about 1908 and from that time his reputation grew. He was represented by three works in the Armory Show of 1913 and in 1914 he held his first one-man show at Gallery 291 in New York. Thus from an early date his influence was felt in the United States as well as in Europe.

These three works are typical. The Kiss, of which he made several versions from 1908 to the 1920s, shows him as a carver and, even in this early work, a fairly ruthless abstractionist; forms are simplified with a tender wit. In the Blond

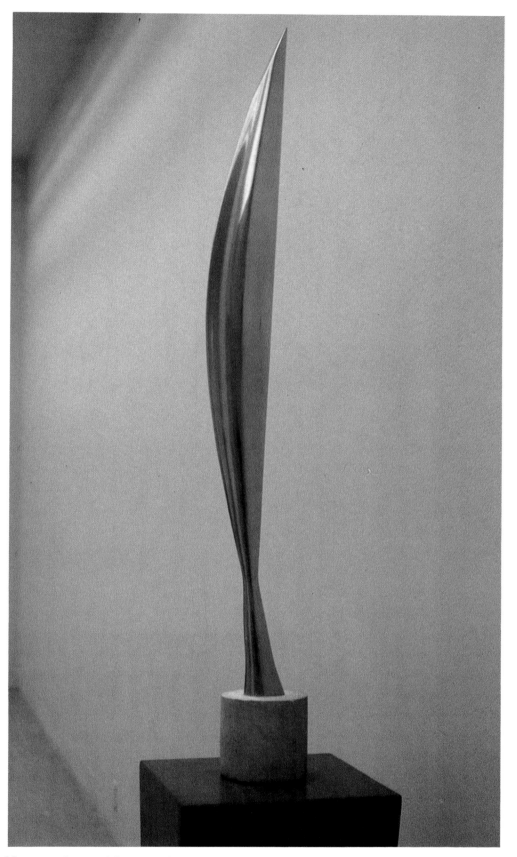

Negress the simplification of form is further refined and the surface highly polished. Many of his works in other media were subsequently cast in bronze and this sculpture is a bronze cast of a piece originally carved in white marble. Its forms are closely related to if simplified from the original head, but in the third work shown here the form is an abstract of

an idea or sensation — that of a soaring bird — and here the refinement of the form is designed to express the notion of freedom in space. Its elegance is purposeful and moving.

Three Men Walking, I, *1948–49.*
Alberto Giacometti (Museum of Modern
Art, New York. Sidney and Harriet Janis
Collection).
The son of a Swiss painter, Giacometti
studied under Bourdelle in Paris, where
he concluded that the close pursuit of
natural form would not capture the
nature of the subject and therefore began
to experiment with reducing and
simplifying form. Around 1930 he

joined the Surrealists, and for five years
produced basically Surrealist sculptures.
In 1935 there began for him a period of
anguished reflection which resulted in ever
smaller works and figures whose stick-like
forms were fixed to the ground in
enormous boat-like feet. All his later work
is of this kind. The three figures walking
in the same place but separately, facing
away from each other, convey a sense of a
desolate and lonely existence.

Female Head, *1911–12. Amedeo*
Modigliani (Tate Gallery, London).
Under the influence of his friend
Brancusi, Modigliani sculpted a number
of heads including this, which also shows
the influence of African sculpture.
Modigliani was a dedicated worker and
his delicate drawings show him to have
been a rare talent. His early death was a
considerable loss to the artistic life of Paris
after the First World War.

The Italian Amedeo Modigliani (1884–1920) was a highly gifted, individual painter and sculptor whose sensational life epitomizes the Parisian *vie bohème*. He was handsome, tubercular, a tremendous womanizer, addicted to stimulants; he announced and fulfilled his intention of drinking himself to death. The finest Italian artist of the century, he always considered himself a sculptor first, though his sensuous paintings, particularly his nudes, are his best-known works. He was influenced by medieval and Renaissance sculpture as well as African art, but his simplified, elongated heads suggest a timeless and remote origin imbedded in primitive imagery.

Modigliani's friendship with Constantin Brancusi (1876–1957), a Rumanian who also worked in Paris, has prompted suggestions that he was influenced in his early work by Brancusi, and there certainly are similarities.

Brancusi developed into one of the most important figures in 20th-century sculpture and the primary influence on one aspect of it – the constant tendency towards abstraction. It has been argued that there is actually no truly abstract art. Brancusi's work is essentially abstractionist rather than purely abstract yet he refines the forms as far towards the abstract as seems possible while retaining any connection with the original objects, and in such works as *Fish* and *Bird in Space* the spirit, feeling and idea are reduced to a single, simple shape. This concern to remove every element extraneous to the essence of the subject and to avoid using it as a symbol distinguishes Brancusi from Rodin, who admired Brancusi's ability and tried unsuccessfully to secure him as an assistant.

Brancusi was fiercely independent and single-minded. To achieve the perfection of surface which was so important to him demanded great technical discipline – and much hard work. Jacques Lipchitz (1891–1973), the Cubist sculptor who for a while had a studio next to Brancusi's, remarked that he could hear the sound of continual polishing, polishing, polishing. 'Polishing', said Brancusi, 'is a necessity required by the relatively absolute forms of certain materials'. This pursuit of absolute refinement of form, producing a machinelike finish, suggests that

there is an absolute, ultimate form which is to be found in the process of reduction, a view which is part of the 20th-century aesthetic. It is not simply a matter of excluding decoration or other extraneous facets, but a belief in the simple image as an end in itself which may also encompass more content than is apparent. An egg may be the beginning of the world, maternity, unrealized life or other imponderables. This philosophy, a great deal older than Minimalism (see page 235), was expressed with enigmatic simplicity in the memorable phrase of Mies van der Rohe, 'Less is more'.

It is this belief, now firmly embedded, that has found its ultimate expression in the showing of a work of art which consists of nothing but its name; the room in which it is contained being totally empty.

This of course does not reflect on Brancusi. On the contrary, the evocative, purposeful refinement of his sculptures is directed towards the presentation of the very opposite of obscurity. His use of materials is always apposite, closely related to the form in which it is shaped, and in a more naturalistic work such as *Seal* romantic overtones are evident. Nevertheless, his choice of materials is not exclusively dictated by the subject, since he sometimes repeats the same subject in different materials.

Brancusi's position in the development of modern sculpture is important and secure. He was, however, the last of the sculptors working in Paris who remains central to the main line of sculptural development. After his death in 1957 French sculpture veered towards a simplified abstraction which echoes the decorative emptiness of much postwar Parisian and, indeed, European painting.

The Swiss-born Alberto Giacometti (1901–1966), who worked in Paris from 1927 until his death, is another sculptor with a highly individual style and a high reputation. He passed through an early Surrealist phase, but thereafter his work is characterized by single or grouped figures which are reduced to almost sticklike form, with rough modelled surface. They present an almost overpowering sense of human isolation. Although pared back to essentials, so that they may seem

close to Brancusi in purpose, Giacometti's figures are rough and imprecise in form and romantically evocative in effect. There is in his sculpture, however, an obsessive repetition that makes the cumulative effect less impressive than his drawings and paintings, which exhibit great pathos and power.

A contemporary, Germaine Richier (1904–59), shares some of Giacometti's qualities, but she conveys an added sense of ominous premonition that gives her work a singular strength. Her figures, seemingly in a process of change from animal to vegetable or humanoid character, inhabit a personal world of irrational fears and forebodings.

The Sculpture of Matisse. Matisse started sculpting about 1900 and it is tempting to see his sculpture as an extension of his developing Fauvist painting. Whilst there is a sense in which this is true, his earliest influence was Rodin. Matisse's first sculpture, *The Serf*, is a standing male nude which resembles Rodin's *Walking Man*, *St John the Baptist* and one of the figures from the *Burghers of Calais* group so closely as to make the debt to Rodin amply evident. His later sculpture, however, has no direct reference. The abstractionist tendency that has been noted in Brancusi and Giacometti, however, is different from that of Matisse.

Matisse's development is best seen in the four bronze sculptures done over the period 1909–30 of a nude female back in high relief. The earliest still shows something of the influence of Rodin in the modelling. The analytical interlocking of forms in the two middle forms in the series demonstrate that Matisse, though never a Cubist, had a thorough understanding of Cubism. The last of the series is a combination of simple, monumental, related shapes which convince us that this is what the sculpture should have been in the first place: the struggle to get there was real and continuing.

Matisse perhaps glimpsed the direction in which his own work would go at his first meeting with Rodin. Afterwards he said that he could see his work 'replacing explanatory details by a living and suggestive synthesis'.

De Stijl

De Stijl is remembered as the Dutch contribution to the modern aesthetic and is associated with the paintings of one of the great modern masters, Piet Mondrian (1872–1944). In fact, the group embraced people of very wide-ranging interests and abilities, including architects, designers, sculptors and one poet, Antonie Kok. The most characteristic work of De Stijl was in architecture, and the Schroder House in Utrecht by Gerit Rietveld (1888–1964) is the purest and most complete realization of De Stijl principles.

The group formed as the result of a meeting between Theo van Doesburg (1883–1931) and Mondrian which resulted in the publication of a magazine *De Stijl*, under the enthusiastic editorship of Van Doesburg in 1917. Van Doesburg was the heart and motivator of the movement and when his health began to fail the original members of the movement tended to drift away. His death in 1931 effectively marks the end of De Stijl.

De Stijl means, in Dutch, 'The Style'; Van Doesburg described how the name was chosen: 'The embryo of what was realized five years later, in the idea and the periodical *De Stijl*, was at the base of the thought I formulated in 1912: strip nature of its forms and you will have style left.'

As with other movements after 1910, De Stijl was formed in awareness of the pictorial complications of Cubism and of Futurism. The artists knew of the first abstracts of Kandinsky and the earliest examples of the new architecture. Their aim was to create a new aesthetic for the 20th century which would span fine art, architecture and design and form a common and universal language. In order to accomplish this it was necessary to remove the local, the incidental, the personal, the traces of Romanticism and of course that deplorable feature of modern attitudes, the 'backward look'. It was easy to see there had to be a radical reconsideration of 'style' in architecture and all forms of decoration.

In the art of painting De Stijl's goal of universal harmony and its enthusiasm for the new led to a nonobjective, nonfigurative image which could not awaken nostalgic reflection and also could not recall a specific and consequently local visual experience.

Only basic elements were acceptable. After much discussion these basics emerged as vertical and horizontal lines; the primary colours, red, yellow and blue, and the 'noncolours', black, grey and white. With these elements most De Stijl members worked exclusively. Paradoxically, the most important expression of De Stijl in painting is to be found in the work of Mondrian after he had left the group and was working in Paris in the 1920s.

The group published its first manifesto in 1981. It began: 'There is an old and a new consciousness of time. The old is connected with the individual. The new is connected with the universal. The struggle of the individual against the universal is revealing itself in the World War as well as in the art of the present day.' There are echoes here of the Futurist concern with time and of Dada disgust with the war, but most important is the emphasis on the universal.

The manifesto was intended as a call to other artists, architects, writers and poets outside the Netherlands, and after the Armistice in 1918 they responded. French, Italian, Belgian and German artists contributed to the magazine *De Stijl*. Van Doesburg added a certain factitious internationalism by adopting a number of pen names for his own articles which suggested different nationalities. His real name, which was Küpper, he never used, but he wrote as I.K. Bonset and Aldo Camini as well as Van Doesburg.

In 1920 Mondrian, who was working in Paris, published his own pamphlet, *Neo-Plasticism*, as well as a dialogue *Natural Reality and Abstract Reality*, which explained his own theory of art. But, essentially, De Stijl existed wherever Van Doesburg

Composition, 1930. Piet Mondrian (Private Collection).
Although the driving force in the creation of De Stijl was Van Doesburg, Mondrian was its most important painter. His own theory of Neo-Plasticism led him to what was then the most austere form of abstraction, employing the simplest of means – red, yellow and blue areas of colour bounded by black vertical and horizontal lines. This work had a profound effect on design and on the general direction of the modern movement, or part of it. In this Composition, completed while Mondrian was living in Paris, the simple elements are combined in a remote and dignified image which still exerts a powerful and direct influence.

happened to be; in 1921 he was in Germany trying to persuade Walter Gropius, who had just been appointed head of the new Bauhaus at Weimar, to adopt his ideas for the design school. For a short time he even contrived to be appointed to the Bauhaus staff, but his influence was temporary in spite of his characteristic assertion that 'at Weimar I have radically overturned everything . . . and have infused the poison of the new spirit everywhere'.

In the next few years a number of architectural works were designed which took the radical designs of Robert van t'Hoff of 1916 (Ter Heide House, Utrecht) to the stage where Rietveld's Schroder House, also in Utrecht, can be seen as a three-dimensional De Stijl painting. In 1924 Van Doesburg claimed, 'The house has been analyzed; it has been dissected into its plastic elements. The static axis of the old construction has been destroyed. The house has become an object; one can circle it on all sides. This analytical method has led to new possibilities of construction and to a new ground plan'.

Top:
Geometrical Composition, *1917.*
Bart van der Leck (Rijksmuseum Kröller-Müller, Otterlo).
The work of the lesser figures in De Stijl tends to enhance the quality of Mondrian's painting. Although imbued with De Stijl theory and the enthusiasm of Van Doesburg, Van Der Leck fails to achieve the taut balance of proportion and scale found in Mondrian. His work seems prosaic and decorative by comparison, particularly when one recalls that it is usually based on a rectilinear translation of a direct visual subject.

Right:
Composition, *1926. César Domela (Galerie Chalette, New York).*
Of a younger generation than Mondrian and Van Doesburg, Domela was a friend of the former. However, when the dispute occurred between Mondrian and Van Doesburg which resulted in Mondrian leaving the movement, Domela gave his allegiance to Van Doesburg and this work is an early example of the use of the diagonal to produce a 'dynamic' image according to Van Doesburg's theory.

Van Doesburg's extrovert and Mondrian's introvert personalities were never really in sympathy and in 1925 Mondrian abandoned the movement altogether, living permanently in Paris until 1938. The disagreement which caused this break is of significance in understanding De Stijl work.

Van Doesburg had propounded a radical extension of De Stijl in what he called Elementarism, which he employed in a design for a cinema and dance hall in Strasbourg. Elementarism was unacceptable to the rigorous art of Mondrian. Van Doesburg wished to introduce diagonal lines which he believed would create a dynamic opposition in the work which the verticals and horizontals of Mondrian would not, being in balance. This quarrel over what might seem to many people a relatively unimportant matter indicates the passion with which the respective views were held.

Of all the formative modern movements, De Stijl has proved perhaps the most difficult to accept. There are vestigial points of reference in some of the work to forms in nature, but they are minimal and, despite some individual work elsewhere (notably the early abstracts of Kandinsky), *De Stijl* can be said to be the first of the modern movements devoted to purely abstract art (as distinct from 'abstractionist').

De Stijl artists were not concerned to present, in whatever form and with whatever personalized distortions, any aspects of the visible world. For them that was a failure to get to the root of things, to reach that universal which Mondrian said was the new and Van Doesburg thought of as style. For Mondrian the universe was an ordered place, and the expression of the order could be attained by the subtle relationships of the simplest elements. None of the De Stijl artists was concerned with incidental aspects of nature or natural form, or with any individual interpretation of them. For Mondrian, 'Man is enabled by abstract aesthetic contemplation to achieve conscious unity with the universal.

'The deepest purpose in painting has always been to give concrete existence, through line and colour, to the universal which appears in contemplation.

'Real life is the mutual interaction of the two oppositions of the same value

but of a different aspect and nature. Its plastic expression is universal beauty.'

And finally, 'Every true artist unconsciously has always been moved by beauty of line, colour and relationship for their own sake and not by what they may represent.'

Although this is by no means a universally held view, it does indicate the intellectual position of De Stijl and Mondrian in particular. The De Stijl artists wished to create an autonomous beauty, independent of the artist's personality which, as one of them, César Domela, put it, would be grasped as readily in Stockholm as in Athens.

These notions did not derive entirely from Cubism and similar contemporary sources. The most significant influence upon Mondrian was the Dutch mathematician and philosopher, M.H.J. Schoenmakers, and most of his ideas and beliefs came from Schoenmakers's books and their conversations. In his *Principles of Plastic Mathematics* Schoenmakers states, 'Plastic mathematics means true and methodical thinking from the point of view of the Creator.' Mondrian's well-known equations of line are also Schoenmakers's. ('Vertical: male – space – statics –

Construction in an Inscribed and Circumscribed Square of a Circle. *1924. Georges Vantongerloo (Peggy Guggenheim Collection, Venice). Vantongerloo (1886–1965) was the one sculptor of the group, although Van Doesburg and the architects Oud and Van Eesteren produced designs which incorporate in basic architectural form the same principles which generated Vantongerloo's sculpture. The masses of rectilinear volumes in an architectonic structure – form penetrating form – became part of the modern architectural aesthetic which continued to dominate architectural practice for succeeding decades.*

harmony. Horizontal: female – time – dynamic – melody'.)

No art to that time had succeeded, as De Stijl did, in producing images so cool and austere. The growing reputation of Mondrian during the 1930s and, after his arrival in the United States in 1940, its consolidation in the forefront of modernism can be seen as a dominant influence in abstraction in that country after the Second World War.

Counter Composition, *1924.*
Theodore van Doesburg (Stedelijk
Museum, Amsterdam).
An early example of Van Doesburg's
Elementarism, this and similar works
provoked a rift between him and
Mondrian, who found them entirely
unacceptable. Van Doesburg, an
aggressive and energetic spirit with

ambitions, perhaps happily unfulfilled, to
convert all art to his beliefs, was
nevertheless an effective propagandist,
and in the magazine De Stijl he
propounded the theories of pure style
which had the effect of initiating
widespread consideration of the nature

and potential of abstraction. His own
painting is less significant than the
architectural drawings he made with Oud
and Van Eesteren, who became
influential modern architects (Mies van
der Rohe, last director of the Bauhaus
and a leading modernist in the United
States from the 1930s, was also a
contributor to De Stijl magazine).

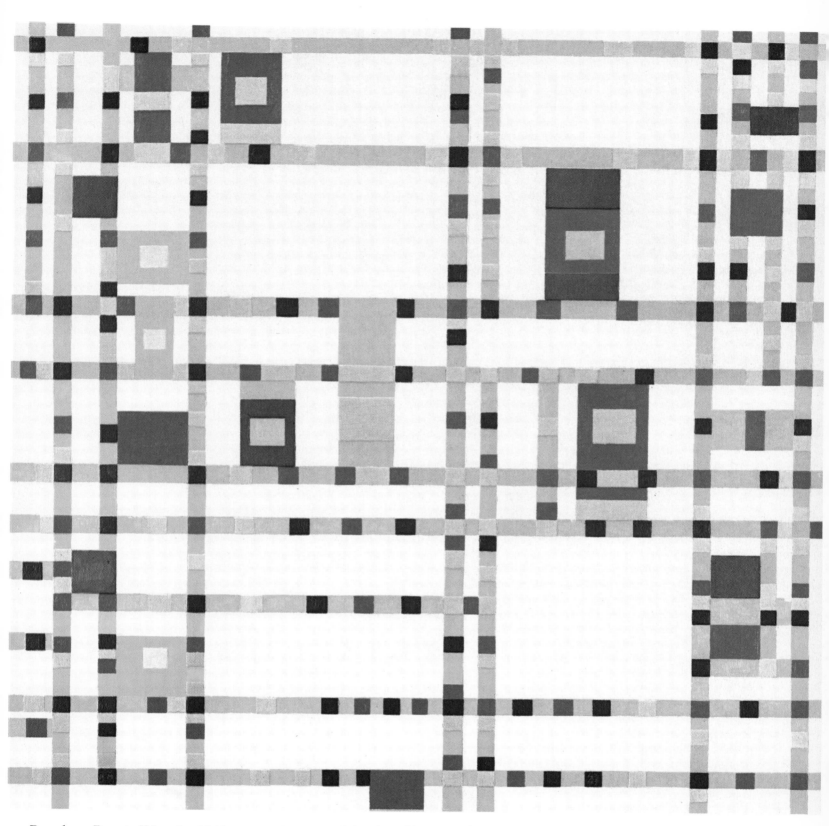

Broadway Boogie-Woogie, 1942– 43. Piet Mondrian (Museum of Modern Art, New York).

The austerity of Mondrian's nature was softened by one lifelong passion – ballroom dancing. In New York at the end of his life his style changed, became freer but more complicated, and he painted two works based on the dance 'Victory Boogie-Woogie'.

Broadway Boogie-Woogie is his last completed work. The painting might be regarded as a choreographic diagram of New York from the air. It is a much more active and lively – one might almost say 'romantic' – work than customary and one wonders whether, had he lived longer, he might have taken this new freedom further.

Dada and Surrealism

The movement known as Dada grew from feelings of mistrust in the moral origins and purpose of the First World War. The Dadaists believed that the war was engineered by the armament manufacturers and other profiteers. It represented one more defeat for the civilization that had bred them and thus for the Classical culture of Europe since the Renaissance. The deaths of the innocent made a bloody mess of faith and hope.

The group which gathered in Zurich in 1915 was composed of poets, writers and artists. In *En avant Dada: a History of Dadaism* (1920) Richard Hulsenbeck, one of the original members, explains that Dada was founded at 'the Cabaret Voltaire, a little bar where Hugo Ball and his friend Emmy Hennings had set up a miniature variety show, in which all of us were very active'. Zurich, a neutral city, was a cultural refuge for a number of dismayed and disillusioned writers and artists and with the Cabaret Voltaire as the centre of their activities they issued a stream of publications, experimental films, sculptural constructions and paintings and graphics.

The Cabaret Voltaire itself became an arts club with a difference as well as an exhibition and lecture hall. The entertainments provided give some idea of the wild irresponsibility and destructive zeal that prompted the movement. These were consciously directed at outraging the uncomprehending public, which, however, observed the antics with fascination. In extraordinary clothes – or occasionally without – the participants recited nonsense poems or created nonsense music with gongs, rattles and other noise-making materials, accompanying the action with obscene posturing. The purpose was to ridicule the human situation, to diminish social pretensions and to force audience self-awareness by attacking their principles and assumptions.

Very quickly, similar manifestations appeared throughout Europe and North America, most notably in Paris and New York. Paris became the centre for Dada activities, and the Dadaists, encouraged by the outraged public response and published attacks, went from excess to excess but nonetheless finally became boring and repetitive, defeating their intentions and alienating those whose sympathies had originally been with them.

Dada was primarily a literary movement, though there were some artistic creations. The collages of Jean Arp (1887–1966), the child machines working hard to no evident purpose of Francis Picabia (1878–1953) and the 'readymade' objects of Marcel Duchamp (1887–1968) had a genuine shock value.

The most notorious of the Dada objects is Duchamp's *Mona Lisa* with added moustache and obscene caption, a deliberate blow at 'old masters' and museum art. This destructive attitude to established standards links Dada – tenuously at least – with other contemporary movements, especially Futurism.

The name Dada, typically given a number of different sources by the Dadaists themselves, probably derives from the French *dada* – a hobby horse, and is said to have been picked out of a dictionary at random.

Surrealism. The origin of the name Surrealism is also rather vague. It appears to have been first used by Apollinaire in describing (1917) a play he had written as *une drame surréaliste en deux actes et un prologue*, and was subsequently abrogated by André Breton (1896–1966).

As defined by Breton, its founder, prophet and most effective propagandist, Surrealism had a more serious cultural purpose and programme than Dada. The Dadaists, it might be said, were apprentice surgeons opening up the tender social body and hacking off a limb or two, while the Surrealists probed the raw wounds with some care and precision. Breton came to believe that Dada was nothing more than a 'rough image of a state of mind which it by no means helped to create' and came to feel little sympathy for their antics or their attitude towards art. He considered that positive creative action, the result of exercising the intellect and – especially – the imagination, was the proper inspiration of a modern art form.

In 1924 Breton issued the first *Surrealist Manifesto* in which he defined Surrealism, as he said 'once and for all' . . .

[Dictionary]
Surrealism. noun. Pure psychic automatism, by which it is intended to express, whether verbally or in writing, or in any other way, the real process of thought. Thought's dictation free from any control by the reason, independent of any aesthetic or moral preoccupation.

Encyclo. philos. Surrealism rests on the belief in the superior reality of certain forms of association hitherto neglected, in the omnipotence of the dream, in the disinterested play of thought. It tends definitely to destroy all other mechanisms and to substitute itself for them in the solution of the principal problems of life.

Thus, Surrealism is not a style in art, like Cubism or De Stijl, it is an attitude to life and society.

During the next two decades the influence of Breton and his fellow Surrealists extended widely through Europe and America. Surrealism appeared in many differing artistic guises, in poetry, fiction, music and in films, two of which by Luis Buñuel and Salvador Dali, *Le chien andalou* (1929) and *L'âge d'or* (1931), are among the most powerful and accessible examples of Surrealist expression.

Throughout the 1930s most countries held exhibitions of Surrealist work and almost invariably these were accompanied by incomprehension and vilification in the popular press. At this time 'Surrealism' became a term to embrace all modern painting, however remote from it, and it has since held a certain currency as synonymous with 'modern art'. There was some support

for the Surrealists among intellectuals in each country, but mystification was the typical response. When the International Surrealist Exhibition opened in London in 1936, the *Daily Express* said it was unfit for the public at large.

Dada Relief, 1916. Hans (Jean) Arp (Kunstmuseum, Basle).
Roughly made of sawn blocks of wood painted and screwed together with no attempt at any refinement, this sculpture reflects the anti-art attitude of the Dadaists. They found easy ways of

fulfilling their desire to shock. Avoidance of the conventional and the valued combined with the elevation of the valueless and the ridiculous was attractive to them. Such objects as this, displayed as art and thus to be respected when they were, they thought, rubbish excited them.

The Hair Navel, (Merz *picture 21B*) *1920 (left). Kurt Schwitters (Lords Gallery, London).* Merzbau, *original version 1945 (below left). Kurt Schwitters (Hatton Gallery, University of Newcastle-upon-Tyne).*
Schwitters's early work combined German Expressionism and Cubism but, working in Germany around 1920, he began making collages which he called Merz out of discarded rubbish – string, bits of paper with words on, etc. The construction of the first of three Merzbau followed. These were three-dimensional interior constructions using a combination of wood, plaster and other 'found' materials. The last Merzbau (shown here), which is 135 sq ft (12.5 sq m) in area, was begun on an isolated farm in the English Lake District and uncompleted at the artist's death.

A supporter of Dada, Schwitters's juxtaposition of unrelated and irrational materials indicates his sympathies. Like the Dadaists he was hostile to traditional art and its attitudes and suggested with his rubbish constructions that anything may be used to make art imagery. He also made one or two collages that anticipate Pop art in their use of comic-strip material.

Right:
Of This Men Shall Know Nothing, *1923. Max Ernst (Tate Gallery, London).*
In this painting the sexuality is obvious and the symbolism clear. The back is inscribed by Ernst with the following: 'The Crescent (yellow and parachutic) stops the little whistle falling to the ground. The whistle, because people are taking notice of it, thinks it is climbing to the sun. The sun is divided in two so that it can spin better. The model is stretched out in a dreaming pose. The right leg is bent (a pleasant exact movement). The hand hides the earth. Through this movement the earth takes on the importance of a sexual organ. The moon runs through its phases and eclipses with the utmost speed. The picture is curious because of its symmetry. The two sexes balance each other.'

Premonition of Civil War, *1936 (above). Salvador Dali (Philadelphia Museum of Art. Louise and Walter Arensberg Collection).* Christ of St John of the Cross, *1951 (right). Salvador Dali (Glasgow Art Gallery and Museum).*

Perhaps the best known of the Surrealists, Dali has always been a successful publicist for the movement and for himself. By employing careful academic draughtsmanship, he makes his distorted and irrational images apparently comprehensible to many who find the more abstract examples of Surrealism bewildering. Whilst his draughtsmanship is commonplace the images he invents

seem, mostly, to evoke a sense of some residual dream memory with all its irrationalities of location, scale and content. In Premonition of Civil War *(painted at the time of the Spanish Civil War) the sensational exhibitionism and overt sexuality of his work is evident. In the* Crucifixion *he treats a traditional subject as a dreamlike image.*

Similar views were expressed in other countries. As time passed, however, two main courses of development appeared, one continuing the nihilism of Dada, the other concerned more with aesthetic construction. At the same time the formerly outrageous behaviour of the Surrealists became increasingly tolerated, and Surrealist artists turned their attention more to producing works and less to striking public attitudes. By the 1940s Surrealists were appearing in mixed exhibitions with little evident incongruity. In short, Surrealism became acceptable, reflecting the fantastic and mystical, and often deviating into emotional pattern-making.

Watches draped over withered tree stumps, animated but dismembered figures, dream evocation, unreasonable and often erotic association of objects in irrational scale, near abstract symbols of sexual reference – these are elements in the form of art known as Surrealism. For the majority of people such material scarcely seemed proper to art, but it is the nature of Surrealism to introduce different subjects, and some measure of its success is that it has managed to achieve their acceptance. Part of the reason for this no doubt lies in the fascination that human nature has for the turned-over stone,

Left:
Mama, Papa is Wounded!, *1927.*
Yves Tanguy (Museum of Modern Art, *New York).*
Born in Paris, Tanguy became a painter *after seeing a painting by Chirico in a gallery window. His work suggests remoteness and isolation like Chirico's, but his subjects seem to be located on the seabed or in an arid desert on a distant planet. The mysticism and irrationality of his strange world is essentially Surrealist. As in many Surrealist works sexual imagery is apparent in this painting.*
Tanguy became a U.S. citizen in 1948, having settled there during the war.

the weird, the half-realized, the dangerous, the unexpected and the fearsome. We are attracted, even while feeling cautious revulsion.

Such distaste and fascination are Surrealist currency and the history of painting abounds in examples of this uncovering of the unconscious and the presentation of the visually impossible – or at least the improbable – in the most visually convincing terms. Sometimes, as in the bestiaries of the Middle Ages, the monster figures stem from a real belief in the existence of the super-real world and a conscious imaginative attempt to personify them. Later, this is extended into an attempt to present a thesis in visual terms which its author is aware is not natural but which he feels to be true in essence – examples are found in the works of Breughel and Bosch. Here the allegory is a justification of the imagery. Sometimes flights of visual fancy have been responsible for a form of Surrealism – the vegetable men of Arcimboldo, the incongruous contiguity of the inmates of the forests in Douanier Rousseau, and even the grotesques of Leonardo.

Perhaps the single most powerful impact on Surrealism was made by psychoanalysis and its revelation of the sexual depths in human nature. The writings and case histories of Freud and his followers provided the Surrealists directly with means of expression. They were aware of the importance of the analyst's inquiry and felt that it provided them with an opportunity to enlarge the language of art, that the art of the day was a dead restraint. The case histories also provided them with a source of shock. Overt sexuality and its expression in art is a surefire public talking point, and the early Surrealists used it extensively.

Another method of shocking public sensibilities, almost as certain of success, was to ridicule the common artefacts of society by destroying their practical utility – hence the fur-lined teacup, saucer and spoon of Méret Oppenheim, the *Cadeau* of Man Ray (1890–1977), a flat iron to the base of which tacks were attached, and Marcel Duchamp's readymades (like the famous *Fountain*, a urinal).

In their efforts to enlarge experience and to question what is obvious and familiar, the Surrealists chose any

number of different methods. As Surrealism is not a 'style', it is limited neither in method nor technique, and the range of expression is considerable. Max Ernst (1891–1976) developed a technique, *frottage*, which, rather like brass rubbing, gave a curious, vague but emotionally loaded evocation of landscape or figure. Salvador Dali deployed a meticulously naturalistic technique in heavily constructed irrationalities, as did René Magritte (1898–1967), while Joan Miro (1893–1984) approached abstraction. Giorgio de Chirico (1888–1978) invented a meditative dream world of eerie conviction. Kurt Schwitters (1887–1948) invented the term *merz* to describe the form of collage he made of rejected bric-a-brac. The list could be extended almost indefinitely.

From Cubism onwards, new pictorial treatments seemed richly available. In this sense it was Picasso, who has been described as 'the greatest agitator Western art has ever known', who initiated modern Surrealism and, as the movement progressed, contributed fruitfully to it. Although not normally identified as a Surrealist, in the late 1920s and 1930s his work included much Surrealist imagery.

On the other hand, Surrealism's preoccupation with dream or fantasy has inspired and lent credence to some mediocre work. Paradoxically, the description 'Surrealist' has come to appear as a stamp of approval.

Underlying all the methods of Surrealist expression is a serious purpose of considerable value: the confrontation with the self. The irrational but figurative treatment of subjects served to increase consciousness of their actuality. There was a social conscience at work – one needs only the slightest acquaintance with the character of a man like Breton to realize that.

However, it is a curious reflection on the course of 20th-century art that at a time when artists were attempting to remove art from the exclusive possession of the privileged and to produce works for a bourgeois society, that not only were the artists (in the case of the Surrealists) appreciated more by the privileged, but they themselves were intent to *epaté le bourgeoisie* – rejecting their conventions and ridiculing their pretensions.

Maternity, *1924 (above). Joan Miro (Private Collection).*
Maternity, *1913 (right). Marc Chagall (Stedelijk Museum, Amsterdam).*
A comparison of these two paintings, both entitled Maternity, *one by the Spaniard Joan Miro and the other by the Russian-born Marc Chagall, reveals the range of*

expression of Surrealist symbolism. In Miro's painting the abstracted forms have a very clear sexual derivation and seem to represent an almost clinical, if imaginative, pictorial diagram of the process of fertilization, with magnified representation of sperm and ovum. The warmth and care of motherhood, seen in

Chagall's equally but differently explicit work, are absent in Miro's. In Chagall the child in the womb is surrounded by rich and varied symbols of life in the world that he is to enter: mysterious and commonplace, full of labour but also of joy.

Art in America: *1900–40*

The story of American art from the
colonial period to the late 19th century
followed a derivative pattern. Even
when in the middle years of the 19th
century the United States was forging
its great industrial power, creating un-
imaginable wealth for a few and a
decent living for the majority, building
great cities and establishing lasting
democracy, it was looking abroad for
its cultural criteria and inspiration. The
artistic life of America was bound up
with art in Europe, and the European
salons and academies gave the young
society its forms and standards.

Although there were many American artists of undoubted ability between the 17th and 19th centuries,
there were none to match the great
genius of so many Europeans in that
period. There are many explanations
for this, including the obvious statisti-
cal one – Europeans were far more
numerous. Moreover, the small population existed in a large area: the East
Coast of North America is as far from
the West Coast as it is from Europe,
and just as European states developed
individual cultures so, to some extent,
did the states of the Union. There was
no single American culture; to this day
European visitors are surprised by the
different character of each region of
what they suppose is a nation like
France or Britain. But the single most
important reason for the United
States's cultural dependence on Europe
was that the people were, or were
descended from (not many generations
before) Europeans.

The growing wealth, the building of
great houses modelled on European
châteaux and mansions and the youthful eagerness of the United States in the
19th century demanded an impressive
and historic art. The bold enterprise
and ready experiment of American
industry was not paralleled in the arts.
Only a few Americans who had studied
in Europe, especially in Paris, were
aware of such new French developments as Impressionism and Post-
Impressionism.

However, in the early years of the
20th century an essentially modern and
incontrovertibly American group of
artists – the first that merited that
description – made its appearance.
This was the Ashcan School, also
known as the Revolutionary Black
Gang and, as a result of their sombre
colour and harsh line, the Apostles of
Ugliness. They were Robert Henri
(1865–1929), George Luks (1867–
1933), William Glackens (1870–
1938), Everett Shinn (1876–1953)
and John Sloan (1871–1951). Their
paintings derived from the realism of
Thomas Eakins (1844–1916) and the
tradition of American genre painting.
They took their subject matter from
urban life, particularly its more squalid
aspects, and painted what they saw.
They were antipathetic both to the
light palette of the Impressionists and
to their lack of subjective commitment.

This was not what the public
wanted, being decidedly short on dignified elegance and hardly suggesting a
long cultural history, but their impact
was nonetheless considerable. They
represent a continuing and lively strain
in American painting. The five members all came from Philadelphia,
though they moved to New York in
1904. Until the First World War they
were the most independent group in
American painting.

America's real awakening to modern
art, however, came on 17 February
1913 with the opening of what was
perhaps the most dramatically effective
exhibition ever mounted. Known as the
Armory Show because it was held in
the large open space of the 69th Regi-
ment Armory in New York, it was later
transferred to Boston and Chicago.
Although there were of course some
young painters who were aware of the
early European movements such as
Cubism, for the art world generally this
show was a revelation, an uncomfortable one too. The artists whose work
was shown included Picasso, Matisse,
Derain, Braque, Brancusi, Kirchner,
Kandinsky and Duchamp, whose

Futurist *Nude Descending a Staircase* was the sensation of the show. Nothing like this exhibition had ever been seen; the public flocked to it, shuddering; the press reviled it.

The show was organized by the newly formed Association of American Painters and Sculptors and also contained works by American painters. It was as much the recognition of the conservatism of native artists, as against the outrageous but exciting work of their contemporaries in Europe, which caused the ensuing revolution in American art. The war temporarily obscured the effects of the Armory Show, but at the end of it a small, effective modern art fraternity was established.

The show had a particular effect upon collectors, and the purchases made then form the basis of many major American collections today. (The prices paid are startling reading: Picasso's *Arbres*, now called *Landscape*, of 1907 was sold for $243, Derain's *La Forêt de Marigues* of 1908–09 for $378, Villon's *Young Girl at a Piano* for $270; Impressionist and Post-Impressionist works by such as Degas, Cézanne and Seurat were similarly valued.)

It is difficult to overestimate the impact of this exhibition on American sensibilities. Galleries suddenly became willing to show experimental work, and in the excitement of the new experience, which could hardly yet have reached the stage of real comprehension, an era of freedom and experiment followed. Much that appeared in the new commercial galleries was not good; study, thought and sensitivity were required from critics, students, gallery owners and collectors. Some collectors now travelled to Europe to buy, and thus Europe as well as America felt the impact of the Armory Show. For the decade which ended with the Stock Market Crash of 1929 and the ensuing Depression, European artists enjoyed a new market of eager, extremely rich, if not always well-informed, American collectors.

The revelation of a new non-American art, of abstraction and an entirely

The Armory Show, *1913. This installation photograph shows Gallery 53, which was devoted to Cubism. Most of the Cubists were represented. A number of the works illustrated in this book were shown at this famous exhibition, including Picasso's sculpture* Head of a Woman *(1909) and Jacques Villon's* Little Girl at the Piano *(1912). The paintings in the photograph include works by Duchamp, Derain, Braque, Gleizes and Picasso. The sculpture is* Family Life *by Archipenko and in the far corner* Torso *by Duchamp Villon.*

different aesthetic, was to cause a number of different responses in the thinking younger artists of the immediate postwar period. The conservatives continued in set paths, disturbed but unconverted; the young recognized that something significant had happened which had to affect them. Two main directions appeared during the 1920s. Firstly, there were those who found in some of the art they saw an inspiration for an art which could use the discoveries of the Europeans but in a way that was American. For them the American scene was the proper subject for American artists, however it might be treated pictorially, and the Ashcan school was a major source of inspiration.

Secondly, there were those who found in the new European art a direct inspiration for their own work – which would be part of world art, not parochial, and would bring America into the mainstream of Western art where, they recognized, it had never been before. Initially, lacking the background of the Europeans, their efforts were not pictorially accomplished and sometimes naive.

For this second group the focus of their activity was what has come to be known as '291'. The photographer Alfred Stieglitz (1864–1946), who was born in New Jersey, studied in Germany and settled in New York, founded in 1905 the Photo-Secession Gallery at 291 Fifth Avenue, New York City. Stieglitz was an extraordinarily sensitive and determined modernist, who imported European artists and showed their work in his attic gallery.

Battle of Lights, Coney Island, *1913.*
Joseph Stella (Yale University Art Gallery, New Haven, Connecticut. Collection Société Anonyme).
Stella abandoned the study of medicine in New York for painting, and on a visit to his native Italy in 1909–12 he met the Italian Futurists. Back in New York he used the experience to interpret his impressions of his new homeland. This is an exhibition piece which uses Futurist and Cubist elements to produce an exciting, aggressive image. It is the first work of its kind in the United States – 1913 was the year of the Armory Show – and in the new atmosphere it gained Stella immediate public recognition.

133

Before the Armory Show, Stieglitz's attic was the only source of information on contemporary European art. American artists were able to see, thanks to the advanced and almost infallible taste of this extraordinary man – who gave Brancusi his first-ever exhibition – the latest work then emerging from Europe.

Thanks to the Realists of the Ashcan School and the modernists of 291, the inferiority complex that had temporarily afflicted American art after the Armory Show began to fade away. By the time of the Depression in the 1930s American art was beginning to achieve its own identity and a number of significant if not yet internationally influential artists were producing work that could be regarded as quintessentially American.

Of course it is important to realize that a painting of an American scene, for instance, or one that employs essentially American objects for abstraction is not necessarily American art, any more than a French painter working in Britain produces British art. What was happening was more significant. Outside influences notwithstanding, the artists were finding the inspiration for their art forms in their own culture. This was the beginning of what became, in the 1950s, the American dominance of Western art.

Right:
Lucky Strike, 1921. Stuart Davis (Museum of Modern Art, New York. Gift of the American Tobacco Company, Inc.). The youngest exhibitor at the Armory Show, Davis was aware of recent developments in Europe and made experiments using the elements discovered through his acquaintance with many of the actual works of the early modern masters. His painting Lucky Strike *combines a number of these influences including the notion of Duchamp's objet trouvé.*

Far right:
Abstraction Blue, 1927. Georgia O'Keefe (Museum of Modern Art, New York. Acquired through the Helen Acheson Bequest).
The floating delicacy of colour sharply divided by the pointed shaft is an example of the move towards abstraction that O'Keefe made in the 1920s. At this time she began the enlargement of details of natural landscape or plant forms to a point where they were no longer recognizable and took on an abstract character. The separated sides carry *different suggestions of cloud and landscape and it has been suggested that she was influenced by her husband Alfred Stieglitz's photographic series of cloud and landscape elements called* Equivalents.

The Armory Show did not convert the public to modern art but, mainly through reproductions and reviews, people were made aware of this strange new phenomenon. It did convert one or two Americans to the new abstraction, among them Stuart Davis (1894–1964) who at 19 was the youngest exhibitor at the Show, with five works. Davis's later importance in the development of modern American art is considerable. Joseph Stella's (1880–1946) *Battle of Lights: Coney Island* (1913), garish and brash in the bright colours that were to become characteristic of his work, was one of the first paintings by an American to employ Cubist and Futurist devices for an essentially American image. He had been a student of Robert Henri, and though he rejected Ashcan realism, the city locations used by Henri were a feature of his early abstractions.

Of American subject painters who did not adopt the European aesthetic, the most important are the Precisionists and the Realists. The Precisionists, of whom Charles Demuth (1883–

1935) and Charles Sheeler (1883–1965) were the leaders, used American industrial products and buildings for their careful, clean, simplified images, somewhat influenced by Cubist simplification of form. Duchamp, who lived in America from 1918, was their principal inspiration – he said that America's art lay in her bridges and plumbing – and they were drawn to familiar manufactured objects.

Duchamp, indeed, became the *éminence grise* of the American art scene for some fifty years between his arrival in 1918 and his death in 1968. Not only his work but his presence at every major art show (including the Happenings of the 1960s) was very important to the young artists of the day. It suggested not only the continuity of art but also its international unity.

The Realists, as the name implies, were concerned with a factual, objective form of painting, which ranged from the meticulous surface observation of Andrew Wyeth, an enormously popular painter with a strong sense of open space (a commodity that Americans are

Above:
'Oriental'. Synchromy in Blue-Green, *1918. Stanton MacDonald-Wright (Whitney Museum of American Art, New York).*
In Paris in 1912 MacDonald-Wright and Morgan Russell developed what they called Synchronism under the influence of Cubism and Delaunay's Orphism. MacDonald-Wright returned to New York in 1916 and the movement lasted until 1920 when he abandoned abstraction as a result of his generally declining interest in modern art.

Above right:
New York Movie, *1939. Edward Hopper (Museum of Modern Art, New York. Given anonymously).*
Hopper lived and painted in New York for most of his life, but it was not the excitement and energy of that great city that excited him, rather the loneliness, the isolation and the moody dignity of run-down buildings. His qualities are well expressed in New York Movie, *where the cold darkness is broken only by the garish light illuminating the salesgirl.*

aware they have in abundance), isolation and timelessness, to the paintings of Thomas Hart Benton (1889–1975), which are careful, subjective depictions of the American scene both urban and rural. Grant Wood's *American Gothic*, a portrait of a stiffly conservative farm couple in a meticulous but patterned technique, has become almost an American icon, exploited by all in the manner of Leonardo's *Mona Lisa*.

The most interesting of the Realists and a painter whose reputation increases steadily is Edward Hopper (1882–1967). In place of Andrew Wyeth's romantic, anecdotal isolation, he had a deeper understanding of loneliness and separateness, manifest in a series of direct images in which the figures, buildings and furnishings seem to have an equal identity and importance in the painting, equally remote from each other and the viewer. There is a melancholy and a mystery which is

powerfully affecting in these apparently straightforward observational works and sets them apart from other Realist paintings. Despite the apparent lack of emotional commitment, Hopper's choice of subject and the arrangement of the image leaves a moving impression of grandeur in the mundane incident of life. With his paintings, the American scene becomes part of the human condition.

Another painter who should be mentioned is Ben Shahn (1898–1969) whose graphic satires were partly inspired by the Expressionist George Grosz's images of disgust. Whilst showing real passion, the illustrational treatment of this master draughtsman makes the quality of his work difficult to apprehend except as illustration.

It should also be noted that after the First World War the focus of art was not so strongly centred on the East Coast (and particularly in New York)

but was giving way to regional developments. The painters of the Mid West or California were interested in depicting their own urban scene or wide open spaces. There were many interesting and talented regional artists, though none that contributed greatly to the development of the modern aesthetic.

To investigate this we must examine further the effect of 291 and Stieglitz's later galleries, the Intimate Gallery and, after 1930, An American Place. Stieglitz's first special group of five painters, John Marin (1870–1953), Marsden Hartley (1877–1943), Arthur Dove (1880–1946), Charles Demuth (1883–1935) and Georgia O'Keefe, whom he later married, were shown with European masters and it was part of his achievement to give a new dignity and sense of purpose to these young artists during the 1920s.

Stieglitz's stable was important as a breeding ground for ideas and as a

source of mutual support at a time when American painting was going through a testing time, before a sense of confidence and identity had been recovered.

Another painter who also exhibited at 291 and in the Armory Show was Stanton Macdonald-Wright, mentioned earlier along with Morgan Russell. They founded the first avowedly modern American movement, Synchromism, based upon ideas similar to Delaunay's Orphism. Macdonald-Wright and Russell studied and worked in Paris and were part of the Parisian art world, having a genuine understanding of Cubism. To the extent that they were Americans and exhibited at 291, theirs was an American movement. Patrick Henry Bruce (1880–1937) and Max Weber (1881–1961), who painted the first truly Cubist American painting in 1909, should also be mentioned.

Unlike the Realists in their surface depiction of the American scene, but with a deep interest in their land, Marin, Hartley, Dove and O'Keefe went to nature for their inspiration, leaving New York for the peace and solitude of the country in their search for the emotional simplification of form and image which they felt the modern aesthetic demanded. In this search they each arrived at a very different and personal understanding of the landscape. Their attempts to create an art modern in idiom but based

upon nature led them towards abstractionism, but not to purely abstract work. Of this group perhaps the most interesting and influential is O'Keefe, whose strange and brooding images evoke a feeling of growth, renewal and permanence in nature.

In the Depression of the 1930s artists suffered with everyone else. In such embattled times ranks close and popular taste is strengthened, elitism and privilege are condemned, the commonplace knits the community and deprivation rejects the unfamiliar. Modern art with its apparent waywardness and lack of concern for practical matters of living had a difficult time, and government aid was given in the first instance to those artists who conformed to popular taste.

In 1933 a government art agency was founded to support artists by putting them to work on mural projects, an alternative preferable to the dole. This was partly inspired by the Mexican muralist revolution (see page 140) and the influence of one of its major figures, Diego Rivera, who was living in New York. Although the Public Works of Art Project only lasted for five months, in that time 4,000 artists produced 15,000 works and introduced a new notion of large-scale works of art which became a notable feature of the 1950s and 1960s. Cautiously, it made the public accustomed to non-realist, large-scale decorative work,

Above left:
Portrait of a German Officer, *1914. Marsden Hartley (Metropolitan Museum of Art, New York. Alfred Stieglitz Collection).*
Hartley first exhibited at Stieglitz's 291 Gallery in 1909, and in 1912 Stieglitz assisted with money to send him to Europe. In Paris he met the Cubists, but he soon moved to Munich where he stayed during the first years of the war. At this time he painted a number of abstractions under the influence of Marc and Kandinsky, which were exhibited in Berlin. This is one of those works; its harsh and strident linear and colour effects have more in common with Expressionism than with the Parisian movements.

Above:
Painting, *1926–28. Patrick Henry Bruce (Whitney Museum of American Art, New York).*
In 1907 Bruce settled in Paris and worked in Matisse's studio. He was also influenced by Delaunay's Orphism. Although he exhibited at the Armory Show he was successful in neither Paris nor New York and became increasingly isolated, so that in 1932 he abandoned painting and destroyed all but 15 of his paintings. This late work is one of his abstractionist still-lifes, which were painted in strong colours and simplified planes.

and the precedent set then resulted in one of the major art ideas exported from the United States to Europe in the years after 1945.

As far as the welfare of the arts was concerned, the main innovation of Roosevelt's New Deal was the Federal Art Project run by the WPA (Works Projects Administration). Between 1935 and 1939, the project provided work for thousands of artists. About 4,000 artists were paid a salary to undertake a variety of work from the painting and drawing of American decorative arts (for the purpose of historical records) to the establishment of and teaching in art-education centres.

The best-known works of this project are the murals in post offices and other Federal buildings, mainly of typically American scenes in the manner of Thomas Hart Benton. Most significant for the future of modern art in America was the fact that a number of young painters who were to take the lead in the dramatic developments of the 1940s and 1950s received a regular income. Among them were Jackson Pollock, Arshile Gorky, Willem de Kooning, Ad Reinhardt, Mark Rothko, Adolph Gottlieb and David Smith. It enabled them to develop free from commercial pressures, so that they burst upon a surprised and impressed world in the immediate postwar years.

As must by now be obvious, the confrontation between artists dedicated to representational imagery and those who adopted pure or near abstract forms of expression went on throughout this whole period. In America during the 1930s representational art, whether that of regional artists representing local culture or of the Precisionists with their more refined imagery, appeared to dominate. Except for a few determined painters like Stuart Davis, abstraction was considered by American painters as too distinctively European.

Yet during this period a new aesthetic was beginning to emerge. In 1936 a Russian emigré who took the name John Graham wrote a treatise called *System and Dialectics of Art*, in which he stated that 'no technical perfection or elegance can produce a work of art. A work of art is neither the faithful nor distorted representation, it is the im-mediate unadorned record of an authentic intellecto-emotional REACTION of the artist set in space'. Experiments with the removal of visual incident while retaining the actuality of experience were part of the purpose of artists such as Pollock and Rothko at this time, though little of this reached the public eye until later.

During the 1930s there was an influx of European artists. They included people associated with the disbanded Bauhaus, refugees, and a number who simply wanted to experience America.

Altogether, they made a dramatic impact. For a start, their presence seemed to signify the acceptance of the United States as an important part, if not the most important, of Western culture. This awareness helped to encourage aggressively forward-looking attitudes in the American art world. Collecting the works of the masters of the early modern movements became a passion, with the result that the United States became the main repository of the modern movements, the Museum of Modern Art in New York today having the finest and most comprehensive public collection of modern art anywhere.

Among the most notable Europeans working in the United States were Matisse (to paint murals for the Barnes Foundation), Léger (to paint murals for the French Line – never finished), Miro (to work in Atelier 17 with the etcher Stanley Hayter), Hans Hofmann and Piet Mondrian. The latter had moved to London from Paris in 1938 but was bombed out in 1940, whereupon he came to New York. He died there in 1944.

As far as the future development of American art is concerned, probably the most significant new arrival was Josef Albers, a former teacher at the Bauhaus. Albers founded Black Mountain College near Asheville, North Carolina, in 1933; it then became the most important teaching centre for modern aesthetics until its closure on Albers's departure in 1950. Many of the artists who were to become well known in the 1950s and 1960s were associated with Black Mountain at one time or another. Albers's teaching, based on Bauhaus ideas, stressed that design and colour could be considered as abstract elements from which prin-ciples of artistic creation derived. It should be remembered that in America – as indeed in most of Europe – art education at this time was academically based and took little account of developments or theories since the Post-Impressionists. Albers's influence continued after the closure of Black Mountain when he went to Yale University as director of art studies.

The disruption of the Second World War obscured the activities of artists from the general view, but when the war ended the scene was set for the American invasion of the international, Europe-based art scene.

Mexican Revolutionary Art

In the 16th century the struggle between the indigenous peoples of Mexico and the Spanish invaders resulted in oppression and deprivation for the former, who felt a deep and bitter antagonism to the Spaniards which lasted to the end of the colonial period in 1821. Thereafter, independent Mexico engaged in turbulent, internecine conflict, during which the peasant population was increasingly exploited, used as cannon fodder by warring leaders and deprived of their land and possessions. By 1876, when Porfiro Diaz became president (in reality dictator), Mexico had also become the battleground for U.S. and European vested interests. Diaz's thirty-year regime expanded the economic possibilities of the country while exercising severe repression.

In 1910 discontent bubbled into rebellion. Diaz's successor was displaced by Huerta, who in turn was overthrown by the popular heroes Carranza, Villa and Zapata. For some years presidents came and went with bewildering speed, revolutionary outbreaks continued, and the people, despite attempts at reform, remained poor, oppressed and exploited. Only in 1940 did Mexico achieve some political stability, agrarian justice and economic independence.

Thus, for thirty years Mexico was permeated by a revolutionary spirit. In the arts its most evident and powerful effect was the extraordinary murals of the period. There is nothing comparable to this elsewhere in 20th-century art. It arose from the passion for social justice, from powerful nationalist feelings ('Mexico for the Mexicans'), and from an unusual degree of government support. The painters responsible were a group whose aims, if not identical, were sympathetic and whose methods were compatible. The strength of their passion and proselytizing zeal were appropriate to the mural method, while the dedication of the government to the idea of expressing Mexican resurgence in large modern buildings offered plenty of wall space on which the artists could work.

They took full advantage of the opportunities, displaying remarkable energy and pictorial inventiveness. Deeply interested in the history of their country, they were incensed by the heartless cruelty of the Spanish conquerors and the later degradation of the indigenous peoples. They saw the resentful acquiesence of the peasants as heroism deserving of record, and the relentless, mechanical massacres as evidence of the Devil on Earth. Their art was not for galleries and museums but

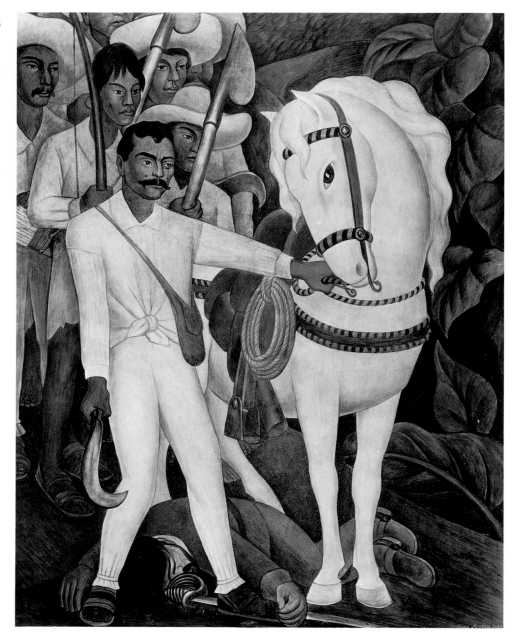

for the people who used the great new public buildings. This was a political-propagandist art, an art expressly for the people.

It is common to regard the European modern movements as proceeding towards 'art for the people' (rather than the elite), but it is probably true to say that the only art of this century that has actually achieved real popular significance and power is that produced by the revolutionary Mexican artists between about 1920 and 1940.

It is also probably true that of all the art of this century this is the least

Left:
Agrarian Leader Zapata, *1931.*
Fresco. Diego Rivera (Museum of Modern Art, New York. Abby Aldrich Rockefeller Fund).
Rivera was the first of the Mexican muralists to achieve success and he painted Creation, *the first of the modern murals, at the Mexico City University in 1922. He had studied and worked in Paris until 1920 and was familiar with the development of Cubism, painting a number of Cubist works himself. Through the next two decades he painted vast historical or allegorical murals containing Marxist elements for the Mexican Ministry of Education. The presentation of the oppressed but dignified peasants which he initiated inspired the revolutionary muralists who were his contemporaries.*

Above:
Zapatistas, *1931. José Clemente Orozco (Museum of Modern Art, New York. Given anonymously).*
With strong revolutionary sympathies, Orozco painted his first mural in Mexico City at about the same time as Rivera and Siqueiros. With these three the muralist programme began. Zapatistas, harsh and forthright in treatment, shows a group of followers of the popular leader Zapata. This constant emphasis on the heroism of the peasants against oppression distinguishes such paintings from most other 20th-century work.

widely known or appreciated by the art public outside its country of origin. One reason is obvious. Murals stay where they are and can only really be appreciated *in situ*. Small-scale reproductions give some idea but cannot convey the power of sheer scale; they tend to reduce them to an image comparable with small cabinet pictures. Moreover, these are not comfortable, 'enjoyable' works, and they do not adopt the forms of the contemporary movements in Europe and the United States. They are gross and aggressive. Essentially Mexican, they appeal to historical knowledge and do not pander to the tasteful. The greedy representatives of capitalism and militarism are the villains, and all gringos are likely to experience feelings of guilt, if only vicariously.

The most important and prolific of these Mexican artists is Diego Rivera (1886–1957) whose early life was spent in cultured Paris and whose first work was Cubist. Of the many others, the most important are José Orozco (1883–1949), David Alfaro Siqueiros (1898–1974) and Rufino Tamayo. Orozco's imagery is powerful and uncompromising. Revolutionary in intent it contrasts the mechanistic forms of authority (men as military machines) with the soft, yielding forms of the masses. His colour is harsh and his tones are strong. His is not an art of acceptance but of violent protest. Siqueiros was politically far enough left to have been imprisoned a number of times. His drawing is powerful and crude, and if his passion is stronger than his talent, the unequivocal directness of his pictorial message makes up for it. Tamayo, using modern forms and later settling in New York, fits more easily into the pattern of modern Western art. It is this very fact which makes him perhaps less interesting than his fellow muralists, despite his subtle colour sense. It also suggests that politically revolutionary attitudes in art need an immediate and straightforward impact.

Animals, *1941. Rufino Tamayo (Museum of Modern Art, New York. Inter-American Fund).*
Tamayo, of a younger generation than Rivera and the others, painted a number of murals which reflected rather the effect of revolution than the revolution itself. He was a more sophisticated practitioner than the others; his work shows the influence of the modern movements, and of Picasso in particular.

The Bauhaus

The Bauhaus was not an art movement. It was a design school, brainchild of the architect Walter Gropius, the form of which was to influence so many later developments in design and art education that it must be considered relevant to a survey of modern art. The fundamental aim of the Bauhaus was to unite all the arts and crafts in a functional programme based on architectural building and mass production of goods. Both indirectly and directly it has affected attitudes and practice in art education since the 1930s, especially in the United States.

The Bauhaus came into existence as the result of a policy of educational reform in Germany after the First World War. Without great natural resources, Germany depended for her growth on the energy and abilities of her people who, in 1919, the year of the opening of the Bauhaus, were demoralized, divided and poor. The Germans felt that the terms of the Versailles peace treaty were both unjust and humiliating, and the new republic set up at Weimar in 1919 in the wake of that treaty had no very propitious beginning and a short life. Hitler's appointment as chancellor at the beginning of 1933 spelt doom. The Weimar constitution was torn up and the Bauhaus, by then a shadow of its former self, was closed by the Berlin police. Its life thus coincided almost exactly with that of the Weimar Republic.

The most famous, most revolutionary art school of modern times lasted a mere 14 years, and during those years there were several changes of direction, much internal strife, and extraordinary pressures from outside – from authority, individuals and the press. Amazement at its success is heightened by the fact that during its short life it inhabited four different building complexes and had three different directors, each of whom reversed or at least modified the direction set by his predecessor. Turnover of staff was also rapid: only one member of the original staff,

Lyonel Feininger, remained throughout.

The closure of the Bauhaus in 1933 had, however, one fortunate result. The widely held assumption, not without foundation, that there was a strong Communist element among staff and students made the Bauhaus anathema to the Nazis, so that those among the staff and students who were able to do so left Germany and settled in other European countries or – a significant number – in the United States. Bauhaus ideas were already famous outside Germany, but with this exodus of Bauhaus members, they became much more effective.

The Bauhaus was located in Weimar from 1919 to 1923, under the directorship of Gropius who was permitted to call his school The State Bauhaus. *Bau* means 'building' and Gropius's intention was to use the combined arts and crafts and fine-art schools as a core for integrating the whole of creative art education into one building school – which, incidentally, at this stage did not include an architectural school.

It consisted of a two-part structure: a fine-art department under what he called 'Masters of Form', and a crafts and practical department under 'Workshop Masters'. The Masters of Form were the artist staff members, and the Workshop Masters were specialist craftsmen directing departments of furniture, ceramics, textiles, etc. They were intended to be of equal status.

From the beginning, Gropius had great difficulty in finding suitable Workshop Masters and those who were appointed resented what was quickly apparent, that the Masters of Form believed themselves, and were held by the students to be, of higher status. Thus from the beginning the emphasis was on fine art although, for some of the best students, the opportunity to explore the possibilities of all kinds of materials and to have the necessity of a commercial future acknowledged was of the greatest possible value.

In 1915 Gropius had married Alma

Mahler, the composer's widow, an extraordinary lady of varied tastes and enthusiasms. Soon after the opening of the Bauhaus she recommended the appointment of a strange but persuasive painter, Johannes Itten. It was Itten's achievement to have incorporated into the courses perhaps the most widely adopted of all Bauhaus innovations – the grounding course which all students should take and in which they should show aptitude and application to justify further studies. This *Vorkurs* was designed to liberate the student's creativity through experience of materials, colours and textures, as well as through study of the works of the past. The now universal and familiar 'foundation courses' that are part of almost all current art education come from the *Vorkurs*.

During the early years of struggle in Weimar the authorities became increasingly unwilling to support Bauhaus methods, while Gropius himself was growing uncertain about the direction in which Bauhaus teaching was going. In about 1923, under pressure from the authorities, the idealistic, artistic, almost Ruskinian philosophy of the school gave way to a more realistic, practical approach. Nevertheless, two years later all state support was withdrawn. Gropius was forced to find another location, but the reputation of the Bauhaus was already considerable and he had a number of invitations. He chose Dessau, transferring there in 1925 and, only a year later, moving into new buildings designed by himself. The Dessau Bauhaus, its building and its teaching programme, is what most people think of when the name Bauhaus is mentioned. But the new school fared no better than its predecessor and the idealistic energy, the determined efforts at creative integration, which were characteristic of Weimar, lost some of their force at Dessau.

In 1928 Gropius resigned and was replaced, on his own recommendation, by Hannes Meyer, a Marxist who saw

Left:
Bauhaus Stairway, *1932. Oskar Schlemmer (Museum of Modern Art, New York. Gift of Philip Johnson). From 1920 to 1929 Schlemmer taught painting, sculpture and stage design at the Bauhaus and ran both ballet and theatre workshops. He was a key figure during its most effective and creative years. His attachment to geometrical solutions appears in his drawings and designs and was also reflected in his teaching. The staircase of the Dessau Bauhaus was painted by him from memory after he had left. The simplification of the figures into basic geometrical shapes is typical of his approach.*

Above:
The Square, *1916. Lyonel Feininger (Leicester City Art Gallery). Feininger was born in the United States and left for Germany to study at the age of 16. He gained early acquaintance with Cubism which he adopted for his mature work. He was the longest serving member of the Bauhaus staff, joining in 1919 and leaving only on its closure in 1933.*

architecture and design only in terms of proletarian social and cultural advantage. It is still unclear why Gropius chose Meyer, but it was damaging to the coherence of the school's teaching. Some staff resigned, students were bewildered or rebelled, and in 1930 Meyer himself resigned, to be replaced by Ludwig Mies van der Rohe, who became one of the fathers of the modern style in architecture. Mies removed the Bauhaus from Dessau, where elections had brought the Nationalists into power, and took it to Berlin, but in the short time left it never recovered its vitality.

In the Dessau years, the industrialization of the workshops and the vital commercial impetus, which led to close contacts with industry, resulted in the experimental production of a range of artefacts that have since become cosily familiar but were, at the time, conceptually novel – such objects as movable reading lights, prefabricated furniture, the fitted kitchen and, most common of all, the tubular steel chair.

In painting and sculpture the influence was no less important though less visible. The teachers at the Bauhaus, the Masters of Form, were among the most significant painters and sculptors of the modern move-

ments outside France. There was a strong Expressionist influence in the early Bauhaus, but in the work of Kandinsky and Klee, it possessed two of the most important abstractionists of the century. Their influence is to be traced through their teaching and that of their students in the United States.

Both Gropius and Mies van der Rohe transferred their activities to the United States, where they continued teaching and designing buildings. Many former staff members also crossed the Atlantic and established the new Bauhaus, later the Institute of Design, under the Hungarian artist-builder Laszlo Moholy-Nagy, in Chicago. Bauhaus principles were also promulgated by Josef Albers at Yale and later at the design school at Ulm originally under the direction of Max Bill.

Sun and Moon, *date unknown. Paul*
Klee (Private Collection).
Klee's importance in the quality of
Bauhaus tuition was central to its effect.
With Itten and Kandinsky he was
involved in the basic information course.
Klee instructed in composition, design and
colour.

European Art in the 1930s and 1940s

It is important to remember that the creators of the modern movements – such artists as Picasso, Braque and Matisse – continued to work productively long after the exciting period of innovation and revolution, some of them well into the era after the Second World War. Some participated in new developments (Picasso, for instance, contributed to Surrealism in the 1930s); others pursued their own individual courses; yet others remained loyal to their first inspiration. All of them contributed to European art in their time.

Throughout the history of art there have always been a number of artists who have not fitted into the current pattern or have made their own special contributions outside the general movement. Between the wars a number of interesting artists were at work who were not part of the modern movements and sometimes not in sympathy with them. It is impossible to include them all in a brief survey of this kind but a few general comments should be

Previous page:
Three Musicians, 1921. Pablo Picasso (Museum of Modern Art, New York. Mrs Simon Guggenheim Fund).
The decorative sophistication of this late example of Picasso's Cubism reveals the possibility for abstract design within Cubist attitudes. It is, however, easy to overlook the careful and sensitive musical quality of the composition, the balance of decorative and simple forms.

Above:
Guernica, 1937. Length 308 in (7823 mm). Pablo Picasso (Prado, Madrid).
It is abundantly evident that Picasso holds a position in the development of 20th-century art that has no parallel. Other masters, such as Matisse or

Braque, have continued to produce work of importance, but Picasso's inventive genius dominates this century as Michelangelo and Rubens dominated theirs. It is in this context that his major works must be examined, for they are the seminal works of their time.

Guernica is central to Picasso's art for a number of reasons. Firstly, it expresses Picasso's protest as a Spaniard at the bombing of the little Basque town of Guernica in the Spanish Civil War and reflects his republican and Communist sympathies. At the time he was not a Communist party member (he joined the French Communist party in 1944) but from this time forward his political commitment recurs in his work, for instance in The Charnel House (1944–45), which again expresses the anguish of the innocent victims of brutal

oppression – the Nazi gas chambers.

A second reason for its importance is the public recognition it received through being exhibited, in the Spanish Republican pavilion, at the Paris Exposition Universelle of 1937. Its large size alone was arresting but, more important, it was a statement by the most famous contemporary artist that modern art could carry a dramatic social message and might be an instrument in the struggle for social justice.

It is also a compositional tour de force. All of Picasso's inventiveness and energy were poured into it. The decorative or exploratory nature of much of his work was abandoned for direct positive statement in a modern iconography. Much has been written of the symbolism in Guernica – of the importance of the bullfight in the symbolism of horse and

bull, of the fragile hollowness of militarism through the soldier figure and so on. It has also been suggested that there is a deliberate Christian pictorial reference deriving from Picasso's familiarity with paintings in the Prado. The restrained colour and the uncompromising line reveal Picasso's emotional involvement in the creation of this work as in no other. Indeed, there is no other work of the century which so clearly establishes the place of the modern aesthetic in society.

made on the art of the time that did not belong to the groups discussed in previous sections.

In the 1920s and 1930s some sensitive artists were still interested in the traditional subject matter of art and the traditional painting methods. Landscape, figure and subject painting still

inspired significant work, and the selection here gives examples.

A painter of great sensitivity and acute colour sense who was mainly devoted to landscape was the English painter Ivon Hitchens (1893–1979). He is part of the strong tradition of English landscape painting, although his style is non-naturalistic.

His use of thin paint in strong though delicate strokes contrasts sharply with the work of Chaïm Soutine (1893/94–1943), who worked mainly in Paris and the French Pyrenees in the 1920s and 1930s. He escaped a poverty-stricken Jewish childhood in Russia and found his way to Paris, where he knew most of the *avant-garde* painters of the day including Picasso, Chagall, Léger and Modigliani. His landscapes and subject studies are painted with thick paint in impassioned brush

strokes which seem to carve the forms into being; the colour is equally strong and aggressive. Soutine's reputation was established after Albert C. Barnes, a formidable U.S. collector and author of books on Cézanne and Matisse, purchased a large number of his paintings (now at Merion, Pennsylvania) in 1923.

Nicolas de Staël (1914–55) was, like Soutine, of Russian origin, though brought up from the age of three in Belgium. He served in the French Foreign Legion in the Second World War and on returning to France settled in Nice. His abstract painting, which derived from Cubism, gradually moved towards a more representational style, achieving a powerful but calm authority. The gradual return to representation conflicted with his theoretical attachment to abstraction and the sharpening division between his art and his

Weeping Woman, *1937. Pablo Picasso (Tate Gallery, London).*
At the time of Guernica Picasso made a number of studies and paintings of a weeping woman, expressing the anguish of human loss. This is the most finished of those works and contains the powerful Expressionist quality of Guernica with *more violent colour. The intensity of pain, concentrated on the central handkerchief, is contained by a combination of clashing reds, greens, violet and yellows. It is remarkable evidence of the Expressionist possibilities of Cubism.*

Right below:
The Divers, II, *1941–42. Fernand Léger (Museum of Modern Art, New York. Mrs Simon Guggenheim Fund). After his early Cubist work Léger used rounded bulky forms often on unpainted ground.*

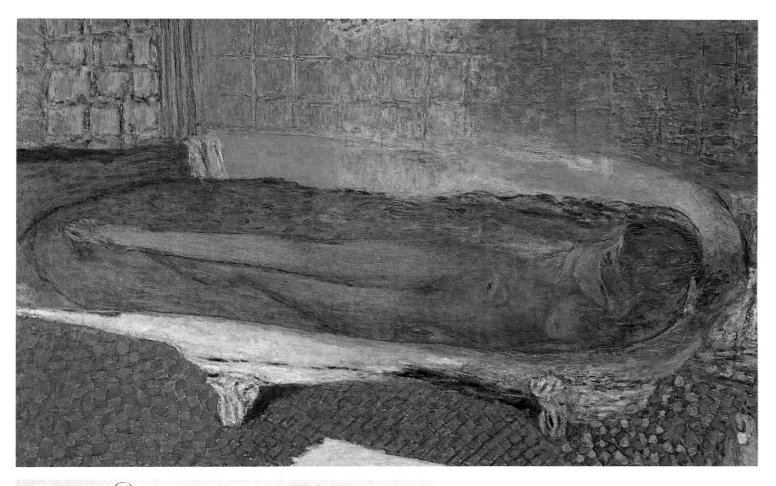

theory helped to drive him to suicide,
tragic evidence of the demands that art
can make on its practitioners.

At first sight the work of the Italian
painter Giorgio Morandi (1890–
1964) seems almost pedantically academic. But within the self-imposed
confines of limited still-life subjects – a
few objects viewed at eye level – he
created a world of calm authority in the
subtlest of colour relationships, using a
very small colour range.

The Second World War inspired a
number of war paintings in the embattled countries, and a number of

The Blue Circus, *1950. Marc Chagall (Tate Gallery, London).*
In 1948 Chagall started to work on two paintings for the Watergate Theatre, London, The Dance *and* The Blue Circus, *but decided not to locate them there and finished them in 1950 after he moved to Vence, near Nice. Chagall's sources and colour have remained the same throughout most of his long career, and* The Blue Circus *is one of his most accomplished compositions.*

representative works, showing a variable emphasis on the effects and horrors of war, appear on adjacent pages. The vicious protest of a George Grosz found little or no place in the art of the Second World War, which is generally observed more in resignation than in protest. The destruction of war and reconstruction in peace is shown in two works by Graham Sutherland (1903–80).

Top:
Reclining Nude, *1919. Amedeo Modigliani (Museo d'Arte Moderna, Rome).*
This unfinished sketch of a female nude has the sinuous, elegant line that is so characteristic of Modigliani's work. His method of working with long nervous strokes separating the forms can be seen at this stage but the refined tautness which characterizes his completed work has yet to appear.

Above:
Winter Stage, *1936. Ivon Hitchens (Tate Gallery, London).*
Essentially a painter of the English landscape, in its many moods and aspects, Hitchens has an intimacy and sensitivity that links him to the strong school of romantic English observation of a greatly loved environment. His work is painted freely, influenced by Matisse, and whilst its range is small each work evinces a real emotional response to its subject.

153

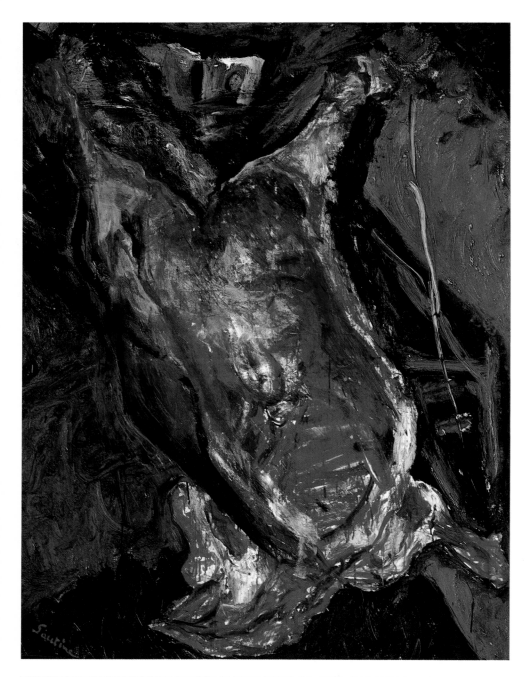

Carcass of Beef, c. 1925. Chaïm
Soutine (Albright-Knox Art Gallery,
Buffalo, New York).
Soutine was familiar with Rembrandt's
The Slaughter House in the Louvre and
inspired by it to create a major work on
the same theme. He did at least four large
paintings from the carcass of a steer
which he bought and kept in his studio.
As the steer putrefied and reds changed to
greens and browns, he paid a model to sit
and fan away the flies that covered it. He
also bought blood to freshen up the colour.
When complaints from neighbours
brought the police Soutine argued that art
was more important than hygiene.
    Painted with Expressionist
involvement, this work shows Soutine's
typically tortured paint handling.

Agrigento, 1953. Nicolas de Stael
(Kunsthaus, Zurich).
A French painter born in Russia, De
Stael was raised and educated in
Belgium, attending the Fine Art School in
Brussels. After the Second World War, in
which he served in the Foreign Legion, he
adopted an abstractionist form for his
landscapes and subject studies. After the
death of his wife he concentrated even
harder on his work but his intellectual
commitment to abstraction was tested by
the increasing pictorial attraction of
representation, leading to personal crisis
and suicide.

Above:
Devastation, 1941: East End, Burnt
Paper Warehouse, *1941. Graham
Sutherland (Tate Gallery, London).
Sutherland was one of those artists with
established reputations who were
appointed to record pictorially the nature
and effect of modern warfare. The burned
paper rolls in a bombed papermill suited*

*his temperament and style and resulted in
this effective work.*

Top:
Still-Life, *1944. Giorgio Morandi
(Musée National d'Art Moderne, Paris).
A solitary man who, unlike most of his*

*Italian contemporaries, never visited
Paris, Morandi devoted most of his
working life to painting a series of simple
still-lifes in muted colour. His only other
significant work was his Metaphysical
painting, which similarly he completed in
Bologna away from the Ferrarese homes
of De' Chirico and Carlo Carra, painters
of the major works of that movement.*

Postwar Europe

Throughout the First World War some cultural interchange continued, even across warring boundaries. In the Second World War, despite greatly improved communications, there was no such interchange. The reasons are plain. The Nazi occupation shut down Europe as effectively as Stalin shut down Russia, while the bombing of civilian targets brought the enemy to everyone's doorstep.

International artistic contacts in Europe ceased at the beginning of the war as all artists with any kind of *avant-garde* reputation beat a hasty retreat (if they were able) from the advancing Nazi forces. These refugees – painters, architects and designers – were those who would build the basic structure of postwar art, especially in the United States. That was not yet apparent, however, at the end of the war.

The Second World War was truly a global conflict: its ultimate result was greatly to increase global contacts, and from that followed global culture. In certain respects, however, integration of world culture had a contrary effect artistically in emphasizing national cultural characteristics. As the United States gained world power, her national identity emerged the more sharply for both native Americans and foreigners.

The war had a more devastating effect in Europe than anywhere else (except Japan) through sheer physical destruction and emotional exhaustion. The hope that accompanied the horror of the First World War, that this was a war to end wars, was never present in the second. The youthful enthusiasm of U.S. soldiers was not in general paralleled in European forces, or among European civilians in the 'front line' of bombing and destruction. War was a beastly business, and peacetime reconstruction was likely to be just as demanding and morally uncertain.

Europe was not only exhausted, it was disillusioned and pessimistic. Intellectual vitality and creative enthusiasm were at a premium.

The reconstruction of art was a slow process. What had once seemed the exciting possibilities of the new art of the early movements looked tired and irrelevant to postwar eyes. Masters like Picasso, Matisse and others had either gone to America or had been submerged. While young artists and students showed some interest in their work, its former sense of direction had been lost. Although the first steps were tentative explorations of such movements as Cubism, Futurism and Surrealism, even in France the work of the prewar Parisian School, while it did

Christ in Glory. 1952–62. Tapestry. Graham Sutherland (Coventry Cathedral).
After the Second World War Coventry Cathedral, which had been bombed, was rebuilt, and many British artists and designers were employed in its decoration. Sutherland designed this great tapestry, which represents Christ in Majesty surrounded at four corners by emblems of the evangelists, to hang above the altar at the east end, from which it dominates the interior.

provoke many derivative works, was not inspiring.

More generally, the first response to the modern movements was rejection: they reflected a dead society where the artist had enjoyed privilege and independence, a status alien to the postwar mood. A new struggle for a form of social justice had become central to politics, with capitalism opposed by communism. The first expression of this concern in art – before the New York School burst upon the scene – was what has come to be known as Social Realism. The first apparent examples came from Paris.

In France there was no idea of surrendering primacy in the world of art. Paris had been the centre of virtually all the most important developments since the 17th century, and all the early movements of modern art, whether French in origin or not, had been represented – and felt it necessary to be represented – in Paris. The first announcement of Italian Futurism, for instance, had been made not in Rome or Milan but in Paris.

A Parisian painter, Bernard Buffet, was an early new talent in postwar France. With the fond approval of the critics, his mannered, almost monochromatic, linear style conveyed an air of depression and deprivation which

Above right:
Self-Portrait, *1954. Bernard Buffet (Tate Gallery, London).*
Buffet had his first one-man show at the age of 19 in Paris and became for some time the representative hopeful of French postwar painting: the loneliness and isolation evident in his work not only reflected the loss of hope and joy in the aftermath of terrible war but also related to the then fashionable Sartrean existentialism. His work now seems commercial – not entirely his fault since he was promoted by cupidinous dealers.

Right:
The Discussion, *1959–60. Renato Guttuso (Tate Gallery, London).*
The strength of Guttuso's social commitment is evident in all his work and he became the leader of a Social Realist school in Italy. The Discussion *suggests heated political argument – a familiar experience in Guttuso's life.*

was taken as the expression of postwar Parisian disillusion. It was anti-abstract and anti-aesthetic. It was, insofar as its somewhat superficial nature would allow, the beginning of social protest. While not directly political, it suggested a stern and undesirable reality. Buffet was much fêted by dealers but his success now seems surprising. The long-term effect of it was to assist in the dethronement of Paris as the sovereign centre of modern art.

Social Realism. A figure of greater impact and significance in the current atmosphere of stern uncompromising Realism was the Italian Renato Guttuso, whose paintings of ordinary people in everyday situations are characteristic of the postwar Italian attempt to portray a society in need of drastic repair – an attempt most notable in the 'Neo-Realist' cinema, with such films as *Open City*, *Bitter Rice* and *Bicycle Thieves*. The ability of the cinema to recreate the dirt and sweat of passing life appeared stronger and more direct than the single image of the painter. For the public in the years after 1945, before the impact of television, the cinema gradually made the

Left top:
Mother Bathing Child, *1953. Jack Smith (Tate Gallery, London).*
The paintings of Jack Smith seemed to condemn the harsh reality of postwar Britain – actually a legacy of prewar Britain – in a poignant, direct imagery in which there is no ambiguity. Smith's colour is confined to dark browns and near blacks and his work also recalls the biting comments of the political cartoonists and earlier observers such as Théophile Steinlen (1859–1923).

Left:
Window, Self-Portrait, Jean and Hands (detail), *1957. John Bratby (Tate Gallery, London).*
Bratby's paintings concentrate mainly on his own life and depict his wife and himself in their own home surrounded by their belongings. He paints in thick impasto with strong linear character which sometimes recalls the technique of Van Gogh.

creation of single images of events, however disturbing, less compelling and effective.

Social Realism came nearest to forming a genuine movement in Britain. The so-called Kitchen Sink School had a short-lived but powerful impact in postwar Britain. Under the socialist government which unexpectedly defeated the wartime hero, Churchill, in the general election of 1945, a serious effort was made towards a more equitable society. The Kitchen Sink School identified the place where the problems started. Jack Smith, who painted a child being bathed in the kitchen sink, John Bratby, who later became an honoured member of the conservative Royal Academy, Edward Middleditch and Frank Auerbach are the representative painters. Their parallel in the performing arts was not the cinema, as in Italy, but the theatre (e.g. John Osborne's *Look Back in Anger*) and the novel.

There was one restraining feature of Social Realism throughout Europe. Although seldom overtly political, it was nevertheless making a social point, and over the cultural horizon there loomed the great Russian Social Realist bear to

Study for one of the figures at the base of a painting of the Crucifixion, *c. 1944. Francis Bacon (Tate Gallery, London).*
Painted over a period of years this central panel with its two companions was first exhibited in 1944. The figure is one of the Eumenides (Greek Furies). With Bacon, a 'sketch' very often means a completed work in the sense that he stopped work on it. It has been suggested that the bandage was inspired by Grunewald's early 16th-century Mocking of Christ. *The figure against a simple orange ground suggests a screaming anguish not uncommon in Bacon's work.*

The Painter and his Model, *1980–81. Balthus (Balthasar Klossowski) (Musée National d'Art Moderne, Paris).*
The mood of isolation and suggestive sexuality that pervades Balthus's work is perfectly calculated and controlled. He is a master of the visual innuendo and his presentation of young girls in innocently suggestive poses creates an atmosphere of effete indulgence. The realism of his work is acutely in keeping with his intention.

frighten artists and others away from too obvious an attachment to the actual world.

Whilst considering forms of Realism, two painters who reached their peak in the 1950s, entirely different in most respects, deserve attention: Francis Bacon in England and Balthus in France. Almost exact contemporaries, their work has one feature in common; for both, the visible world carries disturbing emotional implications.

Francis Bacon's is a social but not a realist art. His paintings are representational to the extent that the shapes he uses add up in curious and distorted form to recognizable objects, usually human. From the stretched and misplaced flesh of his subjects, which are metamorphosed like 1930s Surrealist objects, there seems to emanate a cry of pain. But the human activity, presented in sparing use of paint on traditional canvas, suggests sometimes furtive sexuality, sometimes despairing isolation. It is appropriate that so many of his subjects are presented with mouth open in anguish. The private terror of individual humanity is nowhere more powerfully expressed.

Bacon's is not an easy or likeable art – he has destroyed many of his paintings because he did not like them – but it is more careful and precise than casual viewing suggests. For him painting 'tends towards a complete interlocking of image and paint, so that the

Opposite:
Study after Pope Innocent X by Velasquez, 1951. *Francis Bacon (Aberdeen Art Gallery and Museum). Although Bacon's series of paintings of Popes was initially taken from Velasquez's portrait of Innocent X, this work seems to be inspired by a photograph of Pius XII in Bacon's possession at the time. Pius XII is being carried in a sedia gestatoria through a room in the Vatican, which explains both the frame and the suggestion of vaulting at the top of the painting. The expression of fear or anxiety already evident in this, the first of the series, increases in later versions.*

Below left:
T54–16, 1954. *Hans Hartung (Musée National d'Art Moderne, Paris). Hartung fled from Germany in 1935 to settle in Paris. His early experience of Expressionism, particularly the work of Nolde and Kokoschka, left him with a strong attraction for emotive line, and his abstraction, which followed an earlier stage of representation, depends on the effect of gestured lines on a stained canvas. He became a leader of French abstraction after the Second World War.*

Overleaf:
Painting, 1956. *Pierre Soulages (Solomon R. Guggenheim Museum, New York).*
A precocious painter, Soulages's early interest was in Romanesque buildings and megaliths. In the 1930s he painted bleak winter landscapes – trees against lowering skies and houses in gloomy isolation. After the war his work became abstract but the influence of these early images can be seen in his black and white linear paintings. He was one of those French postwar abstractionists whose work seems less purposeful in retrospect than it did at the time.

Below right:
Sacking and Red, 1954. *Alberto Burri (Tate Gallery, London).*
Burri's early training in medicine and his experiences as doctor in a prisoner-of-war camp seem to have determined his subsequent career when after the war he was attracted to painting and produced a number of works in which the surface skin of raw materials (sacking and other textiles) is torn or cut and pulled aside to reveal a raw, dark or living wound. The implicatory shock of these works, originally effective, has diminished and they have come to seem more decorative and patterned than emotive.

image is the paint and vice-versa. Here the brush stroke creates the form, does not merely fill it in. Consequently every movement of the brush on the canvas alters the shape and implications of the image. That is why real painting is a mysterious and continuous struggle with chance . . .' The value of each

Below:
Large Painting, *1958. Antoni Tàpies (Solomon R. Guggenheim Museum, New York).*
In his earlier work Tàpies attempted to produce the effect of walls with mysterious overlays of obscure graffiti entirely through painted effects, but from about 1950 he has used a variety of materials, usually mixed with paint, to create the crusted surfaces characteristic of his work. Based in Barcelona he has been the leader of a group of Catalan artists since the Second World War.

brush stroke and the advantage of chance, a powerful element in Bacon's art, are what give his work its characteristic precision.

The precision of Balthus is a different quality. His figures, preponderantly of young girls, are drawn with realist accuracy in careful perspective interiors. Born in Paris of Polish descent, Balthus presents brooding and suggestive images with an almost Surrealist strangeness. The isolation of the figures is internal, their personal *angst* indeterminately located. A curiously unreal light illuminates the urban rooms inhabited in isolation by nubile, erotic girls. One feels that something unpleasant is likely to happen – but what?

Although the great masters of the early movements seemed to belong to a past age their very remoteness gave them an aura of mammoth achievement. Picasso, it was dimly realized

then and soon became blindingly apparent, was one of the greatest creative forces in the history of art. It is not surprising therefore that he and the other masters should eventually inspire a number of followers in postwar Paris who seemed to be the inheritors of the modern aesthetic. It was certainly the hope of the dealers who promoted them with determined enthusiasm. They included such painters as Maurice Esteve, Jean Bazaine and especially Edouard Pignon, a follower of Picasso who was promoted as his successor – while Picasso was still working! These painters had absorbed the decorative surface of such movements as Cubism and Fauvism but not the content, and they lacked true creativity. Their work, superficially attractive in pleasant colour, could not maintain Parisian supremacy once the attack of the Americans from the beginning of Abstract Expressionism was launched

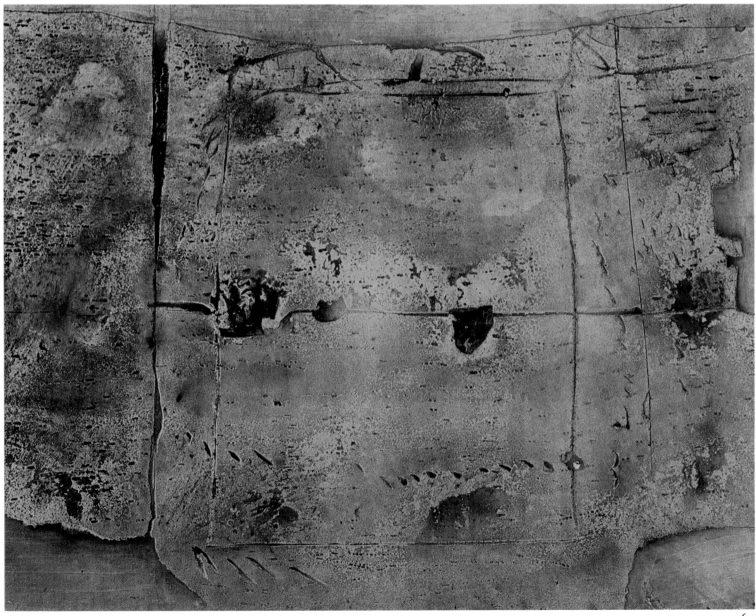

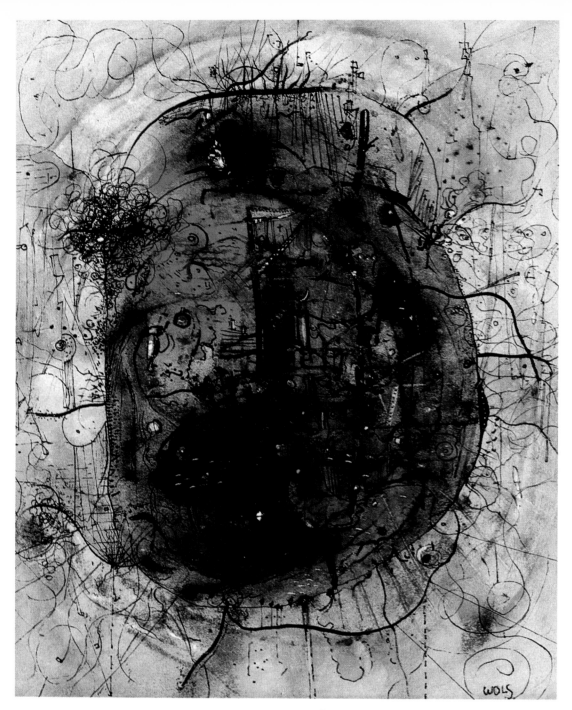

in the 1950s. The downgrading of Paris thus became inevitable, though the seriousness of British art, where the beginnings of the extraordinary phenomenon of Pop were already evident, at one point indicated that London might be the new centre. In the event it was New York.

Nevertheless, Paris was not utterly devoid of creative activity. In a different, though in some ways comparable, development to Abstract Expressionism in the United States, a number of abstractionists were at work. The short-lived pioneer was Wols (1913–51), born Alfred Shulze, who studied photography at the Bauhaus and, when it closed, moved to Paris where he made contact with the Surrealists. He painted centrally placed, biomorphic images in a close-knit lattice of delicate lines.

Above:
Composition V, *1946. Wols (Alfred Otto Wolfgang Schulze) (Musée National d'Art Moderne, Paris).*
Wols and Fautrier are linked in the creation of the form of painting known as Tachisme, which had a considerable vogue in Paris in the 1950s but was eclipsed by the more vigorous and expansive works of the Abstract Expressionists. Tachisme – touch/mark painting – was in opposition to the more geometric abstraction then current. Although attempts were made to identify it with such artists as Pollock it remains essentially French. Wols, who sadly died young, used a fine calligraphy with a free form of abstraction to evoke his effects.

Right:
Tête d'Otage No. I, *1943. Jean Fautrier (Private Collection).*
This painting is one of a series that Fautrier painted in the last years of the Second World War of the heads of hostages that he had seen shot. The matière of the surface and the thinly drawn paint show his interest in the abstract qualities of material, and his principal preoccupation was with abstraction. Although intended to be emotionally compelling, his Parisian sophistication threatens to reduce the work to mere decoration.

164

Les Capétiens Partout (detail), 1954.
Georges Mathieu (Musée National d'Art
Moderne, Paris).
Mathieu, like Wols and Fautrier, is
associated with Tachisme since his work is
also a free form of abstraction. His images
are, however, very different both in scale
and in method. His large paintings, often
completed publicly (linking him with
Happenings and Performance art), are
constructed with broad gestures of linear
paint squeezed directly from the tube, as
can be seen in this detail. As a result his
style is sometimes described as Tubism!

The paintings show vigour and energy,
but the usually central image has a strong
element of the purely decorative which
seems to rob them of significance.

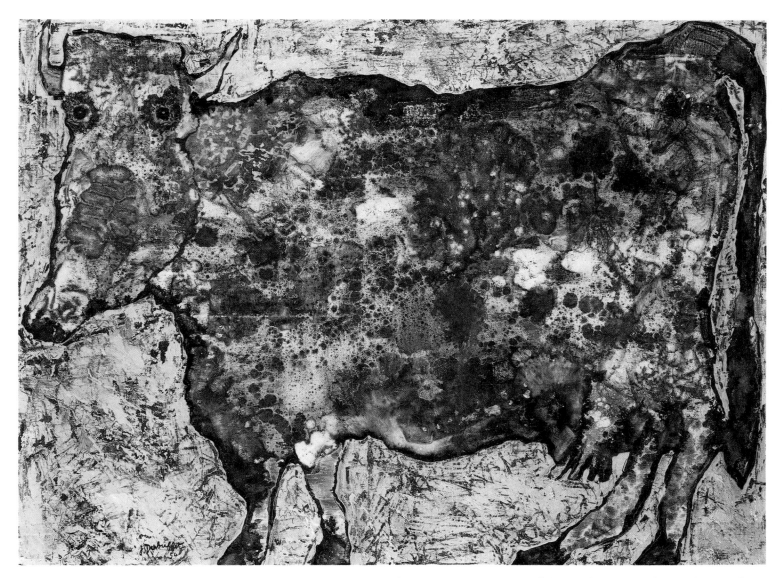

His example gave birth to a school of Parisian painters in the 1950s who resembled neither the Realists nor the

The Cow with the Subtile Nose, 1954. Jean Dubuffet (Museum of Modern Art, New York. Benjamin and David Scharps Fund).
Dubuffet was over 40 when he decided to devote himself to painting and his first works were representational views of Paris in garish colour. In 1949 he held the first exhibition of Art Brut, the name with which his work is usually associated. Two visits to the Sahara seem to have been influential in establishing his interest in materials and surface; with a childlike directness he manipulates surfaces to produce undefined, gradually emerging forms. In this painting earth and subject combine to produce a charming image.

abstractionists found in the galleries. A number of different names were attached to them, including Tachistes, a label that has also been stuck on certain 19th-century Impressionists as well as Pollock and the gestural Abstract Expressionists. The critic Michel Tapie wrote of *un art autre*, claiming it was different in kind from its contemporaries. Other artists associated with Tachisme were Jean-Paul Riopelle, a French-Canadian whose decorative paintings with heavily impasted surface had something of a vogue, and Hans Hartung, an expatriate German whose gestural paintings on a thin stained ground gained him a reputation, although in retrospect the gestures seemed somewhat pointless.

It is perhaps decorative intention rather than serious search that is characteristic of Parisian art in this period. Two other painters who suggest this are Jean Fautrier and Henri Michaux. Fautrier produced a number of central images in which the impasto

of the surface, the subtle colour and added materials produced an evocative, almost mystical quality which helped inspire the development known as *art informel* (without form).

The exploration of the evocative quality of the surface through the application of a variety of materials and textures became a European fashion. In Spain Antonio Tapies used sand stained with dull colour to produce images of a much-used wall on which generations of graffiti had formed indecipherable but evocative messages. Another Spaniard, Manolo Millares, made pictures out of thick, rough canvas tied in lumps or torn, gashed and splattered with paint, red and black predominating – passionate images suggesting debris in the aftermath of conflict. In Italy Alberto Burri, a doctor who gave up his practice for art, made works of sacking and rags which have dark, torn openings with blood-red areas like wounds (he had been a prison-camp doctor).

Left:
La Hollandaise, 1969. *Karel Appel (Galerie Ariel, Paris).*
The violent Expressionist attack of Appel's powerful and often large-scale work is in some part a reaction against the austere geometric abstractions of De Stijl which, as the one important Dutch contribution to the modern aesthetic, had dominated art in the Netherlands up to and after the Second World War. As with many action painters there is some question concerning the content of his strongly coloured work – but it cannot be denied that Appel's work has a vitality which evokes sympathetic responses.

Top:
The Tower, 1954. *Pierre Alechinsky (Stedelijk Museum, Ostende).*
Pierre Alechinsky, a Belgian member of COBRA, shows Surrealist features and an underlying mysticism which is perhaps not fully in sympathy with the work of the COBRA artists in general. His colour too is less strident and his line more sensitive.

Right:
Green Ballet, 1960. *Asger Jorn (Solomon R. Guggenheim Museum, New York).*
The Danish painter Jorn, another member of COBRA and its most powerful and influential figure, was an abstract Surrealist in Denmark before the Second World War, but after the war he settled in Paris, where his violent and deeply felt Expressionism gained him a considerable reputation. Strongly opposed to what he saw as the aridities of Functionalism and Mondrian's Neo-Plasticism, he believed that the violence of modern society demanded a violent response.

Although the intention of all these works may have been to express protest and disgust, or to confront us with the shocking problems of the postwar world, the commonest effect in retrospect is (as with the Paris School) a residual feeling of decorative and effete good taste. For this, perhaps the impact of fresh energy and enthusiasm from New York is largely responsible.

The contrast between Old World and New can be demonstrated by a comparison of two individual Europeans with their American counterparts.

Georges Mathieu paints canvases in which interweaving lines and colour on a coloured ground are painted with great vigour, *con brio*. They produce a knitted pattern suggesting the drip paintings of Jackson Pollock, yet they lack the emotional density that Pollock's overall image produces. Mathieu's centrally placed and isolated forms suggest energy in plenty, but energy without purpose.

Incidentally, Mathieu painted his canvases in a public theatre, and in this respect he should be given some credit for anticipating the 1960s American fashion for Happenings.

The second Paris-based artist is another abstractionist, Pierre Soulages.

His paintings, which carry no title except the date they were painted, echo Franz Kline's strong linear canvases. Yet Soulages's patterns of thick lines are unconvincing, decorative and quaintly charming but without direction or goal.

The dead hand of Parisian aestheticism overlays the efforts of both Mathieu and Soulages; but from this pressure the Americans escape.

A French artist in a different category, indeed a category of his own making, is Jean Dubuffet, who worked for some time in the United States. Dubuffet has an affection for what he calls *art brut*, i.e. amateur art, especially

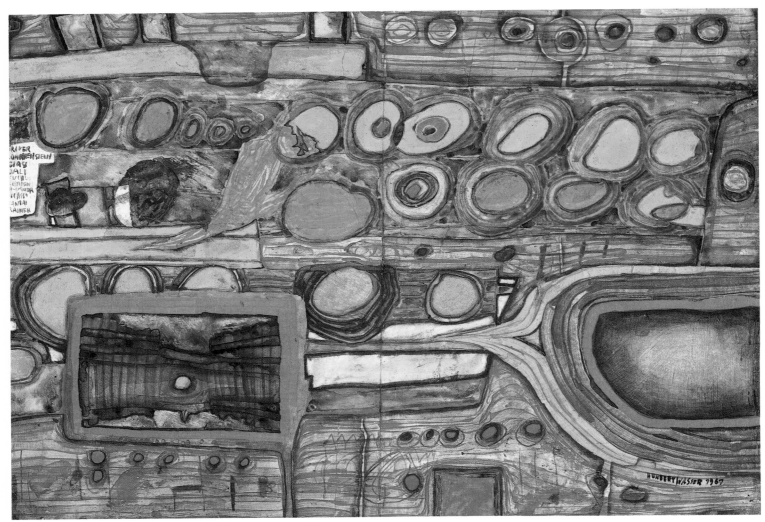

of children and the mentally ill. Like the Surrealists, he rejects the historical continuity of art and the whole Western aesthetic as a superficial gloss supporting conventional cultural attitudes. He believes that the spontaneity of the amateur is preferable to the skills of the professional artist – he has a fine collection of graffiti – and his own works are constructed out of debris, variously manipulated into crudely human forms. His work is related to the Surrealists and to *materiel* painters like Tapies and Burri, but Dubuffet goes further in his search for the strange and awkward image. Childlike as his images are, they relate surface to subject in highly compelling compatibility. Though strange, they look inevitable – always a sign of creative originality.

Other aspects of postwar European art are discussed in later chapters, but there is one final group of painters which, since it had a clear identity and a positive programme, deserves consideration here.

The COBRA Group was an international movement which took its name from the cities of Copenhagen, Brussels and Amsterdam. Its members included Asger Jorn (Danish), Corneille (another one-name artist) and Pierre Alechinsky (Belgian), and Karel Appel (Dutch). Often described as Abstract Expressionist, their work is not quite abstract nor truly figurative; recognizable forms suggesting legendary figures emerge from thick paint and strong pattern. The COBRA artists are interested in mythology and symbolism but their belief and method incline them towards the direct expression of feeling and fantasy, humorous or sinister. While they do not reject the painterly tradition, their use of it does not restrict them to conventional imagery. The result is not always apparent in coherence of aim but they avoid that decorative overlay of the postwar Paris school.

Although not members of the group, the Scottish artist Alan Davie and the Austrian Fritz Hundertwasser reflect the international appeal of COBRA. Indeed, Davie is the one British artist who seems closer to the continent than to the United States at a time when the English Channel was wider than the Atlantic.

The Hokkaido Steamer, 1961. Watercolour and chalk on rice paper. Hundertwasser (Fritz Stowasser) (Joachim Harel Management, Vienna). Although associated with COBRA through personal contact and in style, Hundertwasser was not a member and his work shows none of the sophistication of the group. He was self-trained and has been described as a naive abstractionist. His works are patterned and brightly coloured. A Viennese, he knew the work of Klimt and Schiele and the influence of their decorative style is plainly evident.

Right:
The Fascination of the Island, 1965. Corneille (Solomon R. Guggenheim Museum, New York). With Appel, Corneille was a founder member of the COBRA group and like him settled in Paris in 1949. His work is less violent than Appel's and more decorative. He is also more attracted to landscape than figure. His colour is strong and there is a linear quality not present in Appel; nevertheless, there is a sympathy of approach between these two Dutch artists.

170

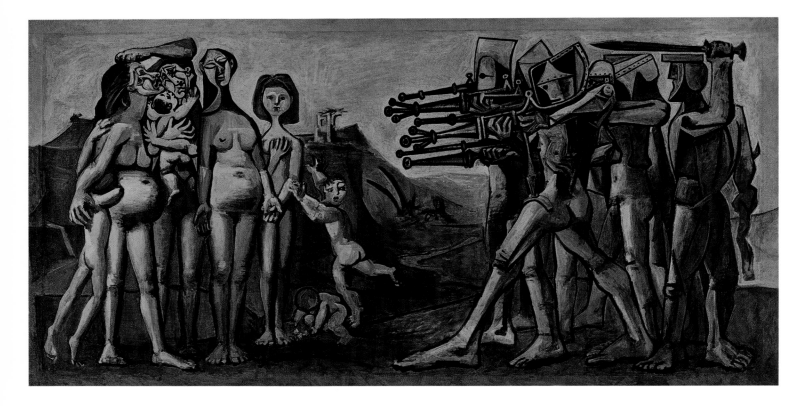

Massacre in Korea, *1951 (above).*
Pablo Picasso. The Snail, *1953 (right).*
Henri Matisse (Tate Gallery, London).
The Garden Chair, *1947–48 (left).*
*Georges Braque (Musée National d'Art
Moderne, Paris).*
*These three near-contemporary works by
three of the greatest masters of the century
reveal the different directions in which
they moved in the period after the Second
World War. The political conviction and
sense of horror that Picasso had displayed
in* Guernica *and* The Charnel House *is
repeated in* Massacre in Korea, *perhaps
less powerfully but no less convincingly.
The echoes of Goya are unmistakable,
and Picasso has used the same restricted
colour range of the earlier paintings.*

*Braque's colour perception and
command, always acute and sensitive,
deepened to become almost physically
attractive. There is a complete assurance
in the handling of all the elements of the
work which makes what might have been
merely decorative strongly moving.*

*With Matisse the change is more
dramatic. In his later years he produced
mainly* papiers découpés *(cut-out paper
of different colours) and this large work,
approximately 113 in (2870 mm) square,
shows his mastery of simple shape and
colour relationships. The vague spiral
shape accounts for the title of the work.*

Art in Australia

In the postwar period the sense of international cultural identity led dealers to look outside the existing European sources for work they could promote and sell. It was a time for new directions and new possibilities, and in the interval before the invasion of Europe by the American Abstract Expressionists, the work of some Australian artists seemed attractive. Among them, Sidney Nolan was outstanding.

Nolan's series of paintings of the life of Ned Kelly, the most famous (at least after his paintings) outlaw in Australian history, achieved a wide popularity for his work and suggested that there might be a new cultural impetus to be found in the Australian subcontinent, generally regarded hitherto as essentially a transplanted and modified British culture. Following Nolan's success other Australians, most notably the brothers Arthur and David Boyd, William Dobell (1897–1970), Russell Drysdale (1912–81), Albert Tucker and Brett Whiteley, achieved European reputations.

Until this period Australian art, much of it the purely topographical or mediocre academic painting produced

Shearers Playing for a Bride, *1957.*
Arthur Boyd (National Gallery of Melbourne. Presented by Tristan Buesst 1958).
Boyd was influenced by Chagall's mystical, dreamlike images in his interpretation of native aboriginal themes. He left Australia in 1960, aged 40, to work in England, but has not produced such interesting work as might have been expected.

Glenrowan, 1956–57. Sidney Nolan
(Tate Gallery, London).
*Nolan studied in Melbourne and exhibited
first in 1938. In 1946 he began the
series of paintings of the legend of the
notorious Australian outlaw Ned Kelly,
which has remained a constant subject
source for his paintings and prints. (It
might be noted that Ned Kelly is more
famous as the result of Nolan's interest
than his career justifies.) Nolan has made
a number of stage designs, including those
for the Australian production of Serge
Lifar's Icarus.*

there as elsewhere, had a largely local
interest. The main artistic contact was
made by Australians who received their
training in Europe, particularly in
London. Most of them subsequently
returned to Australia where a reputation might be more easily acquired
than in England. But after 1945 the
process was often reversed. The postwar art scene in Europe and North
America increasingly attracted Australian artists who had been trained in
Australia and came to London or New
York to exhibit, but often remained to
live and work.

The effect was unfortunate for the
development of Australian art, since
the most talented artists were generally
the ones who remained abroad. Sidney

Nolan is an example. His vitality is best
expressed in the Ned Kelly series (prior
to that he had been an abstract painter).
After he settled in London, was knigh-
ted and became part of the art establishment, his work lost the internal
drive which his Australian subject
matter had inspired. While he remained an influential artist, he became
simply a figure of the international art
scene, in which local inspiration,
though not absent, inevitably suffers a
certain dilution.

Madonna and Child, *1943–44.*
Hornton stone. Henry Moore (St
Matthew's Church, Northampton).
Moore's work developed gradually from
early representational pieces to the
simplification and abstraction that has
increasingly characterized it. Dominant
formative influences were Egyptian,
African and Pre-Columbian sculpture,
and the work of Brancusi, Archipenko
and Picasso. During the Second World
War he sculpted this tender group of the
Madonna and Child, which was one of his
first major commissions.

Modern Sculpture in Britain

Historically the British Isles have produced very few sculptors of the highest rank, and the distinction of this art in the past generation or so is a surprise. It is largely due to the influence and example of one man, Henry Moore.

In the aftermath of the Second World War a number of new starts were made and new directions taken in the arts. In Britain the destruction of cities was such that a great deal of rebuilding had to be undertaken. The British were only marginally aware of recent continental developments in architecture: Le Corbusier, Gropius and Mies van der Rohe, the great masters of the modern architectural revolution, were known to only a few, and commissions for 'modern' architecture were rare.

While traditional forms were still demanded for public buildings, the gradual release from wartime restraint sponsored growing enquiries into architectural form. New technology in building, much advanced by war pressures, was available and in the first decade after the war many new buildings of an indecisive kind, neither unashamedly modern nor confidently traditional, were put up.

The visual arts of painting and sculpture were summoned to provide decorative embellishment, in a style commensurate with the architecture. For modern buildings this usually meant Cubist or Expressionist work.

In sculpture, no strong Classical tradition existed outside the Academy schools, but there was a modern sculptural development of considerable importance. Its master, one of the great figures of 20th-century sculpture, was Henry Moore, who with Barbara Hepworth (1903–75) and Ben Nicholson (1894–1982) was fully abreast of European developments and had already arrived at his mature style.

Moore was born in Yorkshire in 1898 and trained first as a teacher then as a sculptor at Leeds School of Art. From the beginning he displayed great interest in the latest aesthetic ideas and seemed to grasp their implications more thoroughly than any of his contemporaries. Roger Fry's *Vision and Design* (1920) made him aware of the latest thinking on practical as well as theoretical matters, and he quickly developed a passion for the traditional materials of the sculptor, stone and wood, and a mastery of their expressive qualities. His first exhibition in 1928 showed his commitment to the modern aesthetic, and resulted in a commission (*North Wind*) for the London Underground Railway building. From 1926 until 1940 he taught at London art schools, where his influence encouraged a generation of young sculptors more forward-looking than elsewhere, who formed a potential school of British sculptors in the postwar period.

Moore's work owes a great deal to the early influence of the sculpture he saw in the British Museum in the 1920s, particularly African wood carving, Etruscan tomb sculptures and Meso-American art. While fully cognizant of Cubism and other continental developments, he pursued his own course and developed, in a series of figures, a style in which form and material blend harmoniously to assert a quality of ultimate rightness. Much of his work is close to abstraction and it was not easily accepted by the general public (a familiar experience for creative artists), but his work during the war as an official war artist helped to establish his international stature.

Moore's drawings of Londoners seeking shelter from air raids in underground stations struck a responsive chord with the public and from that time on he has had a special place in the regard of his countrymen (even those nonplussed by his major works). He is an artist almost universally esteemed and liked.

Like Moore, Barbara Hepworth was born in Yorkshire and attended the Leeds College of Art and the Royal College of Art in London. Her work has often been associated with Moore's on the superficial evidence of the carefully rounded shapes pierced with holes which are a feature in common. Fundamentally, they are not particularly close. Hepworth is always sharply aware of participating in the Cubist movement and her work is more abstract. She was a friend of many of the leading Parisian figures and her sculpture is closer to that of Brancusi and Jean (Hans) Arp (1887–1966) than to Moore's. Her emotional responses are expressed in simple, swelling forms, sometimes suggesting musical instruments. Her work in Paris and London is different from her work when she settled in Cornwall during the war or the sculptures that came from her frequent visits to Greece.

Ben Nicholson, who was married to Barbara Hepworth for nearly twenty years, is better known as a painter. Influenced by Cubism and Vorticism, he produced abstractionist paintings with careful linear and colour control, soft and unaggressive. His main sculptural work consists of a number of geometrically constructed reliefs in which a balance of elements combine to produce a cool, satisfying pattern.

Victor Pasmore is also primarily a painter and, like Moore, an inspiring teacher. He made a number of reliefs in wood and plastic but regarded them as a natural extension of his painting rather than sculpture.

In 1953 an international competition was held for a monument to commemorate unknown political prisoners. The entrants included most of the well-known figures from the 1930s as well as some younger sculptors just beginning to make their reputations. The winner was Reg Butler (1913-81), an architect turned sculptor, who submitted a small wire frame set on a piece of rock with three small figures. Named *The Watchers*, it was a model for a piece 100 feet (over 30m) in height.

Butler's success in the competition helped to draw attention to British sculpture, and to indicate to a surprised world that possibly exciting things were happening there. Several sculptors of the generation following Moore and Hepworth gained an international reputation, and this comparatively new tradition has continued to thrive. Kenneth Armitage, Lynn Chadwick and Ralph Brown are perhaps the best-known members of the middle generation.

Below:
1967 (Tuscan Relief), *1967. Ben Nicholson (Tate Gallery, London). Nicholson was the son of the painter Sir William Nicholson (one of the Beggerstaff Brothers, who specialized in posters in the 1890s). A precocious draughtsman, he was early influenced by Cubism; in 1933 he met Mondrian, who exerted a decisive influence on his work, inspiring him to produce a number of careful low reliefs based on the square and circle, works which encompassed his dual talents as painter and sculptor.*

Right:
Four Squares with Two Circles, *1963–64. Height 124 in (3150 mm). Barbara Hepworth (Rijksmuseum Kröller-Müller, Otterlo). With Moore, Hepworth led the British sculptural 'renaissance' which was considered to have taken place after the Second World War. Whilst her reputation does not equal Moore's and her work shows similarity with his, there is no doubt of her own individual achievement.*

Locking Piece, 1963–64. Height
116 in (2934 mm). Henry Moore
(Millbank, London).
*In the 1960s Moore's work became
increasingly abstract and he produced a
series of large bronzes which appear to
derive from human or mechanical joints.
They have a bone-like quality and suggest
that while they are articulated together
they also are in opposition.*

Right:
St Sebastian III, *1958–59. Height
87 in (2210 mm). Eduardo Paolozzi
(Rijksmuseum Kröller-Müller, Otterlo).*
Paolozzi has participated in much of the
thought and action in British art since the
1950s. His creative inventiveness was
early evident in his contribution to the
formation of the Pop art aesthetic
although he cannot be confined under the
Pop label. He has made prints, sculptures
and paintings, and his style has varied
widely. It is difficult to identify him with
any one work but this standing figure
represents a number of his qualities and
interests. He is not dominated by the
Moore aesthetic and uses machine parts
and textured surfaces to build his
aggressive, almost heraldic figures.

Below:
Piece LXXXII, *1969. Anthony Caro
(Tate Gallery, London).*
The use of girders and sheet steel, welding
and forging, spray paint, etc. have become
commonplace in modern sculpture. Their
general use began in the postwar period
and by the 1970s had become almost
academic practice. The use of
nontraditional methods and materials is
now so generally accepted that it seems
almost unnecessary to consider them as
special, determining elements. One of the
pioneers in Britain, influenced by the
American David Smith, is Caro. He was
once an assistant of Henry Moore's, but
now rejects Moore's aesthetic.

Art in America: 1940-60

The Museum of Modern Art in New York was founded in 1929 and the Museum of Non-Objective Painting (later to become the Guggenheim) in 1939. In the decade from the stock market crash to the beginning of the Second World War, art in America was growing in confidence and acquiring a clearer sense of identity. The arrival of such artists as Albers and Hofmann from Europe, as we have seen, forged a link with the then-dominant French School. The rise of Nazism and the outbreak of war speeded the exodus of established European artists to America, and most of them lived in or near New York City. Almost to a man the whole Surrealist fraternity arrived just after the outbreak of war, André Breton, founder and chief theoretician, Max Ernst, Roberto Matta, André Masson and the great publicist Dali among them. Marcel Duchamp was of course already there; so was Picabia and the American Surrealist and photographer Man Ray, who went to work in Hollywood.

Not surprisingly in the liberal, stimulating environment of New York they experienced a new burst of creative activity, and soon began to have a considerable influence on native artists. Surrealist ideas became part of the American scene in 1940–41 and when Peggy Guggenheim opened her gallery, The Art of This Century, in October 1942, it became the immediate focus for *avant-garde* artists. Although its impact was not comparable with the Armory Show, it was nevertheless remarkable. The Americans responded eagerly to the new European influences inherent in Surrealism which became, through Peggy Guggenheim's gallery, one of the inspirations of what was known during the war as the New York School and later as Abstract Expressionism. As we have seen, labels of movements do not necessarily say anything about the work they are applied to, and can sometimes be actually misleading. A great deal of the work of the New York School in the 1940s was abstract, but in the way we have considered the term, it was not Expressionist. Many consider Abstract Surrealism a better name.

Another influence was the existentialist philosophy of Jean-Paul Sartre and Gabriel Marcel which, as opposed to traditional philosophy, gave primacy to existence over essence: 'I am therefore I think and do' over 'I think therefore I am'. This sense of man outside system and belief, compelled to find his personal salvation in his own actions, denied objectivity and asserted subjectivity: everyone's life is a personal odyssey. The sense of personal responsibility was sympathetic to the American spirit of self-reliance and enterprise, and contributed to the developing self-confidence of American artists and intellectuals.

The end effect was that immediately after the war the new American art burst upon a war-exhausted world with dramatic effect. The result of the war polarized power between the two superpowers of the Soviet Union and the United States, with the latter dominant in terms of wealth. Europe, however, was severely damaged physically and morally. The large, brash, evidently assured work of the New York School brought a message of hope which the weary aesthetics of the Paris School could no longer offer. From this time on the United States provided an alternative, more attractive to young artists, to the depleted, repetitious activity of French art.

Thus, in 1945 the centre of the story of modern art shifted across the Atlantic.

The importance of the United States Information Services in Europe should not be overlooked. The new postwar sense of identity in the United States evoked a desire to propagandize American culture, and the USIS arranged lectures and exhibitions and published a great variety of documents in pursuit of the hope that, having won the war, the Americans would win the peace. The United States would no

Right:
Summation, 1947. Arshile Gorky (Museum of Modern Art, New York. Mr and Mrs Gordon Bunshaft Fund). Gorky, a native of Turkish Armenia, studied first in Russia and emigrated to the United States in 1920. He worked on the WPA Federal Art Project in the Depression and explored a number of European styles, including Picasso's Cubism and Kandinsky's abstraction. In 1939 he met a number of the Surrealist immigrants and from that time his work carried Surrealist overtones while retaining references to the natural world in biomorphic forms.

Summation, a large preparatory study, is one of his last works and the title, given after his death, suggests that it represents a conspectus of his ideas. It is certainly full of Gorky's typical forms, elegant and mysterious.

Right:
Gotham News, *1955. Willem de Kooning (Albright-Knox Art Gallery, Buffalo, New York. Gift of Seymour H. Knox, 1955).*
De Kooning was born in Holland in the same year as Gorky, whom he met soon after his arrival in New York in 1926 and who exerted a considerable influence on his work. He had seen the abstractions of De Stijl as a youth and his work after his meeting with Gorky became abstractionist Surrealist. Whilst he was preoccupied with the human form (particularly female), during the 1950s he also painted a number of bold, gestural abstractions of which Gotham News *is one. These works, with dense, overpainted layers of colour, seem to imply a deep struggle to arrive at a release of emotion through colour.*

Convergence, 1952. 93 × 155 in
(2375 × 3937 mm). Jackson Pollock
(Albright-Knox Art Gallery, Buffalo,
New York. Gift of Seymour H. Knox,
1956).

*The extreme individualism of Pollock's
work and the originality of his technique
has made it recognizable to many for
whom the process and the reasons for it
remain obscure. Pollock is the first*

*quintessentially American painter with
a world reputation, and as a founder-
leader of the Abstract Expressionist
movement he contributed largely to the
artistic dominance of the United States*

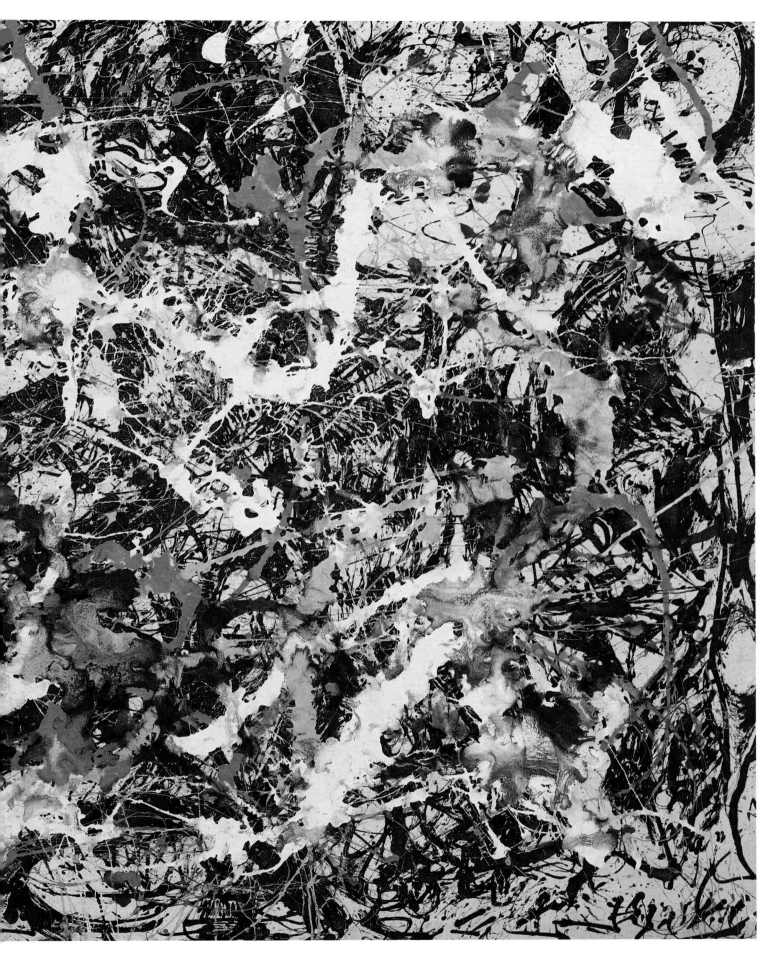

in the postwar period.

His mature technique of dripped paint on large canvases in generous, gestural patterns of overlaid lines characterized his painting until near the end of his life. It is sometimes described as 'action' painting, a suggestive term in Pollock's case. If the individual reveals his nature and understanding in all his actions, his deepest qualities may be expressed when control is removed and the painter engages in free activity unrestricted by idea or technique. Pollock's drip paintings are part of this desire to allow free communication to the spirit.

longer remain a culturally derivative offshoot of Europe. Without the aid and influence of the USIS the works (the massive dimensions of many of them created problems of transportation if nothing else) of the New York School would probably not have been shown in the main public galleries of Europe during the decade after the war.

Of the many artists who in their own persons provided a link between European art and the New World, Arshile Gorky is outstanding. An American who came to the United States in 1920, Gorky was a private spirit of dramatic appearance. Julien Levy, Gorky's dealer and friend, described him as 'a very camouflaged man' and recalled that a woman once took him

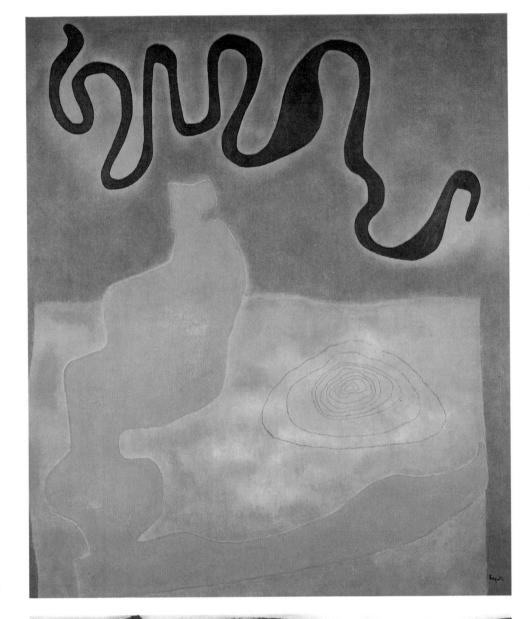

Above right:
Congo, 1954. William Baziotes (Los Angeles County Museum of Art. Gift of Mrs Leonard Sperry).
One of the chief figures of American postwar art movements, Baziotes never achieved the public recognition of some of his contemporaries. His subtle colour sense and almost mystical use of biomorphic forms to create what often seem to be totemistic images give his work interest. He is included here as representative of a number of American painters who gave the postwar scene its energy and variety.

Right:
Chief, 1950. Franz Kline (Museum of Modern Art, New York. Gift of Mr and Mrs David M. Solinger).
Within Abstract Expressionism lay the notion that the gesture is a deeply revealing aspect of creativity. It inevitably expresses (it is held) the inner state, and it requires little reflection to establish that each individual uses gestures to reinforce the expression of ideas. Kline represents this gesturalism in his bold and aggressive, calligraphic brush strokes, which create a pattern, in his earlier work in black over white, of compelling simplicity. In later works with colour, the decorative effect of the colour combinations seems to reduce the impact.

186

The Frozen Sounds, No. 1, 1951.
Adolph Gottlieb (Whitney Museum of
American Art. Gift of Mr and Mrs
Samuel M. Kootz).
Essentially a New Yorker, Gottlieb
received his first training at the Art
Students League and later participated in
the WPA projects of the New Deal.
Associated with the Abstract
Expressionists he also came into contact
with the expatriate Surrealists, and in the
New York atmosphere of revolt against
European geometrical or decorative
abstraction his work became increasingly
mystical. His compulsive use of floating
discs is almost a signature in his work.

for Jesus Christ. Gorky pursued his
enthusiasm for Cézanne and, even
more, Picasso to the point of imitation,
and admitted it. 'I was *with* Cézanne
for a long time and now naturally I am
with Picasso.' The beginnings of his
own most characteristic work appeared
in 1940 and from that time until his
suicide in 1948 he deepened and
extended his language of near-abstract
Surrealist imagery to become one of the

most important figures of the New York
School. Supported by André Breton,
who admired his tense line and strong
personal colour sense, the complexity
and density of his imagery became
impenetrable but, curiously and un-
questionably, always moving and affecting. His influence on such contemporaries as Jackson Pollock (1912–56)
and Willem de Kooning was profound.

It was actually Pollock who really
caught the public attention and produced the most obviously powerful
new work. Early Abstract Expressionism has been divided into two
groups – the gestural painters and the
colour/field painters. Pollock is the
leading figure of the former movement,
which the critic Harold Rosenberg
described as Action Painting (a term
no longer in favour).

The so-called 'biomorphic' forms
encountered in near abstraction in such
painters as Miro and Yves Tanguy
(1900–55) in early Surrealism seem to
have a visceral or sexual reference to
human parts which emerge indistinctly
from a painted ground. This biomor-

phic Surrealism is also found in Gorky,
in the earlier Pollock, in Mark Rothko
(1903–70), Robert Motherwell, Clyfford Still (1904–80) and William
Baziotes (1912–63). In Pollock these
images are given Classical or mythological titles, to express enduring
human emotion in given circumstances. Pollock's art moved on in the
1940s in pursuit of a need to escape
those traditional, Classical associations.
He and his contemporaries abandoned
the methods and even the materials of
traditional art in order to distance
themselves from the past. For Pollock,
Surrealist and existentialist ideas played
a part in this development.

In talking of the European Surrealists Pollock said, 'I am particularly
impressed with their concept of the
source of art being the Unconscious.'
Elsewhere he described his method:
'My painting does not come from the
easel. I hardly ever stretch my canvas
before painting. I prefer to tack the
unstretched canvas to the hard wall or
floor. I need the resistance of a hard
surface. On the floor I am more at ease.

I feel nearer, more part of the painting', and 'I continue to get further away from the usual painter's tools such as easel, palette, brushes etc. I prefer sticks, trowels, knives and dripping fluid paint . . . When I am *in* my painting I am not aware of what I am doing.' The relationship with Breton's automatic writing and the existential concern with the self is clear enough in these remarks.

Five years before his death by suicide Pollock said, 'When I am painting I have a general notion of what I am about. I *can* control the flow of paint: there is no accident, just as there is no beginning and no end.' But to the public at large Pollock's mature work appeared to have no artistic precedent, to be uncontrolled, exhibitionistic and meretricious. Since then our understanding of his aims and achievements has advanced, to reach a consensus of opinion that not only is he the foremost painter of the school but also, perhaps, the first truly 'All-American' artist of the highest rank.

The Abstract Expressionists, Pollock and his associates, were making significant statements about the possible nature of art, the creative force of the unconscious, the identity of the self in any situation. It may be thought of as Narcissistic or self indulgent, but it is certainly one view of the universality of art. Pollock's art, though immediately recognizable, is not easy. The multiplicity of activity reflected in the complex weaving of lines created a changing ambiguity of space which draws the observer into personal self-experience. The pleasure of the pattern is seductive and easy; further exploration is harder but may be deeply revealing.

In Rothko's large and sombre, sensitively and softly coloured areas the colour/field form of Abstract Expressionism reaches its highest expression. His mystical art uses extremely limited means; two or three rectangular shapes float indeterminately on a coloured ground. The paint is applied thinly and the shapes are not defined, seeming to hover behind or in front of the ground colour. The subtlety of Rothko's delicate colour sense together with the large scale of the works make an almost spiritual impact.

In Rothko's words, 'Pictures must be miraculous: the instant one is

completed, the intimacy between the creation and the creator is ended. He is an outsider. The picture must be for him, as for anyone experiencing it later, a revelation, an unexpected and unprecedented resolution of an eternally familiar need'. One is reminded here of Paul Klee's remark that a painting is finished when *it* looks at *you*.

The two trends in Abstract Expressionism, the 'unfinishable' of Pollock and the 'resolved' of Rothko, characterize other members of the New York School, who nevertheless arrived at various different and separate solutions. There is no obvious visual coherence in the work of the whole group – if it can be called a group – and they are of greatly varying quality. From the slick and spurious to the sensitive and profound, all shades of creative ability are represented, and not all observers will find themselves able to respond positively to *all* the work of *all* the New York artists. But perhaps that is true of any other school in any other time or place.

One of the most highly regarded of the Abstract Expressionists is Willem de Kooning. Born in Holland, De Kooning came to the United States as an adult. His work partook of the biomorphic Surrealist imagery and was close to that of Gorky, whom he revered. But his later paintings, larger and more aggressive, exhibit a vigorous gestural quality; his numerous paintings of women are thrust firmly and eagerly on the canvas with only traces of the biomorphic in the emphasis of features – an enlarged eye or assertive breast. These images are essentially American in feeling; at once brash and sensitive, they leer at the observer, demanding attention.

The outsize linear gestures of Franz Kline (1910–62), suggesting details of Chinese calligraphy, are close to De Kooning in their attack, but the source of their real inspiration is not clearly apparent. Motherwell's work, clearly inspired by Surrealism, is more intellectual. It has a literary content absent from most Abstract Expressionist

work. His series *Elegy for the Spanish Civil War* suggests modern icons, with dark, sonorous and phallic forms on a recessive space.

Motherwell's place is somewhere between the gestural and the colour/field painters, which perhaps helped to establish him as the voice of Abstract Expressionist artists (not the critic, that is Harold Rosenberg) in general.

Among other representative colour/ field artists are Adolf Gottlieb (1903– 74), Philip Guston (1913–80), Sam Francis and, perhaps most important for the future, Barnett Newman (1905–70) and Ad Reinhardt (1913–67). The simple, close-knit imagery of Newman and Reinhardt presages the later development known as Minimalism. Newman is not concerned with making images within – or without – traditional ideas of art. Like Pollock's, his work is a realization of the unconscious in its most elevated form. He explains it thus: 'I believe that here in America, some of us, free from the weight of European culture, are finding

Left:
1957-D No 1, 1957. Clyfford Still (Albright-Knox Art Gallery, Buffalo, New York. Gift of Seymour H. Knox, 1959).
After an early association with Surrealism, Still has continued to make large paintings in the idiom that he developed in the 1940s while he was teaching in California. An early Abstract Expressionist, his paintings consist of areas of colour in flat sheets which intermingle to give a rich and vibrant effect. In most of his work one colour, usually dark, covers most of the picture area.

Right:
Elegy to the Spanish Republic No. LV, *1955–60. Robert Motherwell (Contemporary Collection of the Cleveland Museum of Art).*
The Abstract Expressionist painter Motherwell is also a sensitive critic and writer who has edited, with Harold Rosenberg, the Museum of Modern Art series of publications called Documents of Modern Art. *He is the most articulate and intellectually motivated of the Abstract Expressionists and his paintings follow a deliberate programme of progression. Best known are those belonging to the series* Elegies to the Spanish Republic, *begun in 1947. A feeling of devout homage and penitential sadness pervades these works.*

Below right:
Painting, *1957. Sam Francis (Tate Gallery, London).*
Francis studied under Clyfford Still in California and lived in Paris for several years. He belongs to the later generation Abstract Expressionists and his work has an airy delicacy owing more to the influence of Pollock than any of the others. He may be described more appropriately perhaps as an Impressionist, and his floating colour is reminiscent of Turner. The elegant charm of his work also relates him to Parisian influence.

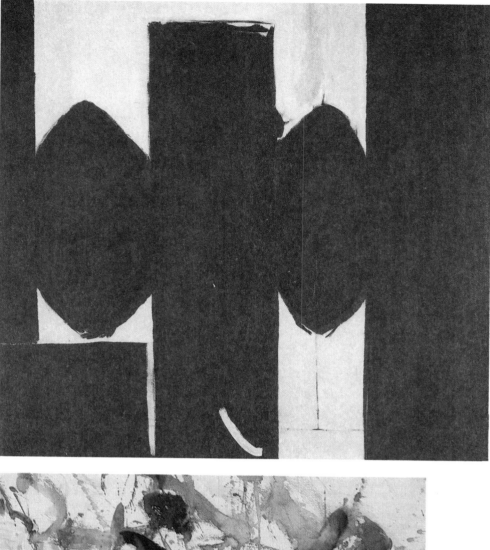

Vir Heroicus Sublimis, 1950–51.
95 × 213 in (2422 × 5136 mm). Barnett
Newman (Museum of Modern Art, New
York. Gift of Mr and Mrs Ben Heller).
This very large canvas is the antithesis of
Abstract Expressionism in avoiding the
emotive implicatory gesture for large flat
sonorous areas of single colour divided by
verticals in careful, subjective
relationship. Colour oscillates and the
very simplicity of the image in relation to
its size indicates an aesthetic that is closer
to Mondrian than to that of Newman's
contemporary Abstract Expressionists.
Like Rothko's work, its effect is lost in an
inevitably greatly reduced reproduction.

the answer, by completely denying that art has any concern with the problem of beauty and where to find it. The question that now arises is how, if we are living in a time without a legend or myths that can be called sublime, if we refuse to admit any exaltation in pure relations, if we refuse to live in the abstract, how can we be creating a sublime art?' His answer is that, 'instead of making *cathedrals* out of Christ, man or life, we are making them out of ourselves, out of our own feelings'. Again, recourse to the inner resource, the unknown self. In Newman's art this expresses itself in simple lines or bands of colour on a single-colour ground. There is a cool remoteness, a process of pure reduction in this which is seen by the later Minimalists as a starting point.

However, there is an important point in connection with this: despite Newman's protests, which are echoed by others, aesthetics – the study of beauty – is just what critics and observers have in mind when considering his work. However, the Abstract Expressionists in general, who are mostly very articulate about their art and have clearly identified their aims in philosophical terms, have shown that, while rejecting tradition and avoiding direct reference to aesthetics, they are deeply

concerned with those areas of creation in which aesthetics traditionally resides. It is indeed sometimes difficult to relate their writings to their works. One is left with the necessity of responding to the work, with or without intellectual comprehension.

Regarding the social acceptance of the work, more significant than the painters' views are the commercial attitudes of dealers, collectors and public galleries. Whether or not the artist places his work within the aesthetic canon, it is certain that it is treated by all these interests as if it is part of the tradition of gallery art. This has perhaps obscured the real difference

between these paintings and the exhibition art of earlier periods, including that of the first decades of this century.

This is, of course, not the fault of the artists themselves, but it does reflect one of the problems of seeing the art of recent years as clearly as one would wish. There is an immediate desire on the part of public galleries and private collectors, enthusiastically encouraged by the dealers, to possess representative work of any new development that seems likely to achieve a significant position in the history of art. Collections include works of artists who do not fulfil expectations and, altogether, the art scene of recent years, especially

in the United States where the collecting passion has grown immensely since the 1930s, has been considerably distorted by these commercial motives.

Abstract Expressionism also became exportable and the immediate postwar years witnessed a general expansion of this century's 'tendency to abstraction'. It was not until the end of the 1950s that the next stage emerged (although it had been germinating for some years). In 1959 Newman had a major show in New York which may be taken as the end of the postwar phase of American art. Next year, something new.

Left:
Cubi XIX, 1969. David Smith (Tate Gallery, London).
David Smith has become regarded as the foremost American sculptor of the century, although he studied to be a painter. Inspired by Picasso's welded sculptures in the 1930s he began to sculpt and after the Second World War (during which he worked as a welder) he produced a series of almost two-dimensional sculpture, drawing free shapes with a welding torch in sheet metal. His later work, of which this is characteristic, became more geometric, and he produced series of arrangements under the same title, using similar geometrical, three-dimensional forms. The dignity and presence of these works has inspired a considerable following in both the United States and Europe.

Above:
Sphere, I, 1963. Arnaldo Pomodoro (Museum of Modern Art, New York. Mrs Simon Guggenheim Fund).
The elegant sophistication of Pomodoro's work is well illustrated by Sphere. The polished outer shell is broken to reveal a structural pattern of seemingly a space age city, or a complicated electronic device. A totally 20th-century image, its physical attractiveness is essentially part of a European rather than American aesthetic. Pomodoro, an Italian, originally worked with his brother Gio making jewellery, and a suggestion of the precious object accompanies the work.

Black Wall, 1959. Wood. Louise
Nevelson (Tate Gallery, London).
Born in Russia, Louise Nevelson grew up
in Maine and studied painting at the Art
Students League, at Munich under Hans
Hofmann and in 1932–33 worked as
an assistant to Diego Rivera. She then
became a sculptor and in the 1950s
began producing the series of boxed
sculptural forms with which her name is
most often associated. Usually painted
black or brown, they convey a mysterious
sense of urban isolation; she called one
series Images of the City. She is now
recognized as one of the most important
American sculptors of recent years.

Lobster Trap and Fishtail, *1939.*
Painted steel wire and aluminium.
Alexander Calder (Museum of Modern
Art, New York).
Calder's name is essentially linked with
the mobile, a name given to Calder's
moving sculptures by Hans Arp. Early in
his career Calder used mechanical power
to move the parts of his sculpture but in

his mature work they hang suspended on
wire moving gently in an unpredictable
pattern through the effect of moving air
agitated by the movements of observers.
There is a delicate playfulness about these
works made, usually, of large plates of
coloured sheet metal; Calder's first essay
in moving sculpture, in the 1920s, was
a toy circus with moving acrobat figures.

The Lobster Trap and Fishtail *was*
commissioned by the Advisory Committee
of the Museum of Modern Art for the
stairwell of the museum.

The 1960s

It is possible to see a certain coherence of intent in the world of art during the period from the end of the Second World War to about 1960. The primary task was one of reconstruction, and it absorbed a good deal of energy and enthusiasm. But the form that reconstruction should take was not commonly agreed. In some countries a natural conservatism predominated; in others a powerful radical spirit was abroad; yet others were marked by a revolutionary zeal springing from the creation of a socialist society. Some of the decisions taken in those years seem to have been justified by time, but elsewhere there have been sharp changes in direction.

The international political situation had changed entirely since the 1930s. The United States and the Soviet Union far outclassed all other states which had formerly considered themselves 'great powers', though the populous countries of the East, such as India and China, had not yet achieved the weight in international affairs that seemed due to them.

In the West at least, there was a great deal of discussion about the purpose and direction of the arts in society, their social role, if any, and their responsibility. In the Soviet bloc, art was firmly enlisted in the service of propaganda, though the presence of the Iron Curtain made it difficult to see what was happening on the other side. In the free societies of the West the government also played a role in the arts by offering financial support, through direct grants or through various tax concessions, and although there was no such thing as political control, the different forms of government support inevitably had some effect on developments in the arts.

One result of the war was to encourage forms of international co-operation, the foundation of the United Nations being the most striking symptom, and in the arts it was apparent that cultural nationalism, which was still a feature of Western art up to 1940, could not survive much longer. Generally speaking, creative people took an increasing interest in relevant work from other countries. The new spirit of internationalism was not welcomed by all, and as with most changes there were some apparent losses as well as gains. On the whole, art has become less internationalized than seemed likely a generation ago.

In the visual arts a battle of some ferocity was fought out in the period immediately after the war, and the area where the fight raged most fiercely, or at least most visibly, was architecture. Architecture is not part of the subject of this book, but it is impossible to ignore it in the postwar contest between traditionalism and modernism. One might think this battle had been fought and won before the war, but the public generally were quite ignorant of the ideas – and the actual buildings, of which there were comparatively few – of the great modernists.

Nevertheless, by about 1960 modernism appeared to have gained the victory. Multitudes of clean-lined, totally undecorated office blocks, hotels, and flats changed the character of many a city. Twenty years later the victory seemed less decisive, or certainly less desirable, but that is another story.

In the traditionalist view, the arts were part of a continuous process of growth, reflecting the fundamental values of the society in which they exist; violent revolutions were not their business, and the revolutionary developments in art since the first decade of the 20th century were regarded with, at best, ambiguity. Traditionalists felt that they had not proved themselves and had not justified their total rejection of proper historical values. A return to those values seemed desirable, but in what form? Here was the difficulty. All but extreme diehards accepted that turning back the clock is as futile a gesture in art as it is in other spheres of life, but there was no agreement on how the old values were to be restored except by returning to abandoned and demonstrably uninspiring forms. Thus, the modernists triumphed because their opponents had no big weapons in their armoury.

Masterpiece Art. For painters and sculptors, another equally fundamental question loomed. From the early Renaissance to the beginning of the 20th century, the acknowledged aim of the artist was to produce a masterpiece. Each individual work aspired to this status, and the success or failure of an artist was measured by the masterpieces he produced, or failed to produce. The Impressionists and the Post-Impressionists had been incorporated within this system, and once they were accepted as masters who produced masterpieces they could be placed on the wall alongside Raphael and Rembrandt.

The leaders of the early modern movements – Picasso, Matisse, Mondrian, Kandinsky, etc. – presented more of a problem. However, their work also took the form of surfaces covered with paint or three-dimensional objects that could be stood on a plinth, and therefore, once they had been accepted, they too joined the tradition of 'masterpiece art'. Picasso is again the crucial figure. By this time he was very widely recognized as a genius, and it followed that anything done by a genius must be a masterpiece. Thus the masterpiece system continued in the period after the Second World War and the majority of artists concurred in it, although less ready to admit it than their 19th-century predecessors. Even the Abstract Expressionists produced finite, assessable works aspiring to masterpiece status, though the size of some of them made hanging a problem. The works of painters and sculptors, up to the 1960s, were designed to be shown in galleries and to find their resting place in a museum or a rich person's home, no less than the works of those working in traditonal style. They might look a little uncomfortable in a museum, but being segregated from earlier work, they settled in.

In the period we are considering, however, the old masterpiece tradition was threatened in a number of different ways and, in the view of the *avant-garde* at least, was destroyed for ever. This conclusion may be somewhat premature, but there is no doubt that in the 1960s and 1970s the idea of the artist and of the role of art has been gradually but dramatically changed. Some of the factors causing the change are mentioned elsewhere, but one immensely important development was the growth of television.

The impact of television has been much more significant for the history of art than the cinema was. Motion pictures had stimulated many creative people to make images in time of a kind that painters and sculptors were obviously not concerned with, and film had been accepted as another art form. Of course, most films had no pretensions to be anything but entertainment, though many of that type have, with time, come to be esteemed for other virtues. That is a minor issue. More important is the fact that seeing a film was something one did much as one might go to a gallery to see a painting, though often anticipating a rather different form of satisfaction.

Television was different. It was *there*, right in the living room, and could be viewed, if one wished, for hours at a time, indeed for more hours than the idlest person had available. Moreover, it was not art, or at least it was not considered an art form in the way that cinema was, its productions largely consisting of journalism of various kinds and low-brow entertainment. (Of course, this argument is not fair: if cinema can be art so can television, and in any case you have more chance of seeing an 'art film' on TV than in a cinema; however, it is attitudes that count.)

And yet, television's social impact was tremendous; no one could dispute that. It was not simply that it usurped much of the traditional role of art; as the prime medium of visual communication it was vastly more important than the fine arts had ever been or could ever be.

Developments since Daguerre have steadily pushed art into a more marginal role in society. Television brought this home to nearly everyone, and it was the necessity of adjusting to their reduced role that occupied the thoughts and affected, in various ways, the works of serious-minded artists in the 1960s.

The decline of the idea of masterpiece art has created severe problems for galleries and museums. When a painting or sculpture was a unique masterpiece to be cherished and conserved, the role of the museum in acquiring and displaying such works was clear and commendable. But in recent years, museums of modern art have found themselves acquiring works which are merely representative of an activity and cannot be recommended for their individual worth. Artists too find themselves in an invidious position, and the general system of art education, which even at its most progressive is still largely backward-looking, has not made it any easier for young artists to find a suitable role in society. Hence the wild profusion of art-related activities of the past two decades.

Pop

One of the results of the American power and presence in Europe after the Second World War and the dominance of Abstract Expressionism in Western art was to make an interest in American culture a proper study for Europeans. Many of them already had considerable enthusiasm for its independent vitality, its easy acceptance of material abundance and its breezy self-esteem. The art community in the United States was somewhat surprised but gratified by the widespread recognition of American artistic leadership, and not inclined to relinquish the pre-eminence it has so recently gained.

In the late 1950s at first in London but soon in New York too, a new and rather surprising development took place. Named Pop art by the British art critic and historian Lawrence Alloway in 1954, it adopted as its subject matter the lowbrow imagery of popular American culture as defined by the powerful advertising industry.

In both character and treatment it could hardly have been more different from the currently supreme abstractionism of the New York School, but during the 1960s it achieved near-universal acceptance as a new and vital art form. It seemed that the visual arts had at last returned to a comprehensible if unexpected type of representational art and, relieved at their release from the esoteric speculation which invariably accompanies abstract art, the public adopted Pop with enthusiasm.

It was energetic, lively, colourful and decorative; it could be easily collected and it fitted pleasantly into modern interiors. Since the 1960s, practised by a long line of followers, it has remained one form of contemporary expression that provokes little adverse comment.

If the matter were as simple as this it would only remain to examine and evaluate the work of the Pop artists and summarize their position in the modern scene. But Pop art is far from being as simple a phenomenon as it first appeared. In two respects at least it is more revolutionary than any movement (including Abstract Expressionism) that preceded it since the early days of Cubism.

Firstly, it was deliberately obsolescent: it was concerned with fashionable images that were of their nature transient. Secondly, it was the first art form in which the lifestyle dictated the art, or indeed *was* the art. Many pop artists lived 'pop' lives: brash, outgoing, self-promoting, commercial. Richard Hamilton, one of the earliest Pop art practitioners, defined the qualities desirable for art as being transient, popular, low-cost, mass-produced, young, witty, sexy, gimmicky, glamorous, and BIG BUSINESS.

Pop was also anti-art, or at least anti-'high' art. It is this that makes the movement so crucial for much that has happened since, whether abstract or figurative. Since the 1960s what, for want of a better term, we still have to call art, has been driving in a totally different direction. The change of direction started with Pop.

The anti-art stance of Pop took the form of a rejection of the aestheticism of abstraction, and of Abstract Expressionism in particular. The Pop practitioners dismissed the arguments of abstraction as elitist and obscurantist, irrelevant when not incomprehensible. They believed that the works did not say what the words suggested they did. But Pop art was not just an expression of anti-intellectualism in terms of a popular art accessible to all because, in fact, many of the artists were themselves highly cerebral; the discussions in which Pop originated were heated and lengthy. All of those involved knew and revered earlier art, whether or not they believed it to be 'relevant' to modern society, and they were fascinated by the work of some of the earlier masters of modern art. Dada, Surrealism and Marcel Duchamp above all were sources of inspiration. Duchamp can be seen as one of the two gurus of Pop (De Kooning being the other). Duchamp himself was of course alive and well and playing chess in Greenwich Village – the last 40 years of his life was artistically nonproductive.

Duchamp's readymades were of special importance, but he was a somewhat unwilling father figure at this stage. He is reported as having written in a letter to the former Dadaist Hans Richter, 'This neo-Dada, which they call New Realism, Pop art, Assemblage, etc. is an easy way out and lives on what Dada did. When I discovered readymades I thought to discourage aesthetics. In Neo-Dada they have taken my readymades and found aesthetic beauty in them.' The importance of the distinction is part of Pop art philosophy. Dada, in the shape of Duchamp's *Bottlerack* for instance, was anti-art in the face of a lingering traditional art which the Dadaists saw as a mockery in the current mayhem of the First World War. For Duchamp a bottlerack was as significant in art terms as any art consciously made as such – or as insignificant. It was art because he said it was.

The anti-art attitude of Pop was somewhat different, however. In the consumer's world of the admen, domestic and commercial objects are made visually attractive, sexy even, but never messy or demanding. It is an anodyne, objective world of induced excitement, fashion and change which inspires a different view of the commercial artefact. A can of soup, in itself no more or less significant than, say, an earthenware jug in a Chardin still-life, becomes, as a readymade, as surely an expression of a lifestyle – of all the elements that Hamilton desires – as Chardin's jug does not. Pop images are not art as visual expressions of a slice of life, they are the chosen symbols, valueless in themselves, which carry at the same time the values of society. They do not, in short, need to be art.

To identify the nature of Pop and its source of imagery is less easy than the account above may suggest, and to describe its development and the relationships between its various practitioners is no less difficult, since Pop is not an art movement with clear motives, aims and style. There is considerable uncertainty as to who are the Pop artists – even among themselves. There are no manifestoes, though plenty of individual statements. It is the only one of the recent developments in art to have achieved general acceptance, but the range of work that has been claimed for it is so wide that it becomes impossible to find any example that can be called typical. It is clear that there are British and American varieties, and also that, inasmuch as Pop exists on the European continents, it is different again there.

The differences between British and American Pop art are discussed below, but there are some important characteristics that they share. Nowhere can Pop artists be regarded as simple observers of the urban scene – or any other scene for that matter. They teach us nothing about the nature of popular culture or social custom. It was a large

Below:
Bottlerack, *1914 (replica, 1964).*
Marcel Duchamp (Galleria Schwarz, Milan).

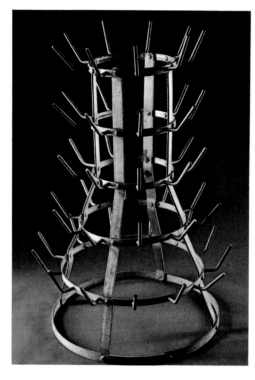

Below:
Campbell's Soup Can with Can Opener, *1962. Andy Warhol (Private Collection).*
Warhol has become one of the best known artists of the last three decades. The range of his work, his personal lifestyle and his determination to remain an inarticulate enigma have made him permanently fascinating to a wide public. His background in commercial illustration perhaps gave him his keen sense of personal publicity and he has certainly

directed his career most astutely. He has chosen to present obsessions, real or induced. Among the first of these was a Campbell's soup can, which he treated in single or multiple images. When asked why he painted them he said, characteristically, 'Because I used to drink it. I used to have the same lunch every day for twenty years'.

Just What is it that Makes Today's Homes so Different, so Appealing?, 1956. Richard Hamilton (Kunsthalle, Tübingen. Collection of Dr Georg Zundel).

Using the artefacts and totems of modern society, Hamilton constructed a collage which is an acerbic comment on modern popular culture. Hamilton studied as an engineering draughtsman and was one of the founders of the Independent Group at the London Institute of Contemporary Arts. This collage was made for the poster and catalogue of the exhibition 'This is Tomorrow', which marked the public appearance of Pop art as discussed by the I.G., and is thus the seminal work of British Pop. Hamilton's intellectual quality and creative curiosity make him not only a leader of Pop but an inspiring figure in the postwar British art scene generally.

part of the task of traditional art, usurped by the camera in the 19th century, to mirror the customs and appearance of the society which gave it birth. Pop does not show how people live. It may comment obliquely on the values of the society that produces it but only through the artist's incidental search for an anti-aesthetic image which cannot be mistaken for 'high' art. While it may appear to glorify the artefacts of popular culture, at the same time and through the same forms it may also ridicule them.

Indeed the role of the artist is a curious and interesting aspect of Pop art. Intellectually aware and specifically anti-aesthetic, he or she nevertheless works in an atmosphere of creative freedom and dedication, and this art may actually be as remote and inaccessible as any Abstract Expressionist's.

Pop Art in Britain. The beginnings of British Pop are to be located in the Institute of Contemporary Arts in London, an institution dedicated to the encouragement of the contemporary – mainly visual – arts. Its president was the Surrealist Roland Penrose, and a tendency towards experimental Surrealism was an early feature of the ICA. In 1952 the Independent Group, a fruitful forum for discussion, was formed at the ICA. It was guided initially by Edouardo Paolozzi, who had a particular interest in scientific images and machinery. From the Group's talks and exhibitions the term Pop arose partly to suggest an art of parallel appeal to pop music. Paolozzi and Richard Hamilton were the most forceful and inventive members of the Group, which included architects, designers, writers and poets. An early work by Hamilton, whose list of desirable qualities in art has already been noted, uses the sort of subject material which was to become common in Pop art. His *Just What Is It That Makes Today's Homes So Different So Appealing?* is a small collage containing images of a cinema, automobile emblems, household gadgets, comic strips and pin-ups (a fair analogy of Pop art), adding up to an almost consistent view of a modern interior. Made in 1956, it is one of the earliest Pop images.

In the 1950s a group of young painters at the Royal College of Art in London gave Pop its first public identity. They included Richard Smith, Peter Blake, Derek Boshier, Allen Jones, Peter Phillips and Joe Tilson. They were followed in the early 1960s by David Hockney, Anthony Donaldson, Patrick Caulfield, Ronald Kitaj, a London-based American, and others. Although they were never formally a group and had no common programme, an examination of their work indicates what British Pop was about.

It was clearly more calculated and more intellectual than anyone was prepared to admit. Such artists as Kitaj,

For Men Only Starring MM and BB, *1961. Peter Phillips (The Calouste Gulbenkian Foundation, Lisbon). Phillips has said that he is interested in painting and uses the familiar elements of his culture in the same natural way as artists of earlier societies used theirs. For him the compelling images are from cinema and pop music. Pinball machines, film stars, customized autos and girls sexy and flaunting are all part of his imagery. His methods include the use of a spray gun, the 'pencil' of the engineering illustrator, and his work epitomizes the image typical of the Pop movement.*

Above:
Got a Girl, *1960–61. Peter Blake
(Whitworth Art Gallery, University of
Manchester).*
*Although Blake has some claim to be the
originator of British Pop, he does not see
himself in this role and has at various
times denied being a Pop artist at all.
This, perhaps, stems from his involvement
with his subjects rather than with Pop
culture. He is not part of the garish Pop
world, translating a throwaway culture
into self-conscious art. The figures that
interest him and the subjects he chooses
are real and important, and he expresses
this feeling with love and care. As a result
his work seems more locked into the
academic process than that of other Pop
artists. He is nevertheless an important
figure in the early development of Pop.*

Right:
OH!, *1963. Joe Tilson (The 180
Beacon Collection, Boston).*
*Visually part of the development of
British Pop, Tilson is intellectually apart
from it, being more interested in language
and awareness, technique and texture
than in the nature of popular culture and
its expression. His OH! is a painterly
work in which the banality of the subject
is changed by the treatment, the careful
technical construction of the O and H also
contributing.*

Hermaphrodite *(detail), 1963. Allen Jones (Walker Art Gallery, Liverpool). Jones evinces a preoccupation with sexy girls and creates images using female anatomical parts in a way that suggests modern preoccupations without being really erotic. Indeed, his subjects are less figures than culture evocations.*

Below left:
If Not, Not, *1975–76. R. B. Kitaj (National Galleries of Scotland, Edinburgh).*
Kitaj, an American who was part of the group at the Royal College of Art in London, has always been difficult to categorize. He uses many elements that are normally recognized as Pop and is particularly interested in the cinematic image. Nevertheless, he does not regard himself as a Pop artist, and the complexity of his allusions and the intellectual basis of his art brings it nearer to a form of Surrealist symbolism than to the standard brash Pop product.

Below right:
After Lunch, *1975. Patrick Caulfield (Tate Gallery, London).*
Caulfield's painting is easily identifiable by the unvarying weight of line, simple colour and areas of painted detail. After Lunch is a typical example. His work raises again the question of the proper subject for art and how should it, now, be treated. His subjects are traditional and usually commonplace. It is his treatment, deadpan and schematic with apparent bursts of meticulously painted local incident, that is different.

whose allusions are as numerous and erudite as T.S. Eliot's, seem hardly to be 'Pop' at all. Kitaj, like Blake and others, is as interested in the qualities of paint in a traditional sense as any academic painter. For some Pop artists, however, the very incongruity of painterly Pop images is attractive.

The fascination with American culture, particularly the cinema, is constantly reflected in their work (John Wayne and Marilyn Monroe are their heroic figures) but quite apart from that there is, most notably in Patrick Caulfield's work, an interest in producing a simplified image of a traditional subject. In this form Pop is making sly comments not only about traditional art forms but also about art values.

The carefully painted pictures of Peter Blake, who does not consider himself to have been a Pop artist, emphasize another aspect of Pop, a genuine affection, even reverence, for popular culture, ranging in Blake's case from the Edwardian Music Hall to Elvis Presley. Although not designed for popular consumption, the images of the Pop artists are often immediately attractive and seemingly simple. Since they were using subjects that were generally familiar, the public, as well as art collectors, were attracted; Pop art became and has remained truly 'popular' in Britain to a degree that it never quite attained in the United States, despite the extraordinarily widespread use of the idiom during the 1960s and later.

Pop Art in the United States. Although Pop may be said to have started first in Britain, since it took much of its material from popular American culture it has obvious affinities with American Pop. Nevertheless, its inspiration, nature and development were very different. American Pop was anti-aesthetic and yet paradoxically closer to the traditional, in a way that British Pop was not. The major spur was found in Abstract Expressionism, which the Pop artists regarded with suspicion and distaste. They came to believe that Abstract Expressionism rested on an obscurantist aesthetic base, particularly inappropriate for the forthright nature of American culture, and that it was an offshoot of European idolization of the great masters of the early movements, Picasso in particular. The gestural energy of, say, Pollock or Kline did not express the modern American way of life, it merely extended the abstractionist tendencies of prewar Europe. Thus the Americans' enthusiasm for American artefacts was more direct than the British, and carried fewer hints of nostalgia or amiable envy.

In spite of their critical view of Abstract Expressionism, for one figure in that movement, Willem de Kooning, they had great respect, and he may be regarded as one of the founding fathers of American Pop. Like all Abstract Expressionists, De Kooning was interested in and exploited the evocative and emotional qualities of paint, but unlike the others, in some of his paintings (particularly the *Woman* series) he suggested a new imagery.

It has been suggested that Pop artists were also traditional painters in some respects; that in their reaction against the aestheticism of Abstract Expressionism they followed traditional pictorial methods. Their treatment and images might be different, but they painted large canvases and made sculptural objects. They operated through the same traditional gallery outlets – and were extremely successful commercially. To some extent it was this commercial success that caused the rapid expansion of the genre and the inclusion in the category of Pop of anyone who could be remotely connected with it.

As in Britain, a sort of proto-Pop first appeared in the 1950s in the work of Jasper Johns and Robert Rauschenberg particularly. Both Johns and Rauschenberg are now firmly attached to Pop, but their earlier work had a serious iconoclastic intent and neither of them were anti-aesthetic, the essence of their work being painterly picture-making. Some of their methods, and certainly their subject matter, were Pop, however. Their works were sensitively painted in a traditional way but

The First Marriage, *1962. David Hockney (Tate Gallery, London. © David Hockney 1962).*
Hockney has always been an independent spirit whose work follows a course determined by his current interests and inspired directly by important events in his own life as well as his acute observation. He has described the origin of The First Marriage *in the Pergamum Museum. He saw his friend standing next to an Egyptian sculpted figure; both looking in the same direction, they seemed united, modern and ancient. It was a marriage of styles, and the bullet-shaped object (bottom left) came in to suggest a Gothic arch and give a religious connotation. The word 'first' was applied because he had painted another picture called* The Second Marriage.

dealt with subject matter of boring inconsequence in a deadpan manner. We shall encounter them again in a later section, on Assemblage.

Later, more truly Pop artists rejected painterly qualities and made the surface treatment deadpan too. The most familiar Pop names, established in the New York scene by 1960 or 1961, were Andy Warhol, Robert Indiana, Roy Lichtenstein, Tom Wesselmann, Claes Oldenburg and James Rosenquist. Among other interesting but less well-known artists were Mel Ramos, Wayne Thiebaud (both West Coast), John Wesley and Allen d'Arcangelo. Other significant figures who were certainly associated with Pop yet stood somewhat apart from the mainstream during the 1960s and 1970s were Jim Dine, George Segal and Marisol.

This far from exhaustive list would certainly touch most of the bases of Pop art, though no single individual could embody the whole range of what constitutes Pop. As in Britain, Pop artists never created a movement like Cubism (perish the thought!) and their motivation was almost as varied as their work. Perhaps the most that can be said is that they shared a feeling of hostility to inaccessible art images and tended to find their own images in the familiar.

Each artist approaches popular culture subjectively and the illustrations of

Peter Getting Out of Nick's Pool. *David Hockney (Walker Art Gallery, Liverpool. © David Hockney 1966). Hockney's preoccupation with the male figure has resulted in some of his most important paintings and drawings. Particularly effective are the delicate and beautifully drawn figures in interiors. In the brilliant sunlight and luxury living of California he found new inspiration, and in his paintings of swimming pools and modern architecture he introduced figures drawn with increasing naturalism. The variety of his activities, including printmaking and designing for plays and opera, have helped make Hockney one of the most interesting and important of contemporary painters.*

their work go far to explain them individually. However, American Pop generally is less 'domestic', more on the overblown scale of advertising, than British or European. As many of the sources are part of a public imagery designed for the masses, the Pop artists enlarge them in detail and thus make them into isolated icons of a sort (e.g. Lichtenstein's enlarged details of strip cartoons, Oldenburg's gigantic plastic hamburger). Such treatment emphasizes the essential unimportance of the object and by extension of the culture that produces it and the art that is made of it. By this token Pop is the first popular art that expresses a real sense of pointlessness in any art that clings to its forms.

Like all truly revolutionary developments, Pop art opened the paths to the future. Much of the Assemblage, Happenings and Conceptual art of the 1970s and 1980s depends upon the underlying propositions first stated in Pop.

Bathtub Collage. No. 3, *1963. Tom Wesselman (Sidney Janis Gallery, New York).*
Wesselman's work is difficult to categorize simply. Although a Pop artist, his methods include collage and assemblage as well as such incidentals as recorded music or sounds, smells and actual objects in sections of interiors. He was concerned in his well-known series of Great American Nudes with painting coolly voluptuous figures in real settings — more real therefore than the figures. The bathroom assemblage here is a good example: the door, towel, basket, curtain and mat are placed in context with the painted nude in an illusionist tiled bathroom. The whole effect is exciting and compelling.

Marilyn, 1967. Screenprint. Andy Warhol (Tate Gallery, London).
There are no very easily distinguishable stages in Warhol's career or artistic development. Since his first essays in art he has been successful, having a genius for constructive publicity perhaps deriving from his days as a commercial illustrator. His first exhibition of shoe drawings secured him a Life magazine spread. He has always been fascinated by pop stars and the tragic glamour of Marilyn Monroe became almost as great an obsession with him as Campbell's soups. He developed a cheap method of printing which gave the effect of newsprint reproduction and made a large number of slightly variant coloured prints: Marilyn is one of such a series. Warhol himself pointed out that anyone could use this technique to make their own images.

Left:
All in One Lycra Plus Attachments,
*1965. Jim Dine (Van Abbe Museum,
Eindhoven).*
*Dine is an artist of varied interests who
has been attached to a number of the more
recent developments by critics and
observers. He began to paint in the
1950s and first exhibited in 1960.
Before this he had also been involved in
Happenings and Environmental
structures. He is sometimes considered one
of the original Pop artists but he himself
does not make these distinctions,
considering that what concerns him – his
environment, studios, personal
experiences, visual enthusiasms – are all
reflected in what he does, whether that is
to paint, conduct a Happening, or make
an Assemblage. His exhibition work
usually consists of objects and paint in
integrated association, as in this example.
His image-making is suave, witty and
compelling.*

Above:
Three Flags *1958. Jasper Johns
(Private Collection).*
*From 1955 Johns began to paint targets,
numbers, alphabets and flags, not in a
straightforward representational way but
so changed that the particular identity of
the subject was confused or extended and
denied its familiar associations. Through
the introduction of texture, spatial effects
and colour change, the paintings became
reflections on the nature and importance
of the subject rather than the subject
itself. It could then be seen as a popular,
unassociated image. This work treats the
U.S. flag respectfully but inventively and
in the process emphasizes its
iconographical importance.*

Overleaf, top left:
The American Dream, I, *1961.
Robert Indiana (Museum of Modern Art,
New York. Larry Aldrich Foundation
Fund).*
*Educated in Chicago at the same school
as Oldenburg, Indiana subsequently
settled in New York. After meeting a
number of painters through working as an
artist's materials salesman, he produced a
number of assemblages in pursuit of the
expression of the great American dream –
the effective and successful functioning
human being, extrovert and uninhibited.
A series of paintings followed, many of
which include short, emphatic injuctions
(EAT, DIE) related to American myths
from procreation to death. They are not so
much paintings which adopt popular
images as subject matter as they are pop
objects in themselves.*

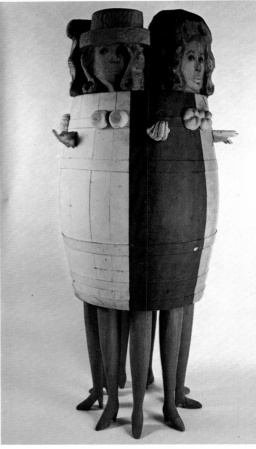

Above:
Ruth, *1962. Escobar Marisol (Rose Art Museum, Brandeis University, Massachusetts).*
Marisol, born in Paris of South American origin, studied first at the Ecole des Beaux Arts and later in the United States at the Hans Hofmann School and the Art Students League. She commenced sculpture around 1953 and her mature work dates from about 1960. Displaying genuine individuality and charm, it is usually an assemblage of painting, carving, plaster casts and man-made objects. The effect of the usually over-lifesize figures is often slightly Surrealist.

Left:
The Last Civil War Veteran, *1959. Larry Rivers (Museum of Modern Art, New York. Blanchette Rockefeller Fund). Although not properly a Pop artist, Rivers uses subject material that is part of the Pop impedimenta and his paintings have the immediacy of most Pop works. But Rivers is interested in the whole tradition of painting and its techniques. He is a figurative painter and his work always shows a desire to exploit the qualities of paint. Like many of his contemporaries, he responds to current stimuli and* The Last Civil War Veteran, *one of a series, was taken from* Life *magazine photographs.*

Marilyn Monroe, I, 1962. James Rosenquist (Museum of Modern Art, New York. Gift of the Sidney and Harriet Janis Collection).

Of all the postwar film stars Marilyn Monroe has proved the most compelling subject for painters of the Pop scene. Her glittering but tragic life, her winsome but powerful sexuality and even her surprising marriage to the playwright Arthur Miller were the stuff of legend, and she was quickly recognized as a symbol of great potential. Rosenquist makes images of details rather than the whole in an irrational arrangement which sometimes recalls half-finished or damaged posters.

Ice, 1966. Richard Lindner (Whitney Museum of American Art, New York).

A refugee from Nazism in Germany, Lindner moved to France in 1933 and from there to the United States in 1941. His work shows many German characteristics, its harsh Expressionist character recalling Beckmann, Dix or Grosz. There is also a relentless exposure, in a form of Pop imagery, of the superficiality of popular culture. Sometimes erotic, sometimes brutal, his analysis of the American scene shows a perception and power which separates him from most Pop art and suggests that his work will be seen in the future as more Protest than Pop.

Motion and Mechanics

One group of distinctly 20th-century developments, which have no direct precedents in earlier periods, are concerned with visual effects produced by the actual materials used by the creator. Early examples consisted of simple experiments with colour, line tones and areas to produce curious optical effects, but the trend became more interesting when extended to new synthetic materials, three-dimensional constructions and to powered mechanisms.

This group of activities has much in common, but no one name exists which covers all of them adequately. Op (short for 'optical') and Kinetic art are two well-known ones, the term 'mechanical art' is sometimes employed when relevant, and certain moving three-dimensional works are known as mobiles.

Many of these works are as purely abstract as one is likely to encounter, many seem motivated by a childlike fascination with machinery, while some use reconstructed natural forms. They are united by one significant characteristic – a desire to extend boundaries, to explore new artistic territory.

Some of the movements in art before 1940, notably Futurism, provided inspiration for these explorations, and their further development during the early postwar years can be traced; but not until after the Pop explosion of the 1950s – and in conscious opposition to it – can anything which may be regarded as a genuine 'movement' be described. The name 'Op', incidentally, was obviously derived from 'Pop'.

A concern with the optical effects in art that can be produced by the elements of colour, line etc., has a long history; indeed, it is part of the whole history of art. A specifically scientific interest in colour and tone effects is found in Seurat and the theory of *pointillisme*, while in this century the work done at the Bauhaus on colour, texture, form and materials provided further inspiration, as did the Surrealist experiments of Marcel Duchamp and Man Ray with motorized effects. The

mobiles associated with Alexander Calder (1898–1976), an engineer by training, also appeared before 1940. Calder's moving sculptures employed the biomorphic shapes of Miró in suspended metal sheets connected by wire rods so balanced as to give a delicate, floating, ever-changing pattern of interrelating forms with every movement of air. The volume inhabited by the work was thus much greater than itself and also constantly changing. Eye-catching, elegant and decorative, these constructions were more attractive than more genuinely significant work.

Op Art. The most easily identified and understood of these developments is Op art. Its concern is with the optical effects of colour, line and shape without reference to any natural source. Squares, circles, rectangles, etc. are explored in combinations of colour. The most familiar figure and the originator of Op art is Victor Vasarély, a Hungarian who studied at the Budapest Mühely Academy, one of the schools that adopted Bauhaus methods, and later worked in France as a graphic artist. He became a painter only in 1943. The striking, often startling, decorative patterns that he produced made him attractive to interior decorators in search of an ultramodern look, and that has obscured the real nature of Vasarély's work, which is as serious as it is experimental.

An earlier painter, Auguste Herbin, had produced a number of paintings in which simple geometric areas of colour were put together and repeated in a series with one element only, either colour or shape, being changed. Vasarély extended the experiments with colour–shape language in order to arrive at what he regarded as a prototype for self-produced images in series. He claimed that the value of such a prototype resides in the distinction of the quality it distils. This is reminiscent of the search of Mondrian for the basic elements of artistic expression. It is

part of that belief, which is yet to be definitively established, that there are values in abstract elements which may transcend anything achieved with elements from the visible world. Vasarély is taking part in the search for a pictorial language that makes meaningful statements and may communicate some specific message, independent of representation.

The attractive images of Vasarély's closely related patterned paintings, made in extensive series in his art factory, do posit some difficulties. The varied responses to individual works in each series as well as to the whole series and the individual nature of perception suggest that if you fashion enough variations on any theme you will eventually evoke every possible response – the monkeys typing Shakespeare theory. This is not to belittle the seriousness of Vasarély's purpose nor that of other Op artists.

Bridget Riley brings a particular method of linear construction to high effectiveness. Her earlier black and white linear paintings were followed by brilliantly coloured paintings, but in both the carefully calculated optical effect produces a sense of movement which becomes emotionally involving. This kinetic effect is an extension of earlier, less sophisticated, Futurist, experiments, e.g. Balla's *Birds in Flight*.

The sense of movement, the kinetic effect, is achieved in a variety of ways for a variety of purposes. Sometimes the movement unfolds with the movement of the observer, either in opposition to his movement or in sympathy with it, as in the works of Yaacov Agam and Carlos Cruz Diez, which are constructed in three-dimensional form, or in that of Richard Anuszkiewicz, Peter Sedgley and Piero Durazio. The fascination with the redeployment of elements for different effect is present in all their work, which shows what remarkable results can be achieved by a small change in a simple process.

The effect of simple objects themselves in repetition can also be dramatic

and a number of Op art objects have been constructed on this basis by Raphael de Soto, Sergio de Camargo, Günther Uecker and others.

Kinetic Art. Kinetic effects employing actual movement rather than optical illusion originate in the experiments of the Constructivists and of Dada and the Surrealists. They involve the use of many different sources of movement and power. Water, sound, light, magnetism, electric and mechanical power – they have all played a part.

The attitude of artists towards technology and science in this century has varied from ecstatic approval to fierce hostility. On the one hand artists have been attracted by the new possibilities offered by scientific discovery and investigation; they have been conscious of the ever-increasing influence of technology in the modern world and aware that the machine has made virtually all hand-crafted objects, including some art objects, more or less obsolete. On the other hand there is a feeling that science is antipathetic to art, dealing only in facts and excluding imagination (though science would not have advanced very far without that quality).

It must, however, be admitted that, in general, the artist has failed to find satisfactory expressions of the relationship, if any, between art and science. The Futurist fascination with modern technology resulted in some charming if naive attempts to express the urgency of modern society. The use of machines in the 1920s and 1930s to move objects to form patterns in space or to perform useless and meaningless actions, whilst it made some connections between the two, was hardly harnessing the power of technology in the cause of art. The use of machine parts or castings of them welded or stuck together may have said some-

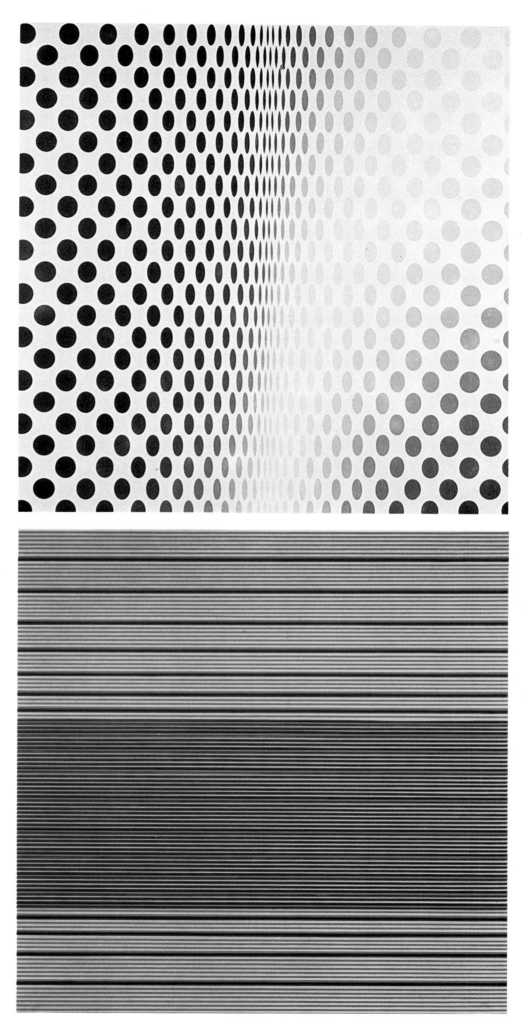

Left:
Arny-C, *1966. Victor Vasarely (Private Collection).*
Even in his early advertising work Vasarely explored optical possibilities. His images in series have a rich visual attraction.

Right:
Loss, *1964. Bridget Riley (Private Collection).*
Bridget Riley is the most consistent of the British Op painters whose work, although different in imagery, comes closest to Vasarely's in its exploration of limited possibilities. Using basic elements of dot and line she extracts the maximum visual changes to produce works which have extreme optical effect. Some are physically difficult to look at for a sustained period so much do they appear to oscillate. She spent some time in Italy and was influenced by the works of the Futurists, particularly Boccioni and Balla.

Below right:
Yellow Attenuation, *1965. Peter Sedgeley (Tate Gallery, London).*
Linear patterns of the kind illustrated are characteristic of Sedgeley's work in the 1960s. He has worked closely with Bridget Riley, with whom he has an obvious affinity. Later, he introduced the centred circular form to produce a series of strange, visually disturbing effects, and recently he has experimented with moving elements and light in his circular constructions.

thing about the power or other qualities of machines, but was essentially using them as still-life alternatives.

There is no reason to believe that a more fruitful relationship cannot be created, but it was not achieved in the work of the Kinetic artists of the 1950s and 1960s. The grinding, grating malfunctions of Tingueley's incompetent machines may have been intended as a form of protest, but they end up rather as large toys. Similarly, the waving metal fronds of Takis, Pol Bury's slowly moving, motorized antennae, Nicolas Schöffers's moving light/space frames all have visual attractions but still seem elaborate playthings.

However seriously intended, the ideas of the Groupe de Recherche d'Art Visuel, started in Paris in 1959 under the influence of Vasarély, often seemed playful and amusing, though also ingenious. The group conducted sophisticated experiments in visual, non-personalized art and achieved some impact through the work of (among others) Julio Le Parc, with his random light effects on suspended, light-reflecting metal squares.

So far, then, most of the work which is inspired by or directly employs contemporary technology has done little more than suggest that the place of art in a scientific society is at best ambiguous.

Today, some people are experimenting with art effects in which lasers provide the technical force. Lasers appear to offer to scientifically directed, creative spirits visual opportunities of a new kind. Maybe from this or some future development a genuinely scientific art will arise, qualitatively different from the external, observing nature of current Kinetic art.

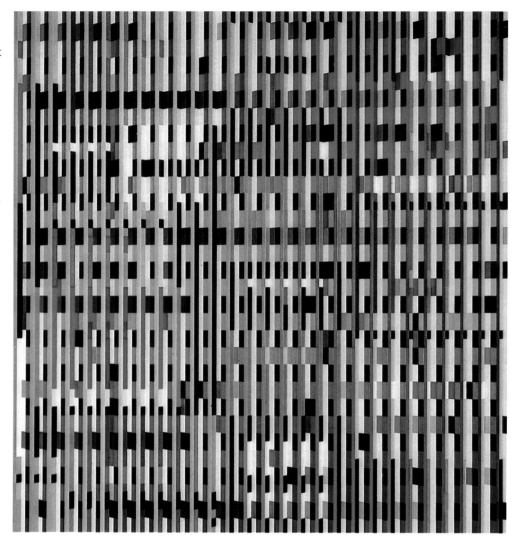

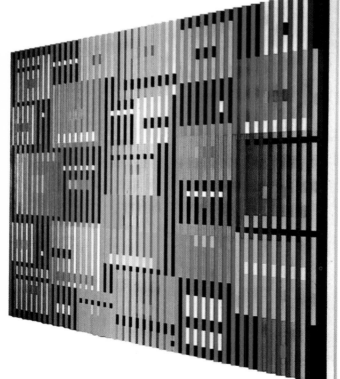

Left and below left:
Double Metamorphosis, 1968–69.
Yaacov Agam (Centre National d'Art Contemporain, Paris).
The two illustrations of this work reveal only part of its nature. Made in relief, it requires the movement of the observer across its face to achieve its total effect. The progressive revelation in Agam's work is often extremely attractive visually, and it is usually found as large-scale decoration in, for instance, office interiors, where it appears at its most effective. Like that of the Venezuelan Carlos Cruz Diez, Agam's work is perhaps halfway between Kinetic and Op.

Below far left:
Luminous, *1963. Richard Anuskiewicz (Private Collection).*
Anuskiewicz studied at Yale under Albers and this appears to have settled the direction of all his subsequent work, including the concentration on square and diamond as his favoured forms. An elegant Op artist, his brilliant control of the elements he uses reveals something of the sense of incompleteness of many Op and Kinetic effects. Once the optical effect, which may be visually disturbing, is experienced, there appears to be a point of disjunction: no further internal contact is made, prompting the question, 'Is that all?' And if so, 'Is it enough?'.

Above right:
Physichromie No. 326, *1967. Carlos Cruz Diez (Wallraf-Richartz Museum, Cologne. Collection Ludwig).*
It is difficult to reproduce the effect of Cruz Diez's work since even the pattern is not apparent until the observer moves across the picture plane. The colour is attached to slats which are at 90° to the picture's surface and some colour is reflected from this. The colours of the slats change and a moving pattern is made.

Below right:
Baluba No. 3, *1959. Jean Tingueley (Wallraf-Richartz Museum Cologne. Collection Ludwig).*
From his student days in Basle Tingueley, a Swiss who settled in Paris in 1952, evinced a curious attachment to the bizarre and unusual. In Paris he began to construct what he called his Métaméchaniques – motiveless mechanized activity by complicated machines which often also produce sounds

and smells. Some of Tingueley's machines self-destruct and thus stand somewhere between mobiles and Happenings, as well as emphasizing Tingueley's happily anarchistic view of life.

Right:
16 Balls, 16 Cubes in 8 rows, *1966.*
Pol Bury (Tate Gallery, London).
Bury, a Belgian painter and sculptor, was an early Surrealist, influenced by Magritte, his fellow countryman. Since 1954 he has been dedicated to Kinetics, and his elegance and technical perfectionism have resulted in works of great tactile attraction, moving slowly in repeating motorized patterns. In this work, the balls and cubes move slowly in a pattern dictated by an electric motor.

Far right:
Signal 'Insect-Animal of Space', *1956. Takis (Takis Vassiliakis) (Tate Gallery, London).*
Takis, a self-taught Greek sculptor, moved to Paris in 1954 where he created his first Kinetic work. His typical constructions consist of tall and slender rods which, fastened to a base, are moved from above by electromagnets, vibrating and swaying in mesmeric patterns of slow and elegant motion. It is of course impossible to illustrate their effect, and photographs cannot do justice to these pleasing and sensitive constructions.

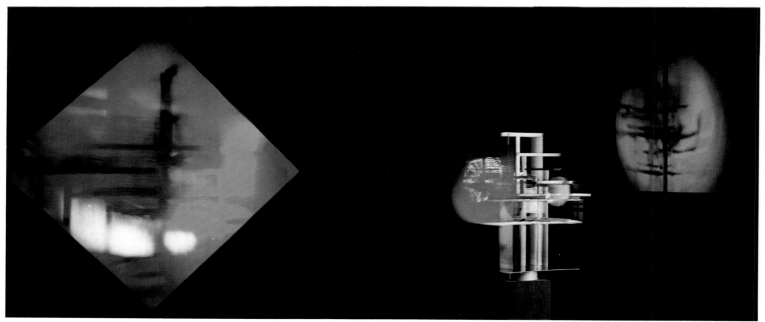

Spatial Dynamic Sculptures, *not dated. Nicolas Schöffer (Musée National d'Art Moderne, Paris).*
It is not possible to reproduce in a static image the effect of this or indeed any Kinetic work composed of moving parts and changing colours, as in this work by Schöffer. This example can be seen as projecting and reflecting changing patterns of colour. These in themselves are exceedingly pleasing and carry something of the fascination of the cinema. It is, however, difficult to categorize the work that Schöffer and other Kinetic practitioners produce since it crosses the boundaries of many disciplines, including acoustics, and borders on Environmental art, Assemblage and Happenings.

Art in America Since *1960*

The new paintings of the 1950s, Abstract Expressionist or others, were soon absorbed by the commercial art world, passing into collections, public and private, and becoming subtly diminished or at any rate less startling in the process. Most of these works were not easily accommodated in an ordinary house or apartment, and their sheer size had other incidental effects.

In the first place, it greatly encouraged the sale of prints, in limited editions signed and numbered. This particular market, though not new, was a real growth area in the 1960s. Secondly, the galleries in which these works appeared were obliged either to extend their premises or to put other works into store in order to accommodate them. The result was to bestow on the Abstract Expressionists a somewhat gratuitous pre-eminence which possibly exacerbated the reaction against them on the part of the new generation.

For time marches on, the revolutionary turns into the conservative, the new grows old. The great works of Abstract Expressionism, screwed firmly in place on gallery walls, came to seem not so much an expression of a new American art as an extension of the European aesthetic. Now that more time has passed, we can see that this is largely true, but we might add that it is inevitable and natural.

However, to young artists like Frank Stella and the progenitors of Pop, such as Johns and Rauschenberg, there was still no art that reflected the true American spirit, the showmanship, the honest vulgarity, the affluent consumer society and the visions of Hollywood.

Post-Painterly Abstraction. Art in America in the 1960s was characterized by a diversity of new attitudes and new movements. Pop, as we have seen, reached its zenith; Minimalism and Post-Painterly Abstraction suggested other preoccupations.

The term Post-Painterly Abstraction encompasses two developments neither of which can properly be called movements. The adjective 'painterly' means the particular visual attraction of the way the paint itself is applied, independent of the subject. This may be the quality by which an artist is most easily identified, and it is characteristic of certain periods or certain artists throughout the history of art since the Renaissance. In itself the quality of paint application may be seductively compelling, so that it may be thought the most significant aspect of the work, or even its sole attraction. Painterliness then is not necessarily a complimentary term, sometimes implying work in which technique replaces content.

Many of the earlier Abstract Expressionists incurred criticism on the grounds that they allowed technique to dominate so that the gestures were empty and self-indulgent. In reaction to that, artists attempted to eliminate personalized expression in one of two ways: first, by making clear, sharp-edged forms in a style known as Hard-Edge; second, by floating the colour on to the surface in what attempts to be an utterly anonymous manner. Both devices purport to exclude that individualized or idiosyncratic quality which might be called a personal style.

This goal cannot be said to have been achieved by either of the methods of Post-Painterly Abstraction. Indeed, the personal identity in the work of Ellsworth Kelly and Morris Louis, respectively exponents of the first and second forms of Post-Painterly Abstraction, is quite evident, and in retrospect their works seem thoroughly assimilated to the postwar abstractionist movement.

The Hard-Edge paintings of Ellsworth Kelly consist of large, simple areas of colour. Al Held and Jack Youngerman, among others, worked in similar style. Their images seem to be parts of some larger abstraction which, if shown, would present an identifiable subject. This is also part of the negative Hard-Edge intention. It is as if they say, not only do you not identify us by

brush-stroke technique but neither do you by subject. This is a cool, 'design' art which insists on attention to shape, non-shape and part-shape, suggesting a significance which it is at pains to avoid stating. Kelly also made sculpture in which the shapes are coloured sheets.

In the other form of Post-Painterly Abstraction, colour is applied in a floated film forming simple areas with no brush strokes visible. Barnett Newman and Ad Reinhardt (see page 190) are the best-known exponents of this style. Reinhardt produced some sombre images which are tonally so close as to seem at first sight one area of colour. They have a sonorous, but restrained quality which influenced Morris Louis.

Although he was born in the same year as Jackson Pollock, in the development of postwar abstraction Louis's work follows Pollock and is characteristic of the 1960s rather than the 1950s. His vague and fluid veils of colour later gave way to parallel strips.

All Post-Painterly Abstraction emphasizes the belief that the subject is the form and the form only is the content. In a deliberate attempt to concentrate attention on the physical presence of the object, these painters avoid any external reference, allusion, metaphor or symbol. The eye of the average observer is of course looking for precisely these characteristics, and it therefore requires an extremely 'cool', anonymous form of art to defeat that expectation. It has accordingly been described as 'single-point Gestalt', since the Gestalt 'will to form' is directed exclusively to the object.

From these general observations it will be seen that American art in the 1960s was moving in two diametrically opposed directions. One sought a remote and rarefied role for art in which familiar elements were removed; the other sought an imagery that was utterly familiar, the more so the better, and appealed, ostensibly, to the common taste. In the event Pop art remained the preserve of the art

fraternity no less than Post-Painterly Abstraction.

Both, incidentally, supplied a great deal of material to the communication media, and this immediate adoption of the latest *avant-garde* development by commercial interests has had a rebound effect on art and artists, often obscuring the artist's most important contributions while effectively publicizing his activity and, of course, applying a spur to the normal process of change.

Study for Homage to the Square: Departing in Yellow, *1964. Josef Albers (Tate Gallery, London). Among all the compulsive obsessions which have seemed to motivate many of this century's painters and sculptors, Albers's dedication to the square was most striking. As early as the 1920s, in a series of glass paintings, he evinced an interest in the form, which became dominant in the late 1930s. For the last 25 years of his life, it was the exclusive theme of his paintings and lithographs. Albers's colour balances and creative juxtapositions which reveal the visual effects of colour make him one of the precursors of Op art.*

Ossippee I, *1966. Frank Stella (Private Collection). In the work of Stella we see the changes that, surprising in themselves, characterize the exploring nature of the creative artist. In his earlier work he tended towards Abstract Expressionism (the current* avant-garde *style) but his first publicly exhibited works expressed a definite repudiation of the free gesture in favour of austerity. In 1958 he exhibited a series of black canvases striped with unpainted lines which related to the canvas edges. The direction was towards a Minimalist form. These austere works were followed by a series of metallic paintings containing fluorescent colours. In 1966–67 he worked on a series of brilliantly coloured paintings using interlacing circles and arcs, as in this example.*

More recently he has made three-dimensional paintings of cutout shapes in brilliant paint mixed with metallic colours (see page 43). This free use of forms and colours suggests a return to the emotional language of Expressionism.

Above:
Red Blue Green, *1962. Ellsworth
Kelly (La Jolla Museum of Contemporary
Art, California. Gift of Dr and Mrs Jack
M. Farris, La Jolla, California).*
*A painter and sculptor, Kelly represents
the Hard Edge School of New York with
his series of precisely defined colour-
ground works, some on canvas and some
in sheet metal. Like so many of the
postwar Americans, he first showed
interest in Surrealism, thanks to the
powerful contingent of European
Surrealists in the United States. Perhaps
the best of Kelly is to be found in the
curved sheet-metal, flat-coloured works he
produced in the late 1960s.*

17th Stage, *1964. Kenneth Noland
(Private Collection).*
*In the course of the development of
abstraction in the postwar United States
the stage known as Post-Painterly
Abstraction seems in retrospect
remarkably unrewarding. The stripe
patterns of Noland in the 1960s are a
good example of the limited means
adopted by those painters who wished to
reduce the elements to themselves alone
without extrinsic connotations. It was
probably a stage through which the
abstractionist process was obliged to pass,
and the questions that remain are
concerned with its residual effect.*

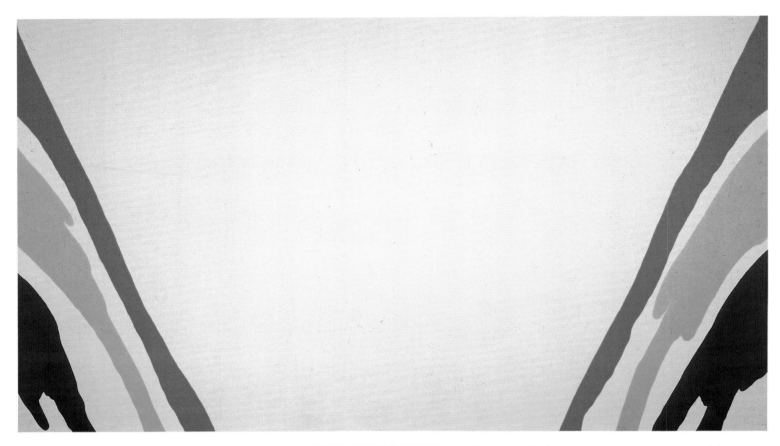

Delta Iota, *1961. Morris Louis (André Emmerich Gallery, New York).*
An austerely dedicated painter, Morris Louis changed his previously somewhat unresolved style in 1954 after a meeting with Helen Frankenthaler, whose painting Mountains and Sea *affected him profoundly. His previous work hardly seems likely preparation for what followed. On sized or unsized unstretched canvas he allowed rivulets of thinned acrylic paint, poured on to the surface, to flow across it, giving a sense of veils of colour floating through the fabric itself. For the remaining years of his life he produced works of great distinction which, like Rothko's, seem to grow in stature with passing time.*

Mauve District, *1966. Helen Frankenthaler (Museum of Modern Art, New York. Mrs Donald B. Straus Fund). Frankenthaler studied art first with the Mexican painter Tamayo and through his form of Surrealist Expressionism was led to Gorky and Kandinsky. Gorky is an evident interest in the main examples of her form of Abstract Expressionism. Her delicate, floating colour, however, is closer to Pollock's trailed paint than Gorky's. Married to Motherwell in 1958, she became a central and influential figure in the movement, and she had special influence on Louis and Noland.*

Happenings and Assemblage

Around 1960 there arose a cultural phenomenon now almost forgotten which for a short time was extremely popular: the Happening. It was dimly related to Pop art, Environmental art and, more nearly, to the performing arts – although rarely taking place in a theatre. A Happening was an occasion for something apparently undirected and unscripted to take place as an art activity rather than narrative play. Its intended appeal was to the visual imagination by the direct stimulation of the senses, particularly by surprise, irrationality, or the provocation of harsher emotions such as disgust and fear. Most Happenings were in fact semiscripted and rehearsed by their organizers.

The antecedents of the Happening can be clearly seen in the Dada performances at the Cabaret Voltaire, in the contemporary performances of the *avant-garde* musician John Cage (themselves rather similar to Happenings) and to various ideas and experiments of the Surrealists. A further important factor was the growing belief that art should have more relevance to direct experience instead of hanging around in galleries. The growth of popular culture following the breakdown of class structures had focused interest on the popular role of art. Although not expressly aimed at the masses, nor of interest to them, the sources of Pop art were in popular culture and did evoke wide public response. It was public response to rearranged familiar experience that the organizers of Happenings wished to evoke.

The main creators of Happenings, Allan Kaprow, Jim Dine and Claes Oldenburg, were Americans, but in Europe the staged events of the Neo-Dadaist Yves Klein (naked girls daubed in paint and directed to roll about on a canvas while an orchestra played a single note for ten minutes) were proto-Happenings, and there were similar, sometimes rather macabre activities in Germany staged by Josef Beuys, among others.

Like the Surrealists, the organizers of Happenings wanted to break through the barriers of automatic, conventional attitudes by striking a blow that penetrated normal emotional defences. Anger, disgust, laughter, or salacity were better than polite cocktails at a gallery opening.

The *enfant terrible* of Pop art, Andy Warhol, used film to extend the Happening. Technical effects were combined with repetition, slow action and irrational connections to achieve a similar assault upon the conventional.

The short (though active) life of Happenings perhaps indicates their uncomfortable nature; in any case, shock tactics are, more than most, subject to the law of diminishing returns. Also, of course, in the current social/artistic metropolitan scene, nothing lasts for long ('we did that last year'). Nevertheless, Happenings do have a place in 20th-century aesthetic inquiry.

During the past twenty years or so, in the United States particularly, a form of work known as Assemblage has become popular. It is found in a wide variety of forms and in no sense is it a style or movement. Many artists of quite different interests have experimented with it. The term itself dates from a 1961 exhibition at the New York Museum of Modern Art called 'The Art of Assemblage'.

Assemblage is not quite painting, nor sculpture, but exists somewhere between the two. Like sculpture it is essentially three-dimensional, but unlike sculpture – at least traditional sculpture – it is unconcerned with the formal unity of the object, being usually preoccupied with the subjective and disparate combination of apparently unrelated elements. Like paintings, assemblages may take the form of a tableau, often coloured with unnatural colour and seemingly amateur in construction – 'bodged up', one might say. They suggest choices made by their creator without any evident rational purpose. They seem to satisfy a certain magpie compulsion while simultaneously evincing a poetic language of combined imagery.

Assemblage has, of course, a long history. Among other things it represents the collecting instinct, and many examples spring to mind. The Victorians were dedicated assemblers – all those birds, flowers, fishes and ferns under glass domes. Historically, the secret cabinet of private delights which is only really comprehensible to the collector has been a common preoccupation of many people of both sexes.

The essential quality of modern assemblage is its nonrational nature. Evocative and intriguing, the associations of object, texture, colour and scale in unfamiliar conjunction owe much of their original inspiration to Dada and Surrealist exhibition objects. The fur-covered tea-set made by Méret Oppenheim or the flatiron with tacks attached to the ironing surface are early and simple forms of modern assemblage. Inevitably, Marcel Duchamp made early assemblages, and one of Picasso's most potent images, his *Bull's Head*, is made from bicycle handlebars and seat.

The use of paint or the attachment of objects to painted surfaces is a modern development primarily designed to inhibit interest in the actual object at the expense of its combination in context with other elements.

An early pioneer in the United States is Joseph Cornell who was making small assemblies in partitioned boxes in the 1930s. His evocative and poetic work echoes the idea of an opened secret cabinet and is composed with a pictorial imagination that leaves a haunting impression of a gentle world of the spirit, far distant from modern technological bustle.

This has, admittedly, little in common with the more brash and aggressive approach of later assemblage, some of which is emotionally disturbing if not frightening. When it is constructed full-size, the observer is often directed to move through or into

it, to become a participant. In Keinholz's *The Beanery*, for example, this
can be a very unsettling experience.

As earlier sections have shown, assemblage art of the 1960s has much in
common with other contemporary developments in Pop art, Happenings,
Kinetic art, etc. Even some Abstract
Expressionism suggests assemblage.
The closest relationship, however, is
with collage. The modern form of
collage is part of the history of Cubism,
but flat-surface assemblage also has a
long history, and in the 19th century a
whole industry of collage postcards
thrived on the fascination of unexpected imagery and contained much
charm, fantasy and humour. Collages
which included pressed flowers and
similar natural objects can be seen as a
halfway stage to three-dimensional
assemblage.

The first figures, the founding
fathers, of American assemblage were
Jasper Johns and Robert Rauschenberg,
who have also been mentioned as
progenitors of Pop. Rauschenberg
works both on flat surfaces, using
silkscreen and painted images, and
three-dimensionally in painted tableau
constructions, either free-standing or
wall-mounted. These works are coarse-
ly painted and roughly constructed –
deliberately 'unprofessional'. They
frequently look as if they have come
together by accident and that Rauschenberg has somehow seen in the
strange juxtapositions some inspirational and poetic associations which he

Untitled (Bébé-Marie), *c.1943. Joseph
Cornell (Museum of Modern Art, New
York).*
*Without formal instruction, Cornell
began painting during the Depression
years in New York and had his first show
in 1932. He is best known for his small
boxed assemblages which carry literary
and historical allusions with suggestions of
geographical location in a way that seems
Surrealist but may be better described as
wistful and nostalgic. In the work known
as* Bébé-Marie, *the doll figure seems
defended against reality by the twig hedge
rather than struggling to get out.*

Target with Four Faces, 1958. Jasper Johns (Museum of Modern Art, New York).

Although Johns is associated in the public mind with Pop art, the refinement and subtlety of his mind is out of sympathy with the brash assertiveness of so much Pop. He adopts popular images so that, using 'the things the mind already knows', he can work on other considerations. The inclusion of elements such as the plaster casts of the lower part of the four faces also makes him one of the founders of modern Assemblage. The target here is surmounted by part of the faces, revealed only by lifting a flap. A disturbing ambiguity: are they the target, or are they a firing party to be revealed at the last moment taking aim at the observer? This arousal of a sense of ambiguity, a Surrealist suggestiveness, is characteristic not only of Johns's work but of much Assemblage art.

is endeavouring to identify. The power of these works often lies in their evocative ambiguities of meaning and method. Their roughness, and the damage inflicted on individual objects, prevent any hint of a pretty arrangement in which each of the elements may be enjoyed. The effect is to remove response to a deeper level of consciousness, to break down the conventional response much as Dada sought to do. This Neo-Dada aspect has occasioned the use of that term for the non-rational art of 1960–70.

It is often difficult if not impossible to find a meaning in Rauschenberg's assemblages that would justify them to many observers, but as statements, positive and aggressively present, they may evoke a considerable if chaotic depth of response – regardless, perhaps, of any conscious aim on the part of their creator.

Jasper Johns's work is quieter and more coherent, and his objects are more directly sculptural. There is a certain blandness in the image-making which also harks back to Dada ideas

and makes them on the surface more easily assimilable than Rauschenberg's. Like Andy Warhol, Johns affects a certain obsessiveness of subject, on which he rings many changes. The series of paintings and reliefs of the U.S. flag are typical examples, suggesting that there is some quality both in the subject and in his response to it that is not easily expressed. Such a manufactured obsession may suggest more commercial acumen than inner creative necessity, but in Johns's case one suspects that his delight lies in technique,

Left:
First Landing Jump *(detail), 1961.*
Robert Rauschenberg (Museum of Modern Art, New York. Gift of Philip Johnson).
A student of Albers at Black Mountain College and at the Art Students League, Rauschenberg has always been an experimental and creative figure who has contributed much to the last twenty years of American art. A founding figure in both Pop and Assemblage art, his visual and painterly sense has enabled him to create dramatic and visually memorable images. His work as a printmaker and designer for the Merce Cunningham Dance Company has extended his influence to other fields and his graphic work includes collage illustrations of considerable distinction for Dante's Inferno. *As with so many assemblages,* First Landing Jump *opens up the ambiguities concerning the proper content of art.*

Above right:
Blue Sponge Relief: RE19, *1958.*
Yves Klein (Wallraf-Richartz Museum, Cologne).
Klein had a particular fascination with blue and, it seems, with the texture of sponges. He made a number of painting reliefs – uncomplicated assemblages – using them. His was a strange visionary personality, attracted to Zen Buddhism, with a flair for personal publicity and a restless, relentless curiosity. His reputation is greater than the body of his work and rests mainly on the ideas he sparked off rather than his realized intentions, which were so varied as to make coherent understanding impossible. His tempestuous career was ended by a heart attack at the age of 34.

Right:
The Museum of Modern Art Packaged, *1968. Model (detail). Christo (Christo Jaracheff) (Museum of Modern Art, New York. Gift of D. and J. de Menil).*
Christo's grandiose packaging schemes know almost no physical bounds. The wrapping up of the physical environment like a Neiman Marcus luxury gift betokens ownership of one's own world. A happy conceit, it nevertheless makes a significant point: any idea may be encompassed and taken into one's care and keeping. The Museum of Modern Art, wrapped, is one object to take home and enjoy.

229

Left:
Fire! Fire!, *1963. Enrico Baj (Tate Gallery, London).*
The assemblages of Enrico Baj depend for their success not on graphic awareness or visual sensitivity but essentially on their wit and intelligence in combining associated elements with the literary subject matter. When he is successful his work has charm and delight, but too frequently it falls short of the qualities of wit and visual appropriateness that can be found in, for instance, the drawings and collages of Saul Steinberg.

Above right:
Compression Diget 4, 1960. *César (César Baldaccini).*
A common feature of modern sculpture is its use of unfamiliar materials, or familiar materials in unfamiliar connections. Since Schwitters, the detritus of technology has become attractive material for the sculptor and it is the throwaway object that César adopts: not the cigarette pack but the machine (even a whole automobile). He uses industrial power tools – crushers, stampers and cutters – to change its shape into a new identity, which may look close to a traditional abstract form. César received traditional training in France in modelling, wood carving and stone-cutting. These skills he uses only as a basis for understanding sculptural form.

and his deliberate use of banal subject matter emphasizes his traditional, painterly preoccupations.

In Europe at the same time a number of artists were creating assemblages. They were associated with a group formed in Paris called New Realism (it had nothing to do with the development described on pages 242–246) which emphasized an awareness of the present and resulted in the sort of attempt to disturb sensibilities that had characterized Dada. The driving force was Yves Klein, whose sense of publicity has already been noted. He arranged a number of public art performances in which the elements of earth, air, fire and water figured, symbols of his preoccupation with the great forces of nature – the ultimate void, spiritual energy. He sought to persuade people into a self-induced state of

ecstatic uncertainty.

Klein was imbued with a degree of undisciplined creative energy that few could emulate though many were inspired. He died young in 1962 and the work he left does not perhaps reflect his true qualities. His residual assemblage is modest but his impact on his contemporaries was considerable. Among these is his closest friend, Arman, whose figures composed of a variety of objects contained within a form have a sculptural unity uncharacteristic of assemblage art.

Enrico Baj reveals another aspect of assemblage – humour. His images of pomposity, made of the elements of his subjects, have a wry attraction and considerable wit. Among other European assemblage makers are César (César Baldaccini) and Zoltan Kemeny. Both these sculptors use a variety of

materials in combination, but there is a difference in emphasis in their work from that of the Americans Johns or Rauschenberg. In Cesar's monolithic metallic constructions the elements of a single machine are often combined to make a different, animal-like form. In some works, all the metal from an automobile is crushed into a single rectangular block. Kemeny also uses metals, usually in the form of rods or wires cut into lengths and welded into reliefs which suggest abstract forces, internal energy and growth. Although classifiable as assemblages, the work of both Cesar and Kemeny has a close affinity with current abstract sculpture.

In the United States, Oldenburg, Christo, Segal and Keinholz form a group of assemblage artists who operate in different ways and have different intentions, though some common

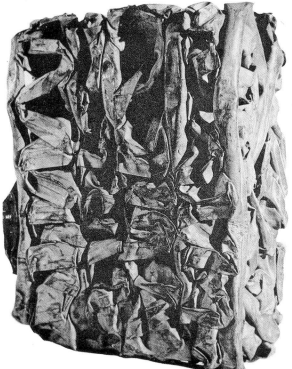

Below:
Glove Torso, 1967. Fernandez
Arman (Wallraf-Richartz Museum,
Cologne. Collection Ludwig).
After exploring the earlier movements of
the century and arriving at a form of
abstract Cubism, Arman abandoned
painting for solidified Assemblage. Objects
in transparent polyester moulds which are
fashioned into specific shapes make up his
later work, such as Glove Torso.

Above:
Sentimentales Gravitations, 1958.
Copper and wood. Zoltan Kemeny (Tate
Gallery, London).
Like Vasarely, Kemeny was a student at
the Budapest Academy of Art and

subsequently a commercial designer,
before becoming a sculptor. Like Vasarely
too, he settled in France, until he moved
to Zurich in 1942. His early sculpture
is constructed from 'found' bric-a-brac,

but later he began to construct sculptured
reliefs from an arrangement of similar
elements – rivets, nails or metal numbers.
These are formed into panels suggesting
landscape visions.

Walk, Don't Walk, 1976. George Segal (Whitney Museum of American Art, New York).

A New Yorker, Segal was one of the creators, with Allen Kaprow, of Happenings when he was still a figurative painter. Having abandoned painting for sculpture he developed a highly personal form of Assemblage using the actual objects and artefacts of the setting to augment the human figures in white plaster cast partly from life which inhabit them. He often includes working elements of the locale, as in this work (the Walk/ Don't Walk signal flashes off and on). The facility to walk around or even within these works gives them a sense of frozen actuality which is powerfully involving to most participants.

Pastry Case, I, *1961–62. Painted*
plaster under glass. Claes Oldenburg
(Museum of Modern Art, New York. Gift
of the Sidney and Harriet Janis
Collection).
Born in Stockholm, Oldenburg was raised
in Chicago and studied at Yale and the
Chicago Art Institute before moving to
New York. At this time he was a painter
but, influenced by Dubuffet, he began to
make objects of deliberately cheap
materials representing consumer goods on
a large scale which emphasized their
actuality much as over-life size
traditional sculpture had done. The
gigantic soft hamburgers, ice cream cones,
a giant ironing board for Manhattan (to
celebrate the garment industry), and a
giant trowel thrust into the earth earned
him the Pop label. His effect in releasing a
generation of creative ideas has been
considerable.

preoccupations.

Oldenburg makes large-scale
replicas, usually in plastic, of
commonplace objects such as
hamburgers, ice-cream cones, light
switches, etc. This work, as we have
seen, is closely linked to Pop art, and
Oldenburg was also one of the organizers of the first New York Happenings.

Edward Kienholz, very different
from Oldenburg in spirit, lives in Los
Angeles and creates assemblages of
everyday objects and environments,
disturbing parodies of contemporary
society, which he finds violent, cynical
and perverted. His constructions – repulsive, decaying – are brutal assaults
on the sensibilities equivalent to those
of the society he is portraying. They
can be almost unapproachable and his
treatment of seemingly ordinary
situations has tremendous emotional
impact.

Finally, two Environmental artists,
Segal and Christo. George Segal is
essentially a sculptor, who uses the
location of his plaster-cast human
figures as part of his environmental
assemblages. His figures set in ordinary
interiors or exteriors create a sense of

abivalence between reality and art by
reversing the usual supportive role of
the environment.

The work of Christo has achieved
wide attention due largely to the scale
on which he often works. He has
packaged landscape locations and
whole buildings. He wraps and ties
objects in plastic sheeting or linen and
makes them into almost anonymous
bundles, as of some amorphous
modern artefact: not quite anonymously, however, since the form can
sometimes be cautiously identified.
The reduction of the object so wrapped
to a useless nonexistence serves to
identify the essential repetitive uniformity of the brand-named modern
artefact. The sense of a loss of identity
is emotionally transferred to the packaged observer, who is unfortunately
similarly interchangeable.

The work of Segal, Christo and
Kienholz offers little hope, joy or aspir-
ation for human institutions. In fact, a
great deal of assemblage art is either
shallowly attractive or depressingly
compelling. Yet there may be, in the
art of assemblage and landscape modi-
fication, a fruitful area to be explored.

Minimalism

An aesthetic attitude – it can hardly be called a theory – developed in the United States during the 1960s which is generally known as Minimalism. Its main recognized exponents were sculptors; they included Donald Judd, Robert Morris, Tony Smith and for a short period Frank Stella.

It often happens that a new idea supplants an older one in direct opposition to it. In this instance Abstract Expressionism was the target. The justification of Abstract Expressionism lay in the belief that in every action or gesture of the artist his personality and intelligence were immanent. Everything he did was a revelation of his own subjective view of the world. Minimalism seeks by a process of reduction to remove all the personal elements, all allusion (or illusion), all external reference, all symbolism and allegory. Everything, in fact, but the object itself. Its reality is only itself. All the acknowledged or unacknowledged overtones or underlying implications present in other works are avoided. Minimalism therefore results in works of stark simplicity. It is closely allied to Post-Painterly Abstraction; indeed, artists such as Kelly and Louis are often described as Minimalists.

In the event, as all others have found, the inspiration for the form comes externally from the individual who makes the form, and however

Left:
The Beanery *(detail) 1965. Edward Kienholz (Stedelijk Museum).*
The disturbing elements of assemblage art which uses dirty and tatty second-hand objects in constructed situational environments are combined in this uncomfortable frightening work with Surrealist elements – clock faces, etc. – to establish the emotive power of Kienholz' imagery. The observer walks through the bar close to the immobile figures almost life size in a state of indefinable apprehension. Kienholz' use of the bric-a-brac of society has more apparent purposive quality than most 'merz' works.

much he may intellectually reject it his activity is subjectively motivated. When Tony Smith says that he likes shapes because they remind him of the plans of ancient buildings he is providing a gestalt framework outside the form. For the observer too such a subjective response is inevitable. What the Minimalist does is merely to minimize the references. The carefully arranged pile of bricks which achieved such notoriety when displayed in the Tate Gallery, London, in 1976 is simply a carefully arranged pile of bricks and Carl André, their arranger, claims no more for them. Why get annoyed at a pile of bricks? The reason lies in the preconceived values one may have about the function of a gallery, or perhaps it is a fear of being conned, or doubts about the Emperor's new clothes. For André, that is your problem; all he has done is pile up some bricks. It is the removal of subjective statement that concerns the Minimalist. He may come close to success but one suspects that it is a Pyrrhic victory.

Although the main strength of Minimalism was in the United States, a number of British sculptors were related to it. Their early leader was Anthony Caro; others were Philip King, William Tucker and Tim Scott. A mixture of Minimalism, Environmental art and Assemblage is found in the work of Richard Long, whose arrangements of stones nevertheless have a very different intention from André's bricks – subjective evocation being their specific inspiration.

In Minimalism as in other recent developments, the dilemma of contemporary art is displayed. The notion that it must be concerned with creating something that is new, something quite distinct from what has gone before, has become engrained in the dealer/gallery/critic award system; novelty becomes the measure of success. One suspects that the allegation levelled against some Abstract Expressionists, that the ability to talk well about the origins of one's work is more important than the

work itself, can still be made.

During the 1960s and early 1970s there was a belief current in art circles that the course of abstraction was almost run. Minimalism offered confirmation of this belief. It seemed improbable that the possibilities of abstraction could be taken further. As one of the most striking, perhaps the most characteristic development of the century, abstraction had played the most significant part in the development of the modern aesthetic. From Cubism, through subsequent styles up to Abstract Expressionism, it had shown an inspiring adaptability. But Minimalism looked like a full stop.

However, the uses suggested in earlier developments such as Surrealism had not been fully explored and abstraction has continued to show remarkable vitality. One of the reasons may be found in the nature of Minimal art. It is exhibition art, constructed essentially for gallery display, and in the 1970s painters and sculptors continued to be attracted to it as a – apparently simple – means to create witty and provoking paintings or objects. Moreover, since it is gallery art and intellectually elitist, it has helped to divert its practitioners from speculating on whether art with any historical connections, traditional forms, etc. has any point in the modern world, and whether the gallery system can accommodate contemporary visual, creative activity.

Minimalist objects or paintings by such artists as the veteran American Milton Resnick or the Briton, Bob Law, are essentially gallery constructions but, increasingly, other work is not only difficult to fit physically into a gallery but loses all inspiration when it is so situated. Richard Long's arrangements of stones may be slightly risible lying around on the floor of a gallery but in a remote and isolated landscape they may have a natural force and appear dramatically evocative, although to appreciate them the observer has to work almost as hard as their creator.

Above:
Equivalent VIII, *1966. 120 firebricks.*
Carl André *(Tate Gallery, London).*
André's pile of bricks became the centre of the discussion on the use of public money for the purchase of works of art in the 1970s. Since the value of the bricks could be more or less precisely assessed and the price paid by the Tate Gallery was known, the difference might be supposed to be the value of the art content. A pretty conundrum. André is nevertheless an interesting artist. A Minimalist, he concentrates on the use of repeated elements in a defined or open area and the space which their presence demands. Like Richard Long, he has created large-scale Environmental works. In an interesting comment he observed, 'Perhaps abstract art has occured in human history every time there has been a total technological change in the organization of society'.

Left:
Spatial Concept 'Waiting', *1960.*
Lucio Fontana (Tate Gallery, London).
Born in Argentina of Italian parents,
Fontana studied in Milan and worked for
a number of years in Paris before
returning to Milan. There he founded
Spatialismo, *which promoted the ideas of*
a new art, concentrating on theory rather
than the realization of works of art. Both
a sculptor and painter, he had Dadaist,
anti-art views, his slashed canvases
deliberately suggesting the destruction of
the exhibited art work which is, in fact,
only a piece of tinted, slashed canvas.

Top:
Untitled, *1968. Steel rectangles.*
Donald Judd (Museum of Modern Art,
New York. Mr and Mrs Simon Askin
Fund).
Influenced by both Rothko and Newman,
Judd has become a leader of Minimalism
in sculpture. He uses industrial materials
(metal and plastic), large and graceless
but dominating 'primary structures' in
repeated geometric shapes. Intellectual
and articulate, he has expressed his view
that paint on surfaces representing three-
dimensional space are inferior to the space
which the three-dimensional object
determines, simply but positively – and
the more simply the more positively.

Above:
119 Stones, 1976. Richard Long (Tate
Gallery, London).
Although this can be seen in a gallery, the
work that perhaps best expresses Long's
spirit is found in landscapes around the
world where he has left his arrangements:
a line of stones in the Himalayas, a
walking line in Peru, stones on Dartmoor
and County Clare, Ireland; all – as he
says – 'looking the ground in the eye'.
What exists for observers is the
photograph of the arrangement he takes
himself. He has said 'I like the idea that
stones are what the world is made of . . . I
like sensibility without technique'.

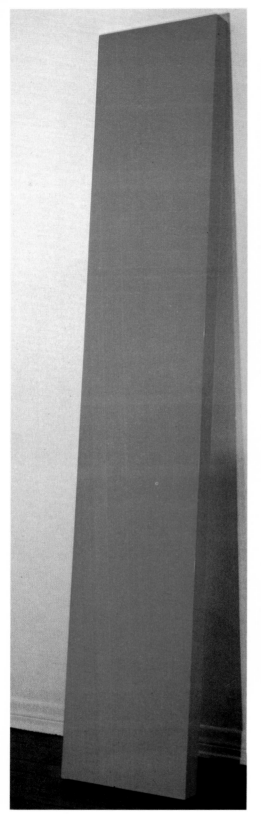

Above:
Red Plant, *1967. John McCracken
(Private Collection).*
*The painted, plank-like forms – often
constructed of plywood or fibreglass – are
at the extreme end of Minimalism or
Structuralism as the group around
McCracken is sometimes designated. In
these works we are close to the blue-
painted canvases of Yves Klein in the
1950s and whilst some pleasure may be
derived from viewing them it may seem as
minimal as the works themselves.*

Top:
Genghis Khan, *1963. Philip King
b.1934.*
*King works in plastic rather than
traditional materials, his sculptural forms
being moulded rather than carved.
Although now an established figure in the
current British art scene (he is presently
Professor of Sculpture at the Royal
College of Art) he first attracted attention
at the New Generation show in 1965 and
has consistently produced a series of
elegant and forceful works since then.
Genghis Khan is a good example of the
imaginative ambiguous imagery that his
simple flat and curved shapes achieve.
Some of the dread and cruel power
associated with the name is immanent in
the work.*

Above:
Untitled, *1970. Robert Morris (Leo
Castelli Gallery, New York).*
*Robert Morris is one of the leaders of
Minimalism. His work shows how the
sculptor, to use the orthodox if
inappropriate term, adopts a material
and exhibits it, allowing the material to
dictate its form and thus to affect the
viewer as itself rather than as the creation
of the sculptor. The Minimal act of
placing it – where and how – is all that
the sculptor determines. Although this is
an unfamiliar and apparently unlikely
way of arriving at an object to be
exhibited, it often produces intellectual or
physical responses akin to some Surrealist
effects.*

Conceptual Art

'The medium is the message': Marshall McLuhan's famous dictum, however unhelpful it may have proved in general terms, did have the positive effect of bringing attention to bear on the intellectual overlays that characterized much contemporary art criticism.

What was art about if it was not about understood content? Who had to understand it to justify it? Perhaps the creator might be expected to do so, and what he said about it ought to have value. Since, however, the visual creative process has baffled most attempts at explanation throughout history – one remembers Turner's comment that 'art is a rum thing' – it was not easy for artists to articulate in words what they were doing in an essentially different medium. Nevertheless, it was important that they should appear to be intelligent and, if it were possible to establish intelligence with words, it could reasonably be assumed that the art the words described was intelligent too. Since, further, the words could not replace the art, they had to form an inspiring if oblique gloss upon it. Theorizing – in profound and complex philosophical terms – became part of the art-creating process, and as the art became less, or more Minimal, the words revealed that the Emperor was naked – or he wasn't there at all. But not always. The creator with what Kandinsky called the 'inner necessity' will say what he has to say anyway, words or not.

Conceptual art or Idea art is a development parallel to Minimalism, and perhaps should be regarded as part of it. The thesis of Conceptual art is that the idea or system is more important than, and ultimately replaces, the work itself. Of course, if you don't know this you may think that the work is the work. Nevertheless, for both creator and observer it is not. The work is what is left after the object has been physically removed. Of course this is true of a Rembrandt or a Cézanne painting, or perhaps of Rembrandt's or Cézanne's work as a whole. The ques-

Chair with Fat, 1964. Josef Beuys (Hessiches Landesmuseum, Darmstadt. Collection Karl Ströher).
It is difficult to illustrate the work of Beuys. Most of his expression has taken the form of activity and the objects that remain seem unrelated or inadequate. However, the Chair with Fat is an example of his one-time preoccupation with the unpleasant nature of the material itself; to build it on to the seat of a chair so invitingly emphasizes this feature.

tion of where art exists – whether in the material object or elsewhere – has been a fundamental question in all recent art theory. It was raised most strikingly in this century by one of modern art's most influential prophets, Marcel Duchamp, and Suzanne Langer, a contemporary theorist, has questioned the need for art to exist at all; what counts is only the artist, or, more precisely, the condition of being an artist.

According to the theory of Conceptual art, as a consequence, the material object has no value in the traditional 'masterpiece' role, but only in the guise of art-historical document, historical evidence, social context, political polemic, etc., as a residual didactic experience. Aesthetics do not come into it.

As will be seen from the above a further stage has been reached in which pictorial or visual considerations, tactile, spatial or painterly qualities, sculptural material, etc. are all banished. Even the smile of the cat has been removed. All that remains is response. Happenings and Environmental art are closely akin to Conceptual art in that the event or the environmental construction are by their nature transitory and exist only in their residual effect.

A link between Conceptual and performance art is found in the activities of Josef Beuys, the German guru of the 1970s, who started as a performance artist. His use (as early as the 1950s) of fat as an art material is explained by

him as follows: most art stimulates or shocks via one sense only, sight. Sculpture from fat, however, is objectionable to several of the senses simultaneously: it looks foul, tastes rancid, feels slimy and smells unpleasant. In addition, it has a psychological impact, suggesting unhealthiness, obesity and greasiness – repulsive human characteristics. All in all its only sympathetic role is as a lubricant. Beuys uses it for making sculptures that recall, but in more deeply affecting form, Méret Oppenheim's fur-covered teacup and its livening effect upon the physical senses. It is the residual effect upon firstly the senses and secondly the mind that is Beuys's concern. His Happenings, which he calls 'Actions', have very strong symbolic intentions and make use of indentifiable objects such as a dead hare, a cross, etc. As in all Conceptualist art, the purpose is to provoke a contextual response, not to create an aesthetic object.

The strength of this development has been evident through the 1970s and continues in the work of such practitioners as Arnulf Rainer, who draws on distorted self-photographs; Richard Long, whose Environmental activities have been mentioned; Walter de Maria and Herman Nitsch, whose Orgies Mysteries Theatre indulges in such repellent activities as spraying blood and guts around the room. Perhaps the nadir is represented by a Viennese, Rudolph Schwartzkogler,

Spiral Jetty, 1970. Robert Smithson (Great Salt Lake, Utah).
Smithson has been a key figure in the development of Environmental situation sculpture. An intelligent, difficult man interested in prehistory, art, science fiction and natural history, particularly geology, he evolved a notion of presenting 'sites and non-sites' in a gallery location. He showed a map of an area with natural materials taken from the area, thus presenting both the location in formal, identifying terms and as a physical presence. This concern with the environment led to his changing the environment with forms that seemed a human creation of maybe prehistoric origin. He saw Spiral Jetty as 'an image of contracted time: the far distant past . . . the remote past . . . and the no-longer valid optimism of the recent past'. The jetty itself has been under water for more than a decade.

who died, Robert Hughes relates, a martyr to his notions in 1969, through the process of slicing himself away, starting with an inch by inch amputation of his penis. Photographs of the event became collectibles in the same way that the board on which Beuys drew diagrams of his theories during a lecture became the art object that 'fixed' the occasion, it being all that the gallery could exhibit, even though without the lecture it was meaningless.

If Conceptual art is the true reflection of current art, the struggle to remove art from its traditional past seems at last to be succeeding. Yet Conceptual art, so-called, is not a visual art at all, except in a quite insignificant sense. But if it is not art, what is it? This is where we came in . . .

The Role of the Galleries
When the Church was replaced by royal or private patrons around four centuries ago, a new trade grew up to guide and supply the secular art buyers. Wealthy men who lacked confidence in their own judgement or simply preferred to delegate a menial task to others became dependent on art dealers to build up their collections. The connoisseur and the critic also appeared on the scene and the history of art became a serious study. In the 19th century a writer such as John Ruskin powerfully affected public taste and proffered critical standards by which all art could be judged.

The royal collections became state collections, great houses allowed visitors to view their treasures, museums were founded, art became a symbol of cultured society. The great American commerical barons, recognizing that the accoutrements of culture could be bought, scoured Europe for masterpieces, and an able, not over-scrupulous dealer like Joseph Duveen made a fortune from their cupidity and ignorance.

By the beginning of this century the art-dealing trade was well-enough established in Paris and London to create a growing demand for art. Most dealers initially resisted the revolutionary developments of the 1900s, whether out of distaste or because they reckoned (correctly at the time) it would not sell. Nevertheless, the demand for all art continued to grow, creating a corresponding demand for new artists which in turn encouraged the foundation of art-training centres, colleges and studios.

Once modern art had become acceptable, the race to supply the new began. Great cities formed modern as well as historical collections. Perhaps the greatest boost came from the foundation in 1929 of the Museum of Modern Art in New York, devoted exclusively to modern work and sponsored by the likes of John D. Rocke-

feller. Most other museums provided special galleries for modern work. The Museum of Modern Art adopted a policy of including all representative work to achieve a total survey of what was happening in the visual arts – which included some commercial design.

Legislation making gifts to museums or public galleries tax-deductible was passed in the United States (not in European countries), enabling the rich to acquire philanthropic reputations with little damage to their pockets. To the galleries, and initially it seemed also to the artists, it was a godsend. It provided the dealers with great opportunities and assured steady employment for artists, once they had acquired a dealer.

The artist's view of dealers and galleries was, on the whole, one of less than total approval. They were inclined to think that the dealers exploited their work and the museums buried it alive. However, for the artist to achieve any public success it was necessary to join the system. Some extreme and independent spirits played games with the galleries; Yves Klein exhibited an empty, plain white gallery, to ecstatic critical response incidentally; but not many artists could have got away with it.

The directions taken by painting and sculpture after about 1945 were increasingly inappropriate to the normal gallery setup. Some artists devised ways of avoiding the system by creating works in the open air which were part of the landscape and could only be seen there. Robert Smithson's location subjects such as *Spiral Jetty* or Michael Heizer's earthwork monument *Complex One* were dramatic examples. These large-scale Environmental works were intended to create an effect which added an emotional dimension that the landscape location would not have had otherwise. The interference with the normal environment which Christo makes is a further example of a new non-gallery form of expression, which dates from the 1960s.

The most significant aspect of the power of museums is that many pieces only 'work' in a gallery and, indeed, cannot be accommodated elsewhere. In some cases they could clearly not be produced or paid for without the com-

mercial support of the gallery system. The sombre and disturbing work of Edward Kienholz or the evocative constructions of George Segal would hardly settle into a domestic interior. The scale of much contemporary sculpture, not to mention the disturbing nature of its imagery, demands display in a gallery where a space of the right size and shape may be constructed for it.

Many Minimalist works require the isolation of a gallery. A plank of wood leaning against a wall, a pile of felt or a neat arrangement of bricks in a builder's yard would be what they are; removed to a gallery, given space and a label of authority they become art.

For the observer of these objects, certain difficulties arise. The mere fact that they have been selected by experts – gallery directors and professional art historians – has an inhibiting effect on the individual's response. Moreover, it is hard to understand the changed role of the gallery in current conditions: the work is not selected for whatever individual excellence it may possess but rather as something representative of a general activity.

Duchamp's readymades delivered a terrific cultural shock, but we may well feel surprised that they were exhibited at all. But Duchamp, apart from being known as a brilliantly gifted as well as controversial artist, was a man of intelligence, sensitivity and force of character. Had he been some stuttering unknown, his bottleracks and urinals would never have got near any gallery. It is frequently, one is tempted to say, almost always, personal knowledge of the artist and his ideas that commends them to the gallery directors. Those ideas may well have merit, but one has only to see the bewilderment on the faces of visitors to realize that they are not getting across to the public. At the same time, the authority of a great institution, standing behind whatever is exhibited, inevitably implies that the observer is deficient in not appreciating what in reality he cannot possibly appreciate. The public galleries are making available in ever-growing quantities the products of art, but the policy of representative display, replacing informed discrimination, has reduced rather than enhanced the role of the art gallery.

Realism and Superrealism

Minimalism represents the current phase of abstraction, which remains a major ingredient of 20th-century art, but it has coincided with a return to forms of Realist painting, inaugurated by Pop art, which might suggest a new revival of traditional figurative art. To many people, unable to come to terms with abstraction and tenaciously holding to the belief that the visual arts should represent the visible world, this may come as a relief. It might even suggest a return to sanity after three-quarters of a century of misdirected experiment.

In fact, the new form of realism does not support that view. It does not look backward to a glorious earlier age, nor is it concerned with the simple representation of modern life. Its images may be familiar, but the forms represented, whether human, animal or still-life, carry overtones which echo and re-echo in subtle ways, both general and specific. Human figures, for instance, may vary from the compelling actuality of Duane Hanson's middle-aged American women shoppers to the erotic suggestiveness of Graham Ovendon or Al Leslie.

The new realism, or Superrealism as a part of it is called in the United States, cannot be regarded as part of the academic tradition, although it is of course true that academic painting throughout this century has been figurative. Photography has changed all that. A great deal of this painting derives from photographic information, and artists use the camera much as their forbears used the sketchbook (hence the term Photorealism). But the new paintings are not photographic alternatives.

Superrealism takes a number of different forms, but one factor in common is that for all of the artists concerned the representational nature of the image-making is a conscious and clear alternative to abstractionism. While these artists are in opposition to the abstractionists they are nevertheless concerned with the same kind of problem, in particular with the question of

Left:

Ansonia, 1977. Richard Estes.
(Collection of Whitney Museum of
American Art, New York. Gift of Frances
and Sydney Lewis).
The photographic realism of this painting
achieved by an astonishing control of
tone and colour could hardly be taken
further. The sharpness of the image of a
familiar street scene from any American
city gives an importance to the subject,
significance which the ordinary pedestrian
walking such streets would hardly notice.

Below:

Paul's Corner, 1970. Ralph Goings
(O.K. Harris Gallery, New York).
The Superrealism of Goings's paintings of
the urban and suburban scene in
California parallels that of Richard Estes
in New York. He concentrates on
automobiles 'on location' in a treatment
that recalls the glossy magazine
advertisement for a new model – but his
cars are always work-horses.

what form art should take (if it is not to disappear altogether). The Realist sees art arising from a visual source, however much modified to produce the image required; the Minimalist and the Conceptualist see it springing from the idea, and they are not concerned with aesthetics or form.

To the extent that they are making pictures to hang on walls and sculptures to stand in space, the Realists are continuing the history of art. But their treatment of their subject matter suggests at least some ambiguity in pursuing this intent.

The United States, which most frequently provides the imagery of non-American artists working in the Realist manner, is also the real home of this style, of which Superrealism and Photorealism are the most dramatic forms.

In sculpture, where the human figure dominates, John de Andrea, Duane Hanson and Mark Prent are

representative. Hanson and de Andrea, make images of specific individuals precisely modelled and highly finished, dressed in real clothes and accompanied by real objects. Hanson's are usually of middle-aged women, de Andrea's of neatly turned out or sveltely nude teenage college types, usually preoccupied with intimations of sex. Prent's figures appear to be suffering emotional tensions. These figures are the equivalent of, say, figures in Dutch 17th-century genre painting or in Hogarth's pictures of 18th-century English society, and they represent elements of mass culture. They are just as potent as images, and Hanson particularly finds images that add up to more than the sum of their parts.

In Britain social comment is sometimes more obvious, as in the work of John Davies. The large, much over-lifesize portraits by Chuck Close are further examples of this precise realism.

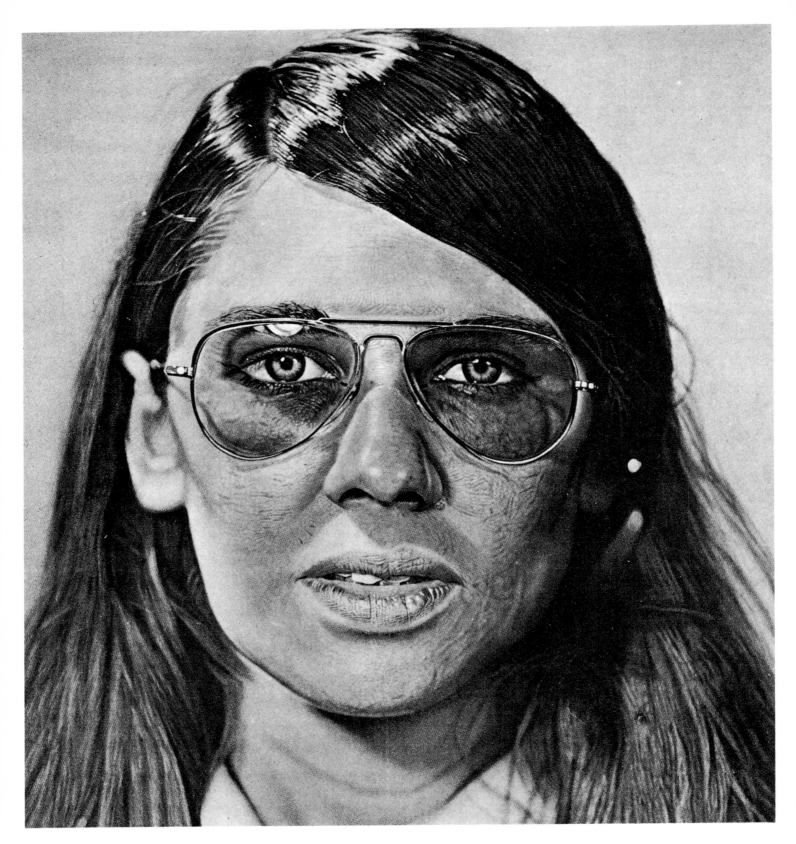

Above:
Susan, *1972. 98 × 88 in*
(2520 × 2265 mm.). Chuck Close (Neue
Galerie, Aachen. Collection Ludwig).
The over-lifesize images of Chuck Close
have a compelling quality which is
related, if distantly, to Rembrandt's
searching analysis of the human face. By
enlargement Close emphasizes each
revealing surface change, each small
blemish, and with deadpan objectivity

tears away the concealing veil. Strangely,
too, the sum of the oversize parts does add
up to a human face of physical unity. This
form of Superrealism has become a
characteristic symptom of the rejection of
what is regarded as the inadequacy of
abstraction as communication.

Right:
Two Seated Models, *1968. Philip*
Pearlstein b.1924.
The uncompromising realism of Pearlstein
paintings of nude male and female models
indicates the continuing source of pictorial
inspiration provided by the human body.
Pearlstein uses photographs and the
photographic image rather than
structural expression is characteristic of
this new form of realist art.

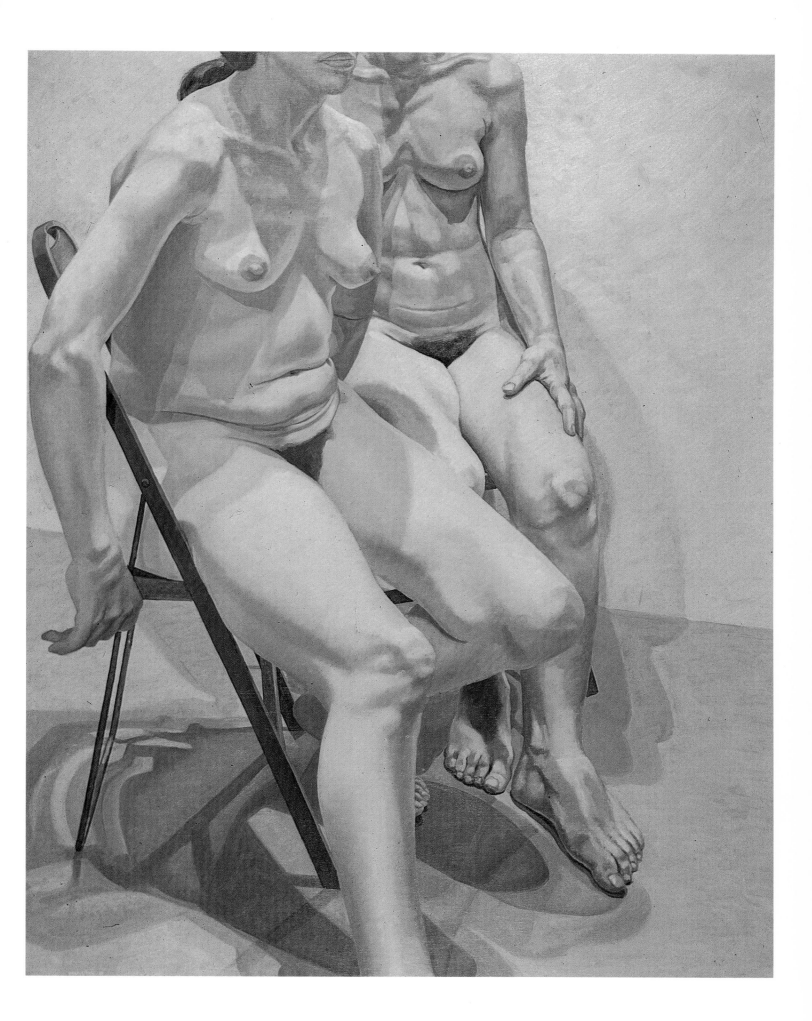

Superrealism in the representation of urban or rural scenes is also found in the work of Richard Estes and Ralph Goings. The paintings have such a clean finish that even the dirt seems to have been given a wash, and it is this concern with every inch of the canvas that distinguishes the Superrealists.

Although their commonest preoccupation, the Realists are not only concerned with painting an everyday scene as such. The early Photorealist work of the British painter Malcolm Morley was completed in small squares with the rest of the work area covered. By painting details he avoids a grand concept and discovers how it all fits together afterwards.

Figurative Realism, whose subject matter is almost limitless, still represents the largest body of work being produced. This does not mean that it is the strongest or most valuable form of current painting. Nor does it mean that because it is so common it has no value.

Values are very tricky commodities in the current art scene. No outstanding talent appears to have been unveiled in the last few years, no special group or movement promises some new Renaissance. It seems that the extraordinary energy of the early years of this century has finally given out and it is hard to see what direction art will take in the future. However, that is not unusual; it is only in retrospect that new developments become predictable.

Above:
Woman with Dog, *1977. Duane Hanson.*
The sculptural equivalent of Richard Estes' street scene, this figure has an actuality that gives the observer a feeling of intrusion on privacy when looking at it. It seems that the process and progress of the art of this century led back to a realism of the commonplace. This is social observation with deadpan comment.

Right:
Couple, *1978. John de Andrea (O.K. Harris Gallery, New York).*
The astonishing sense of actuality produced by these life-size figures is characteristic of the form of sculptural Superrealism which is one aspect of current American work. De Andrea usually represents young American co-eds, and here the juxtaposition of the cool clothed youth with the affectionate nude girl reflects, in an almost disinterested if not uninterested way, current sexual mores. Like other Superrealist sculptors, de Andrea uses real hair, glass eyes and actual clothes over life-cast figures. However traditional in subject matter, these works are not traditional in conception or method.

246

Conclusion

A book dealing with any subject which, like art, is part of the ever-changing fabric of human culture can never be brought to a final conclusion. In the current atmosphere of rapid change, the most widely informed opinion is inevitably out of date before it becomes general knowledge – if only because it takes a year or more to produce a book after the words have been written.

The story of art runs on, and will surely continue for as long as there are human societies remotely like ours. Those who attempt to chronicle this story must always look backwards, or at best sideways. The artists lead; the writers follow. To forecast the future is as hazardous in this area as in any other, and, as the account presented in this book may have suggested already, in art you must expect only the unexpected. Who in 1940 could have foretold the importance of the United States in the art scene a decade or so later? Who a generation ago, when abstraction seemed synonymous with 'modern' art, would have prophesied the recent development of Superrealism?

Dramatic and often puzzling new developments in the visual arts have formed the subject of this book but they have not suggested themes which can be confidently projected into the future. The emphatic swing of the last few years in favour of representational forms of expression, welcome though it may be to those who regard most modern art as mad or meaningless, cannot be interpreted as a permanent rejection of those earlier, less 'readable' movements, nor does it preclude future developments more obscure, perhaps more disturbing.

By the time this book reaches its readers, Superrealism may already seem no more than a temporary aberration, and the trends picked out in the latter chapters may have proved less significant than others which have received less notice – for there are many recent works that do not fit into any of the categories mentioned, vague though those categories necessarily are.

It is easy to become cynical about allegedly 'new' developments. The appetite of the communications industry is so voracious that any work which appears slightly different, arcane – or potentially offensive – is seized on with a zeal and enthusiasm which are often quite inappropriate. Nothing that can be easily promoted is neglected, and the inflation or distortion that goes on frequently dismays the unfortunate creator, carried away helpless on puffs of publicity. Modern forms of communication indeed, however valuable generally, can carry dangers for creative spirits. More than ever today we should be wary of equating the new with the good.

The essential unpredictability of the visual arts is one of their most exciting characteristics. We may think we see a movement towards uniformity in the development of a world culture embracing East and West and all that lies between, and this process, though more evident so far in the world of international business or science, will surely produce far-reaching social and political changes affecting the arts as well as every other aspect of human culture. But although the arts form a vital part of culture, it is important to remember that the actual works of art are created by individuals, privately, and their effect is equally a matter of individual, private response.

As the appreciation and enjoyment of art is essentially a private matter, the value of art can in the last analysis be judged only by its effect on each one of us personally. The understanding and responses expressed in this book are likewise personal, and while it is to be hoped that they may be helpful, their value extends only so far as they may be incorporated in the understanding and feelings of the reader. There is no substitute for direct personal response to a work of art, and for that reason the reader is urged to concentrate on the works themselves which are here reproduced. The text that accompanies the illustrations is intended to assist comprehension and evaluation but not to present ready-made, prepacked, value judgements.

Better of course than pictures in a book are the actual works of the painters and sculptors, when it is possible to see them. Although modern colour reproduction has reached a high standard, book illustrations cannot replace the direct visual experience. They are valuable references for style and content but otherwise may give a misleading impression. They tend, for example, to be much smaller but, more important than that, they fail to convey the enormous physical differences of the originals – from a Paul Klee measuring a few inches to a Jackson Pollock extending to several yards – while sculpture by its nature is unsatisfactory in a two-dimensional image and (as we have seen) some modern art activities are by design impossible to reproduce.

In spite of some obvious variations in quality and significance, developments in art during the 20th century have opened the way to new visual awareness and enhanced opportunity for the enjoyment and understanding of art generally – at least, this book has been written in that belief. And in spite of the limitations mentioned above, the story of modern art is a coherent whole. It is a story of dramatic and often iconoclastic change. A century ago, 'fine' art was the province of a tiny cultural elite, and most artists communicated exclusively with that elite, in a language only the elite was expected to understand. From the Impressionists onwards, however, successive developments or movements have made their various contributions towards an art involving a far larger segment of society, an art which in intention at least is accessible to all and, perhaps more successfully, an art based on far wider social concerns, reflecting every facet of contemporary society. The modern art movements may have failed to achieve many of the aims their practitioners subscribed to, but they have certainly had the effect of placing art in the area of public debate and of arousing powerful emotions, ranging from dizzy delight to disillusioned despair, in an ever-expanding throng of observers.

Bibliography

GENERAL

Arnason, H.H. *History of Modern Art*. New York, London, 1968.

Arnheim, Rudolf. *Art and Visual Perception: A Psychology of the Creative Eye*. Berkeley, Cal., University of California Press, 1954.

Ashton, Dore. *A Fable of Modern Art*. New York, Thames & Hudson, 1980.

Baigell, Matthew. *History of American Painting*. New York, Praeger, 1971.

Banham, Reyner. *Theory and Design in the First Machine Age*. Praeger, 1960.

Barr, Alfred H., Jr., ed. *Masters of Modern Art*. 2nd ed. New York, The Museum of Modern Art, 1955.

Bowness, Alan. *Modern European Art*. New York, Harcourt, Brace, Jovanovich, 1972.

Bradbury, Malcolm and McFarlane, James (eds). *Modernism 1890–1930*. London, Penguin Books, 1978.

Breunig, LeRoy C., ed. *Apollinaire on Art: Essays and Reviews, 1902–1918*. New York, Viking, 1972.

Brown, Milton W., and others. *American Art: Painting, Sculpture, Architecture, Decorative Arts, Photography*. New York, Abrams, 1979.

Brown, Milton W. *American Painting from the Armory Show to the Depression*. Princeton, N.J., Princeton University Press, 1955.

Buckle, Richard. *Diaghilev*. New York, Atheneum, 1979.

Burnham, Jack. *Beyond Modern Sculpture: The Effects of Science and Technology on the Sculpture of this Century*. New York, Braziller, 1968.

Charlot, Jean. *The Mexican Muralist Revolution*. New Haven, Yale University Press, 1963.

Chipp, Herschel B. *Theories of Modern Art: A Source Book by Artists and Critics*. Berkeley and Los Angeles, University of California Press, 1968.

Geldzahler, Henry. *American Painting in the Twentieth Century*. New York, The Metropolitan Museum of Art, 1965.

Gombrich, E.H. *The Story of Art*. London, Phaidon, 1972.

Greenberg, Clement. *Art and Culture: Critical Essays*. Boston, London, 1961.

Haftman, Werner. *Painting in the Twentieth Century*. New ed. New York, Praeger, 1965.

Hamilton, George Heard. *Painting and Sculpture in Europe 1880–1940*. Rev. ed. Baltimore, Harmondsworth, 1972.

Hammacher, A.M. *The Evolution of Modern Sculpture: Tradition and Innovation*. New York, Abrams, 1969.

Heron, Patrick. *The Changing Forms of Art*. London, Routledge, 1955. New York, Macmillan, 1956.

Hughes, Robert. *The Shock of the New*. London, BBC Publications, 1980.

Hunter, Sam, and Jacobus, John. *American Art of the 20th Century: Painting, Sculpture, Architecture*. New York, Abrams, 1974.

Kramer, Hilton. *The Age of the Avant-Garde: An Art Chronicle of 1956–1972*. New York, Farrar, Straus & Giroux, 1973.

Lucie-Smith, Edward. *Movements in Art Since 1945*. London, Thames & Hudson, 1969.

Lynton, Norbert. *The Story of Modern Art*. Ithaca, Cornell University Press, 1980.

Malraux, André. *The Psychology of Art*. New York, Pantheon, 1949.

Read, Herbert, *A Concise History of Modern Painting*. Rev. and enl. ed. New York, Praeger, 1968.

Read, Herbert. *A Concise History of Modern Sculpture*. New York, Praeger, 1971.

Rose, Barbara. *American Art Since 1900: A Critical History*. Rev. ed. New York, London, 1975.

Rothenstein, John. *Modern English Painters*. London, MacDonald, 1974.

Russell, John. *The Meanings of Modern Art*. New York, Harper & Row, 1974.

Schapiro, Meyer. *Modern Art, 19th and 20th Centuries: Selected Papers*. New York, Braziller, 1978.

Scharf, Aaron. *Art and Photography*. London, Allen Lane, 1968.

Shattuck, Roger. *The Banquet Years: The Origins of the Avant-Garde in France, 1885 to World War I*. Rev. ed. New York, Vintage Books, 1968.

Stangos, Nikos (ed). *Concepts of Modern Art*. London, Thames & Hudson, reprint 1983.

Steinberg, Leo. *Other Criteria: Confrontations with Twentieth-Century Art*. New York, Oxford University Press, 1972.

Sypher, Wylie. *Rococo to Cubism*. New York, Vintage Books, 1960.

Walker, John A. *Glossary of Art, Architecture and Design Since 1945*. 2nd rev. ed. Hamden, Conn., Linnet Books, 1977.

MOVEMENTS

IMPRESSIONISM, POST-IMPRESSIONISM

Herbert, Robert L. *Neo-Impressionism*. New York, Solomon R. Guggenheim Foundation, 1968.

Pool, Phoebe. *Impressionism*. New York, Praeger, 1967.

Rewald, John. *The History of Impressionism*. 4th rev. ed. New York, The Museum of Modern Art, 1973.

Rewald, John. *Post-Impressionism: From Van Gogh to Gauguin*. 3rd ed. rev. New York, The Museum of Modern Art, 1978.

Roskill, Mark. *Van Gogh, Gauguin and the Impressionist Circle*. Greenwich, Conn., New York Graphic Society, 1970.

SYMBOLISM

Delevoy, Robert L. *Symbolists and Symbolism*. New York, 1978.

Jullian, Philippe. *Dreamers of Decadence: Symbolist Painters of the 1890s*. New York, 1971.

Lucie-Smith, Edward. *Symbolist Art*. London, Thames & Hudson, 1972.

Milner, John. *Symbolists and Decadents*. London and New York, Studio Vista/Dutton Paperbacks, 1971.

FAUVISM

Crespelle, Jean-Paul. *The Fauves*. Greenwich, Conn., New York Graphic Society; London, Oldbourne, 1962.

Duthuit, Georges. *The Fauvist Painters*. New York, 1950.

EXPRESSIONISM, DIE BRÜCKE, DER BLAUE REITER

Grohmann, Will. *Expressionists*. New York, Abrams, 1957.

Dube, Wolf-Dieter. *The Expressionists*. London, Thames & Hudson, 1972.

Myers, Bernard S. *The German Expressionists: A Generation in Revolt*. New York, McGraw-Hill, 1963.

Roethel, Hans K. *The Blue Rider*. New York, Praeger, 1972.

Roh, Franz. *German Art in the 20th Century*. Rev. ed. Greenwich, Conn., New York Graphic Society, 1968.

Selz, Peter. *German Expressionist Painting*. Berkeley and Los Angeles, University of California Press, 1957.

CUBISM

Apollinaire, Guillaume. *The Cubist Painters*. New York, Wittenborn, 1962.

Barr, Alfred H., Jr. *Cubism and Abstract Art*. Reprint. First publ. 1936. New York, Arno for The Museum of Modern Art, 1967.

Cooper, Douglas. *The Cubist Epoch*. London, Phaidon Press (distributed by Praeger), 1971.

Fry, Edward F. *Cubism*. London, Thames & Hudson; New York, McGraw-Hill, 1966.

Golding, John. Cubism: *A History and an Analysis, 1907–1914*. Rev. ed. New York, London, 1972.

Rosenblum, Robert. *Cubism and Twentieth-Century Art*. New York, Abrams, 1968.

FUTURISM

Apollonio, Umbro, ed. *The Futurist Manifestos*. New York, London, 1973.

Kirby, Michael. *Futurist Performance*. New York, Dutton, 1971.

Marinetti, Filippo Tommaso. *Selected Writings*. R.W. Flint, ed. New York, 1971.

Martin, Marianne W. *Futurist Art and Theory, 1909–1915*. New York, Oxford University Press, 1968.

Taylor, Joshua C. *Futurism*. New York, The Museum of Modern Art, 1961.

Tisdall, Caroline, and Bozzolla, Angelo. *Futurism*. New York, Oxford University Press, 1978.

ORPHISM

Spate, Virginia. *Orphism: The Evolution of Non-Figurative Painting in Paris, 1910–1914*. New York, Oxford University Press, 1979.

VORTICISM

Cork, Richard. *Vorticism and Abstract Art in the First Machine Age*. Berkeley, University of California Press, 1976.

DADA

Barr, Alfred H., Jr. *Fantastic Art, Dada, and Surrealism*. Reprint, First publ. 1937. New York, Arno for The Museum of Modern Art, 1970.

Bigsby, C.W. *Dada and Surrealism*. London, Methuen, 1972.

Foster, Stephen C., and Kuenzli, Rudolf E., eds. *Dada Spectrum: The Dialectics of Revolt*. Madison, Wisc. Coda Press, and Iowa City, Ia., University of Iowa, 1979.

Hülsenbeck, Richard, ed. *Dada Almanach*. Millerton, N.Y., Something Else Press, 1966.

Motherwell, Robert, ed. *Dada Painters and Poets*. New York, Wittenborn, 1951.

Richter, Hans. *Dada: Art and Anti-Art*. New York, London, 1965.

Rubin, Williams S. *Dada and Surrealist Art*. New York, London, 1969.

Verkauf, Willy, ed. *Dada: Monograph of a Movement*. New York, Wittenborn, 1957.

SUPREMATISM, CONSTRUCTIVISM

Bann, Stephen, ed. *The Tradition of Constructivism*. New York, Viking, 1974.

Barron, Stephanie, and Tuchman, Maurice, eds. *The Avant-Garde in Russia, 1910–1930: New Perspectives*. Exhibition catalogue, Los Angeles County Museum of Art. Cambridge, Mass., MIT Press, 1980.

Bowlt, John E. *Russian Art 1875–1975: A Collection of Essays*. New York, 1976.
Bowlt, John E., ed. *Russian Art of the Avant-Garde: Theory and Criticism, 1902–1934*. New York, Viking, 1976.
Elliott, David. *Rodchenko and the Arts of Revolutionary Russia*. New York, Pantheon, 1979.
Gray, Camilla. *The Russian Experiment in Art: 1863–1922*. London, New York, 1971.

DE STIJL
Jaffé, Hans L.C. *De Stijl*. New York, Abrams, 1971.
Jaffé, H.L.C. *De Stijl, 1917–1931: The Dutch Contribution to Modern Art*. Amsterdam, Meulenhoff, 1956.
Overy, Paul. *De Stijl*. New York, Dutton, 1969.

BAUHAUS
Bayer, Herbert; Gropius, Ise; and Gropius, Walter. *Bauhaus, 1919–1928*. Introduction by Alfred H. Barr, Jr. New York, London, 1938.
Gropius, Walter. *The New Architecture and the Bauhaus*. Shand, P. Morton, tr. First publ. 1936. Boston, Charles T. Branford, 1955.
Itten, Johannes. *Design and Form: The Basic Course at the Bauhaus*. New York, Reinhold, 1964.
Itten, Johannes. *The Elements of Colour*. New York, Nostrand Reinhold, 1970.
Naylor, Gillian. *The Bauhaus*. London, Studio Vista; New York, Dutton, 1968.
Neumann, Eckhard, ed. *Bauhaus and Bauhaus People*. New York, Nostrand Reinhold, 1970.
Roters, Eberhard. *Painters of the Bauhaus*. New York, Praeger, 1969.
Whitford, Frank. *Bauhaus*. London, Thames & Hudson, 1984.
Wingler, Hans M. *The Bauhaus: Weimar, Dessau, Berlin, Chicago*. Cambridge, Mass., MIT Press, 1969.

SURREALISM
Breton, André. *Manifestoes of Surrealism*. Seaver, Richard, and Lane, Helen, tr. Ann Arbor, University of Michigan Press, 1972.
Breton, André. *Surrealism and Painting*. Watson Taylor, Simon, tr. New York, Harper & Row, 1972.
Jean, Marcel. *The History of Surrealist Painting*. New York, London, 1960.
Levy, Julien. *Surrealism*. Reprint, First publ. 1936. (Co-publ. by Worldwide Reprints.) New York, Arno, 1968.
Lippard, Lucy, ed. *Surrealists on Art*. Englewood Cliffs, N.J., Prentice-Hall, 1970.
Nadeau, Maurice, *The History of Surrealism*. London, Cape, 1968.
Read, Herbert. *Surrealism*. New York, Praeger, 1972.
Tomkins, Calvin. *The Bride and the Bachelors*. Enl. ed. New York, The Viking Press, 1968.
Waldberg, Patrick. *Surrealism*. New York, McGraw & Hill, 1966.

NEW YORK SCHOOL
Ashton, Dore. *The New York School: A Cultural Reckoning*, New York, Viking, 1973.
Geldzahler, Henry. *New York Painting and Sculpture: 1940–1970*. New York, The Metropolitan Museum of Art, 1969.
Hobbs, R.C. and Levin, Gail. *Abstract Expressionism: The Formative Years*. New York, Whitney Museum, 1978.
Janis, Sidney. *Abstract and Surrealist Art in America*. Reprint. First publ. 1944. New York, Arno, 1970.
Rosenberg, Harold. *The Tradition of the New*. New York, Horizon, 1959.

Sandler, Irving. *The Triumph of American Painting: A History of Abstract Expressionism*. New York, Praeger, 1970.
Sandler, Irving. *The New York School: The Painters and Sculptors of the Fifties*. New York, Icon/Harper & Row, 1978.
Tuchman, Maurice, ed. *American Sculpture of the Sixties*. Los Angeles, Los Angeles County Musem of Art, 1967.
Tuchman, Maurice, ed. *The New York School: Abstract Expressionism in the 40s and 50s*. London, Thames & Hudson, 1970.
Weller, Allen S. *Art USA Now*. New York, The Viking Press, 1963.

POP AND AFTER
Bann, Stephen: Gadney, Reg; Popper, Frank; and Steadman, Philip. *Four Essays on Kinetic Art*. St. Albans, Britain, Motion Books, 1966.
Barrett, Cyril, S.J. *Op Art*. New York, 1970.
Battcock, Gregory, ed. *Minimal Art: A Critical Anthology*. New York, Dutton, 1968.
Battcock, Gregory, ed. *The New Art*. New York, Dutton, 1966.
Battcock, Gregory, ed. *Super Realism: A Critical Anthology*. New York, Dutton, 1975.
Benthall, Jonathan. *Science and Technology in Art Today*. New York, Praeger, 1972.
Davis, Douglas. *Art and the Future*. New York, Praeger, 1973.
Hulten, K.G. Pontus. *The Machine*. New York: The Museum of Modern Art, 1968.
Kirby, Michael. *Happenings: An Illustrated Anthology*. New York, Dutton Paperbacks, 1966.
Lippard, Lucy. *Pop Art*. New York, London, 1966.
Lippard, Lucy . *Overlay: Contemporary Art and the Art of Prehistory*. New York, Pantheon, 1983.
Lucie-Smith, Edward. *Art Today – from Abstract Expressionism to Superrealism*. Oxford, Phaidon, 1983.
Lucie-Smith, Edward. *Art in the Seventies*. Oxford, Phaidon, 1983.
Meyer, Ursula. *Conceptual Art*. New York, Dutton, 1972.
Pincus-Witten, Robert. *Postminimalism*. New York, Out of London Press, 1978.
Popper, Frank. *Origins and Development of Kinetic Art*. Greenwich, Conn., New York Graphic Society, 1968.
Rosenberg, Harold. *The De-Definition of Art: Action Art to Pop to Earthworks*. London, Secker & Warburg, 1972. New York, Horizon Press, 1972.
Rosenberg, Harold. *Art on the Edge: Creators and Situations*. London, Secker & Warburg, 1976. New York, Macmillan, 1975.
Russell, John, and Gablic, Suzi. *Pop Art Redefined*. New York, Praeger, 1969.
Seitz, William C. *The Art of Assemblage*. New York, The Museum of Modern Art, 1961.
Seitz, William C. *The Responsive Eye*. New York, The Museum of Modern Art, 1965.
Selz, Peter. *Directions in Kinetic Sculpture*. Berkeley, Cal., Berkeley University Art Museum, 1966.
Walker, John A. *Art Since Pop*. New York, Barron's, 1978.
Wescher, Herta. *Collage*. New York, Harry N. Abrams, 1971?

Picture Information

YAACOV AGAM
Double Metamorphosis. 1968–69. Paint on wood structure. 50 × 73 in (127 × 188 cm).
JOSEF ALBERS
Study for Homage to the Square; Departing in Yellow. 1964. Oil on board. 30 × 30 in (76.2 × 76.2 cm).
PIERRE ALECHINSKY
The Tower. 1954. Oil on canvas. 32 × 45¾ in (81 × 116 cm).
CARL ANDRÉ
Equivalent VIII. 1966. 120 firebricks. 5 × 27 × 90¼ in (12.7 × 68.6 × 229.2 cm).
JOHN DE ANDREA
Couple. 1978. Cast vinyl polychromed in oil. Lifesize.
RICHARD ANUSKIEWICZ
Luminous. 1963. 24 × 24 in (61 × 61 cm).
KAREL APPEL
La Hollandaise. 1969. Oil on canvas. 51 × 38 in (130 × 97 cm).
FERNANDEZ ARMAN
Glove Torso. 1967. Mixed media in cast polyvinyl. 33 in (85 cm).
ARMORY SHOW
Installation photograph showing Cubist paintings. 1913.
HANS (JEAN) ARP
Dada Relief. 1916. Painted wood. 9½ × 7 × 2 in (24 × 18.5 × 5 cm).
FRANCIS BACON
Study for one of the figures at the base of a painting of the Crucifixion. c.1944. Oil on board. 37 × 29 in (94 × 73.7 cm).
Study after Pope Innocent X by Velasquez. 1951. Oil on canvas. 78 × 54 in (197.8 × 137.5 cm).
ENRICO BAJ
Fire! Fire!. 1963. Oil and Meccano on furnishing fabric. 50⅝ × 38¼ in (128.6 × 97.2 cm).
GIACOMO BALLA
Dynamism of a Dog on a Leash. 1912. Oil on canvas. 35⅜ × 43¼ in (91 × 110 cm).
Flight of Swallows. 1913. Tempera on cardboard. 19½ × 26¾ in (49 × 69.5 cm).
BALTHUS (BALTHASAR KLOSSOWSKI)
The Painter and his Model. 1980–81. Casein and tempera on canvas. 89¼ × 91¾ in (226.5 × 230.5 cm).
WILLIAM BAZIOTES
Congo. 1954. Oil on canvas. 71¼ × 59¾ in (181 × 151.7 cm).
MAX BECKMANN
Self-Portrait. 1914. Oil on canvas. 37 × 24 in (94 × 61 cm).
JOSEF BEUYS
Chair with Fat. 1964. Mixed media with animal fat. 18 × 16 × 39 in (47 × 42 × 100 cm).
PETER BLAKE
Got a Girl. 1960–61. Oil on hardboard with wood, photo-collage and gramophone record. 27 × 61 in (69 × 155 cm).
UMBERTO BOCCIONI
Development of a Bottle in Space. 1912. Silvered bronze (Cast 1931). 15 × 12⅞ × 23¾ in (38.1 × 32.7 × 60.3 cm).
Elasticity. 1912. Oil on canvas. 39⅜ × 39⅜ in (100 × 100 cm).
Unique Forms of Continuity in Space. 1912. Bronze.
DAVID BOMBERG
In the Hold. c.1913–14. Oil on canvas. 77¼ × 91 in (196.2 × 231.1 cm).

PIERRE BONNARD
Nude in a Bath. 1937. Oil on canvas. 36½ × 58 in (93 × 147 cm).
Women with a Dog. 1891. Oil on canvas. 16 × 12¾ in (40.6 × 32.4 cm).
ARTHUR BOYD
Shearers Playing for a Bride. 1957. Oil on canvas. 59 × 69 in (150 × 175.3 cm).
CONSTANTIN BRANCUSI
Bird in Space. 1928. Polished bronze. 54 in (137 cm) high.
Blond Negress. 1933. Version II, after a marble of 1928. Bronze. 15¾ in (40 cm) high. On a four-part pedestal of marble, limestone, and two wood sections (carved by the artist). 55½ in (141 cm) high.
The Kiss. c.1922–40. Yellow stone. 28¼ in (71.8 cm).
GEORGE BRAQUE
Bottle, Glass and Pipe. 1914. Oil on canvas. 19⅛ × 25½ in (48 × 65 cm).
Clarinet. 1913. Pasted papers, charcoal, chalk and oil on canvas. 37½ × 47⅜ in (95.2 × 120.3 cm).
L'Estaque. 1906. Oil on canvas. 23½ × 28½ in (60 × 72 cm).
The Garden Chair. 1947–48. Oil on canvas. 23¼ × 20½ in (59 × 51 cm).
The Portuguese. 1911. Oil on canvas. 45⅞ × 32⅛ in (116 × 83 cm).
JOHN BRATBY
Window, Self-Portrait, Jean and Hands. 1957. Oil on board. 48 × 144 in (121.9 × 365.8 cm).
PATRICK HENRY BRUCE
Painting. 1926–28. Oil on canvas. 35 × 45¾ in (88.7 × 116.1 cm).
BERNARD BUFFET
Self-Portrait. 1954. Oil on canvas. 57⅝ × 44⅞ in (146.4 × 114 cm).
ALBERTO BURRI
Sacking and Red. 1954. Sacking, glue and plastic paint (vinyl) on canvas. 34 × 39½ in (86.4 × 100.3 cm).
POL BURY
16 Balls, 16 Cubes in 8 Rows. 1966. Motorized construction of stained wood and plywood. 31½ × 15¾ × 7⅞ in (80 × 40 × 20 cm).
ALEXANDER CALDER
Lobster Trap and Fishtail. 1939. Hanging mobile: painted steel wire and sheet aluminium. 102 × 114 in (260 × 290 cm).
ANTHONY CARO
Piece LXXXII. 1969. Forged steel with found steel elements, painted. 17½ × 47½ × 57½ in (44.5 × 120.6 × 146 cm).
CARLO CARRA
Funeral of the Anarchist Galli. 1911. Oil on canvas. 78¼ × 102 in (198.7 × 259.1 cm).
PATRICK CAULFIELD
After Lunch. 1975. Acrylic on canvas. 98 × 84 in (248.9 × 213.4 cm).
CÉSAR (CÉSAR BALDACCINI)
Compression Diget 4. 1960.
PAUL CÉZANNE
The Château Noir. 1902. Oil on canvas. 27½ × 32¼ in (70 × 82 cm).
MARC CHAGALL
Maternity. 1913. Oil on canvas. 76⅜ × 45¼ in (194 × 115 cm).
The Blue Circus. 1950. Oil on canvas. 13¾ × 10½ in (34.9 × 26.7 cm).
GIORGIO DE CHIRICO
The Rose Tower. 1913. Oil on canvas. 28¾ × 28¾ in (73 × 73 cm).
CHRISTO (CHRISTO JARACHEFF)
The Museum of Modern Art Packaged. 1968. Scale model: painted wood, cloth, twine, and polyethylene. 16 in (40.3 cm) high, on painted wood base 2 × 48⅛ × 24⅛ in (50 × 122 × 61 cm).

CHUCK CLOSE
Susan. 1972. Synthetic polymer paint and ink on canvas. 98 × 88 in (252 × 226.5 cm).
CORNEILLE (CORNELIS VAN BEVERLOO)
The Fascination of the Island. 1965. Oil on canvas. 63 × 51 in (161.3 × 129.5 cm).
JOSEPH CORNELL
Untitled (Bébé-Marie). c.1943. Construction. 23⅜ × 12⁵⁄₁₆ × 5¼ in (59.1 × 31.1 × 13.3 cm).
CARLOS CRUZ DIEZ
Physichromie No. 326. 1967. Mixed media. 47 × 70 in (120 × 180 cm).
SALVADOR DALI
Christ of St John of the Cross. 1951. Oil on canvas. 80 × 45 in (204.8 × 115.9 cm).
Premonition of Civil War. 1936. Oil on canvas. 43¼ × 33⅛ in (110 × 83 cm).
STUART DAVIS
Lucky Strike. 1921. Oil on canvas. 33¼ × 18 in (84.5 × 45.7 cm).
EDGAR DEGAS
After the Bath. c.1895. Pastel. 30 × 32½ in (76.2 × 82.6 cm).
ROBERT DELAUNAY
Circular Forms. 1912–13. Oil on canvas. 39⅜ × 26¾ in (100 × 68 cm).
ANDRÉ DERAIN
The Houses of Parliament. 1906. Oil on canvas. 31⅛ × 38⅝ in (79 × 98 cm).
JIM DINE
All in One Lycra Plus Attachments. 1965. Mixed media. 47 × 59 in (120 × 150 cm).
OTTO DIX
Portrait of the Artist's Parents. 1924. Oil on canvas. 46 × 51¼ in (116.5 × 130.2 cm).
THEO VAN DOESBURG
Counter Composition. 1924. Oil on canvas. 39¼ × 39¼ in (100 × 100 cm).
CESAR DOMELA
Composition. 1926. Oil on canvas. 31¾ × 20 in (81 × 51 cm).
JEAN DUBUFFET
The Cow with the Subtile Nose. 1954. Oil and enamel on canvas. 35 × 45¾ in (88.9 × 116.1 cm).
MARCEL DUCHAMP
Bottlerack. 1964. (replica of 1914 original). Actual object in metal. 26 in (66 cm).
Nude Descending a Staircase, No. 2. 1912. 37¾ × 23½ in (96 × 60 cm).
MARCEL DUCHAMP AND RICHARD HAMILTON
The Large Glass or *The Bride Stripped Bare by her Bachelors, Even.* 1915–23, replica 1965–66. Oil, lead wire, lead foil, dust and varnish on glass. 109¼ × 69¼ in (277.5 × 175.9 cm).
RAYMOND DUCHAMP-VILLON
The Horse. 1914. Bronze, cast c.1931. 40 × 39½ × 22⅜ in (101.6 × 100.1 × 56.7 cm).
RAOUL DUFY
La Rue Pavoisée (Street Decorated with Flags). 1906. Oil on canvas. 21⅝ × 18⅛ in (55 × 46 cm).
JACOB EPSTEIN
Rock Drill (full reconstruction). 1973–74. Figure in polyester resin. Drill in metal. Drill bit in wood. 80½ × 55½ in (205 × 141.5 cm).
MAX ERNST
Of This Men Shall Know Nothing. 1923. Oil on canvas. 31⅝ × 25⅛ in (80.3 × 63.8 cm).
RICHARD ESTES
Ansonia. 1977. Oil. 48 × 60 in (121.9 × 151.3 cm).
JEAN FAUTRIER
Tête d'Otage, No. 1. 1943. Plaster on canvas stained colour. 14 × 11 in (35 × 27 cm).
LYONEL FEININGER
The Square. 1916. Oil on canvas. 29 × 35½ in (74 × 90 cm).

LUCIO FONTANA
Spatial Concept 'Waiting'. 1960. Colour print. 36⅝ × 28¾ in (93 × 73 cm).
SAM FRANCIS
Painting. 1957. Watercolour on paper. 24¾ × 19⅛ in (62.9 × 48.6 cm).
HELEN FRANKENTHALER
Mauve District. 1966. Synthetic polymer paint on canvas. 103 × 95 in (261.5 × 241.2 cm).
NAUM GABO
Head of a Woman. c.1917–20, after a work of 1916. Construction in celluloid and metal 24½ × 19¼ in (62.2 × 48.9 cm).
HENRI GAUDIER-BRZESKA
Bird Swallowing a Fish. c.1913–14. Bronze. 12½ × 23¾ × 11 in (31.8 × 60.3 × 27.9 cm).
PAUL GAUGUIN
Nave Nave Mahana (Days of Delight). 1896. Oil on canvas. 37⅜ × 51⅛ in (95 × 130 cm).
ALBERTO GIACOMETTI
Three Men Walking, I. 1948–49. Bronze. 28½ × 16 × 16⅜ in (72.2 × 40.5 × 41.5 cm) including base, 10⅝ × 7¾ × 7¾ in (27 × 19.6 × 19.6 cm).
ALBERT GLEIZES
Woman at the Piano. 1914. Oil on canvas. 57⅝ × 44¾ in (146 × 113.6 cm).
RALPH GOINGS
Paul's Corner. 1970. Oil or acrylic on canvas. 47 × 74 in (120 × 189.4 cm).
NATALIA GONCHAROVA
Cats. 1913. Oil on canvas. 33¼ × 33 in (84.4 × 83.8 cm).
ARSHILE GORKY
Summation. 1947. Pencil, pastel, and charcoal on buff paper mounted on composition board. 79⅝ × 101¾ in (202.1 × 258.2 cm).
ADOLPH GOTTLIEB
The Frozen Sounds, No. 1. 1951. Oil. 36 × 48 in (91.3 × 121.8 cm).
JUAN GRIS
Still Life Before an Open Window. 1915. Oil on canvas. 45¾ × 35 in (116 × 89 cm).
GEORGE GROSZ
Metropolis. 1917. Oil on cardboard. 26¾ × 18¾ in (68 × 47.6 cm).
RENATO GUTTUSO
The Discussion. 1959–60. Tempera and oil on canvas. 86⅝ × 97⅝ in (220 × 248 cm).
RICHARD HAMILTON
Just What Is It that Makes Today's Homes so Different, so Appealing? 1956. Collage. 10¼ × 9¾ in (25 × 26 cm).
DUANE HANSON
Woman with Dog. 1977. Cast polyvinyl, polychromed in acrylic, with mixed media. Lifesize.
MARSDEN HARTLEY
Portrait of a German Officer. 1914. Oil on canvas. 68¼ × 41⅜ in (173.3 × 104.8 cm).
HANS HARTUNG
T54–16. 1954. Oil on canvas. 51⅛ × 38⅛ in (130 × 97 cm).
BARBARA HEPWORTH
Four Squares with Two Circles. 1963–64. Bronze. 124 in (315 cm) high.
IVON HITCHENS
Winter Stage. 1936. Oil on canvas. 23¼ × 61¼ in (59.1 × 155.6 cm).
DAVID HOCKNEY
Peter Getting out of Nick's Pool. 1966. Acrylic on canvas. 84 × 84 in (214 × 214 cm).
The First Marriage. 1962. Oil on canvas. 72 × 84¼ in (182.9 × 214 cm).
EDWARD HOPPER
New York Movie. 1939. Oil on canvas. 32¼ × 40⅛ in (81.9 × 101.9 cm).

HUNDERTSWASSER (FRITZ STOWASSER)
The Hokkaido Steamer. 1961. Watercolour on rice paper, with a chalk ground. 18⅞ × 26 in (44 × 66 cm).
ROBERT INDIANA
The American Dream, I. 1961. Oil on canvas. 72 × 60⅛ in (183 × 152.7 cm).
ALEXEI VON JAWLENSKY
Peonies. 1909. Oil on canvas. 40½ × 30 in (103 × 76 cm).
JASPER JOHNS
Three Flags. 1958. Oil on canvas. 31 × 45 in (78.4 × 115.6 cm).
Target with Four Faces. 1958. Mixed media. 29 × 26 in (75.6 × 66 cm).
ALLEN JONES
Hermaphrodite. 1963. Oil on canvas. 72 × 24 in (182.8 × 61 cm).
ASGER JORN
Green Ballet. 1960. Oil on canvas. 56 × 79 in (144 × 199.7 cm).
DONALD JUDD
Untitled. 1968. Five open rectangles of painted steel spaced approximately 5⅛ in (13 cm) apart, each 48⅜ × 120 × 120¼ in (122.8 × 30.5 × 514 cm); overall, 48⅜ × 120 × 121 in (122.8 × 30.5 × 307.6 cm).
WASSILY KANDINSKY
Black Lines. 1913. Oil on canvas. 50⅜ × 50⅜ in (128 × 128 cm).
Yellow, Red, Blue. 1925. Oil on canvas. 50 × 78¾ in (127 × 200 cm).
ELLSWORTH KELLY
Red Blue Green. 1962. Oil on canvas. 83 × 154 in (213 × 396 cm).
ZOLTAN KEMENY
Gravitations Sentimentales. 1958. Copper elements on copper backing with wooden support. 33⅞ × 27⅞ in (86 × 70.8 cm).
ED KIENHOLZ
The Beanery. 1965. Mixed media. Lifesize.
PHILIP KING
Genghis Khan. 1963. Purple plastic and fibreglass. 84 × 144 in (213.4 × 365.8 cm).
ERNST LUDWIG KIRCHNER
The Artist and Model. 1907. Oil on canvas. 59 × 39⅜ in (150 × 100 cm).
R.B. KITAJ
If Not, Not. 1975–76. Oil on canvas. 60 × 60 in (152.4 × 152.4 cm).
PAUL KLEE
A Young Lady's Adventure. 1922. Watercolour. 17¼ × 12⅝ in (43.8 × 32.1 cm).
Sun and Moon.
YVES KLEIN
Blue Sponge Relief: RE19. 1958. Mixed media. 78 × 64 in (200 × 165 cm).
GUSTAV KLIMT
The Kiss. 1907–08. Oil on canvas. 70¾ × 70¾ in (180 × 180 cm).
FRANZ KLINE
Chief. 1950. Oil on canvas. 58⅜ × 73½ in (148.3 × 186.7 cm).
OSKAR KOKOSCHKA
The Tempest. 1914. Oil on canvas. 71¾ × 86⅜ in (181 × 220 cm).
WILLIAM DE KOONING
Gotham News. 1955. Oil on canvas. 69 × 79 in (175 × 200.5 cm).
Woman I. 1950–52. Oil on canvas. 75 × 57 in (192.7 × 147.3 cm).
FRANTIŠEK KUPKA
Ranging Verticals. 1912–13. Oil on canvas. 23 × 28½ in (58 × 72 cm).
MIKHAIL LARIONOV
Glass. 1912. Oil on canvas. 41 × 38¼ in (104.1 × 97.2 cm).

BART VAN DER LECK
Geometrical Composition. 1917. Oil on canvas. 39¾ × 39¼ in (101 × 100 cm).
FERNAND LÉGER
The Divers, II. 1941–42. Oil on canvas. 90 × 68 in (228.6 × 172.8 cm).
The Wedding. 1912. Oil on canvas. 101 × 81⅛ in (257 × 206 cm).
PERCY WYNDHAM LEWIS
Composition. 1913. Watercolour drawing. 13½ × 10½ in (34.3 × 26.7 cm).
ROY LICHTENSTEIN
M-Maybe. 1965. Oil and synthetic polymer paint on canvas. 59 × 59 in (152.4 × 152.4 cm).
RICHARD LINDNER
Ice. 1966. Oil on canvas. 69 × 59 in (177.8 × 152.4 cm).
EL LISSITZKY
Proun 99. c1924. Oil on wood. 50¾ × 39 in (128.9 × 99 cm).
RICHARD LONG
119 Stones. 1976. Stone. Approximately 6 × 276 × 231 in (152 × 701 × 586.7 cm).
MORRIS LOUIS
Delta Iota. 1961. Acrylic on canvas. 103¼ × 175½ in (262.2 × 445.8 cm).
JOHN McCRACKEN
Red Plant. 1967. 101 × 18 × 3 in (259 × 45 × 7.5 cm).
STANTON MACDONALD-WRIGHT
'Oriental'. Synchromy in Blue-Green. 1918. Oil. 36 × 50 in (91.3 × 126.9 cm).
AUGUST MACKE
Landscape with Cows and Camel. 1914. Oil on canvas. 18½ × 21¼ in (47 × 54 cm).
RENE MAGRITTE
Time Transfixed. 1939. Oil on canvas. 57½ × 38⅜ in (146 × 97.3 cm).
ARISTIDE MAILLOL
The Mediterranean. 1902–05. Bronze. 41 in (104.1 cm) high.
KASIMIR MALEVICH
Head of a Peasant Woman. 1913. Oil on canvas. 31½ × 37½ in (80 × 95 cm).
Suprematist Composition. c.1915. Oil on canvas. 23 × 19 in (58.4 × 48.3 cm).
EDOUARD MANET
Olympia. 1863. Oil on canvas. 51¼ × 74¾ in (130.5 × 190 cm).
FRANZ MARC
Fighting Forms. 1914. Oil on canvas. 35⅞ × 51⅝ in (91 × 131 cm).
FILIPPO TOMMASO MARINETTI
Zang-Tumb-Tuum (page from the book). 1914.
ESCOBAR MARISOL
Ruth. 1962. Mixed media. 65 in (167.2 cm).
GEORGES MATHIEU
Les Capétiens Partout. 1954. Oil on canvas. 115 × 234 in (295 × 600 cm).
HENRI MATISSE
Female Nude. 1907. Bronze. 13½ × 19¾ × 11¼ in (34.2 × 50.2 × 28.6 cm).
Landscape at Collioure (Study for 'Bonheur de Vivre'). 1905. Oil on canvas. 18 × 21½ in (46 × 55 cm).
Luxe, Calme et Volupté. 1904–05. Oil on canvas. 37 × 46 in (94 × 127 cm).
The Dance. 1910. Oil on canvas. 102½ × 154 in (260 × 391 cm).
The Dessert, Harmony in Red. 1908. Oil in canvas. 71 × 86½ in (180 × 220 cm).
The Snail. 1953. Gouache on paper. 112¾ × 113 in (286.4 × 287 cm).
JEAN METZINGER
Dancer in a Café. 1912. Oil on canvas. 57½ × 45 in (145.9 × 114.2 cm).

JOAN MIRO
Maternity. 1924. Oil on canvas. 36½ × 28¼ in (93 × 72 cm).
AMEDEO MODIGLIANI
Female Head. 1911–12. Stone or marble. 25 × 5 × 13⅞ in (63.5 × 12.7 × 35.2 cm).
Reclining Nude. 1919. Oil on canvas.
PIET MONDRIAN
Broadway Boogie-Woogie. 1942–43. Oil on canvas. 50 × 50 in (127 × 127 cm).
Composition. 1930. Oil on canvas. 18 × 18 in (46 × 46 cm).
CLAUDE MONET
The Bridge at Argenteuil. 1874. Oil on canvas. 23⅝ × 31½ in (60 × 80 cm).
The Lily Pond. 1899. Oil on canvas. 34¼ × 36¼ in (88.3 × 92.1 cm).
HENRY MOORE
Locking Piece. 1963–64. Bronze. 115½ in (293.4 cm) high.
Madonna and Child (St Matthew's Church, Northampton). 1943–44. Hornton stone. 59 in (149.9 cm) high.
GIORGIO MORANDI
Still-Life. 1944. Oil on canvas.
GUSTAV MOREAU
Jupiter and Sémelé. 1894–95. Oil on canvas. 83¾ × 46½ in (213 × 118 cm).
ROBERT MORRIS
Untitled. 1970. Felt. 71 × 95 in (183 × 244 cm).
ROBERT MOTHERWELL
Elegy to the Spanish Republic No. LV. 1955–60. Oil on canvas. 70 × 76⅛ in (177.6 × 193.1 cm).
EDVARD MUNCH
The Dance of Life. 1899–1900. Oil on canvas. 49¼ × 79¾ in (125 × 202 cm).
LOUISE NEVELSON
Black Wall. 1959. Wood painted black. 104 × 85¼ × 25½ in (264.2 × 216.5 × 64.8 cm).
BARNETT NEWMAN
Vir Heroicus Sublimis. 1905–51. Oil on canvas. 95⅜ × 21¾ in (242.2 × 513.6 cm).
BEN NICHOLSON
1967 (Tuscan Relief). 1967. Oil on pavatex carved on relief, mounted on board. 59¾ × 66 in (151.8 × 167.6 cm).
SIDNEY NOLAN
Glenrowan. 1956–57. Ripolin on hardboard. 36 × 48 in (91.4 × 121.9 cm).
KENNETH NOLAND
17th Stage. 1964. Polymer paint on canvas. 95 × 83 in (244 × 213 cm).
EMIL NOLDE
The Windmill. 1924. Oil on canvas. 28¾ × 34⅝ in (73 × 88 cm).
GEORGIA O'KEEFE
Abstraction Blue. 1927. Oil on canvas. 40¼ × 30 in (102.1 × 76 cm).
CLAES OLDENBURG
Pastry Case, I. 1961–62. Enamel paint on nine plaster sculptures in glass showcase. 20¾ × 30⅛ × 14¾ in (52.7 × 76.5 × 37.3 cm).
JOSÉ CLEMENTE OROZCO
Zapatistas. 1931. Oil on canvas. 45 × 55 in (114.3 × 139.7 cm).
EDUARDO PAOLOZZI
St Sebastian III. 1958–59. Bronze. 87 in (221 cm) high.
PHILIP PEARLSTEIN
Two Seated Models. 1968. Oil on canvas. 60 × 48 in (152.4 × 122 cm).
MAX PECHSTEIN
The Harbour. 1922. Oil on canvas. 31½ × 39¼ in (80 × 100 cm).
ANTOINE PEVSNER
Maquette of a Monument Symbolizing the Liberation of the Spirit. 1952. Bronze. 18 × 18 × 11½ in (45.7 × 45.7 × 29.2 cm).

PETER PHILLIPS
For Men Only Starring MM and BB. 1961. Oil on canvas. 108 × 60 in (274.3 × 152.4 cm).
PABLO PICASSO
Guernica. 1937. Oil on canvas. 138 × 138 in (350.5 × 350.5 cm).
Head of a Woman (Fernande). 1909. Bronze. 16¼ in (41.3 cm) high.
Les Demoiselles d'Avignon. 1907. Oil on canvas. 96 × 92 in (243.9 × 233.7 cm).
'Ma Jolie' (Woman with a Zither or Woman with a Guitar). 1911–12. Oil on canvas. 39⅜ × 25¾ in (100 × 65.4 cm).
Massacre in Korea. 1951. Oil. 43¼ × 66¾ in (110 × 169.5 cm).
Seated Woman (Nude). 1909–10. Oil on canvas. 36¼ × 28¾ in (92.1 × 73 cm).
Still-life with Guitar. 1922. Oil on canvas. 32½ × 40¼ in (83 × 102.5 cm).
The Violin. 1914. Oil on canvas. 25½ × 18 in (65 × 46 cm).
Three Musicians. 1921. Oil on canvas. 79 × 87¾ in (200.7 × 229.9 cm).
Weeping Woman. 1937. Oil on canvas. 23½ × 19¼ in (59.7 × 48.9 cm).
CAMILLE PISSARRO
The Côte des Boeufs at L'Hermitage, near Pontoise. 1877. Oil on canvas. 45¼ × 34½ in (114.9 × 87.6 cm).
JACKSON POLLOCK
Convergence. 1952. Oil on canvas. 93½ × 155 in (237.5 × 393.7 cm).
ARNALDO POMODORO
Sphere, I. 1963. Bronze. 44¾ in (113.5 cm) diameter, on base ½ in (1.2 cm) high, 7⅜ in (18.5 cm) diameter.
ROBERT RAUSCHENBURG
First Landing Jump. 1961. 'Combine painting': cloth, metal, leather, electric fixture, cable, and oil paint on composition board; overall, including car tyre and wooden plank on floor, 89⅝ × 72 × 8⅞ in (226.3 × 182.8 × 22.5 cm).
ODILON REDON
The Cyclops. c.1894. Oil on panel. 25⅛ × 20 in (64 × 51 cm).
AUGUSTE RENOIR
Spring Landscape. 1877. Oil on canvas.
BRIDGET RILEY
Loss. 1964. Emulsion on board. 46 × 46 in (117 × 117 cm).
DIEGO RIVERA
Agrarian Leader Zapata. 1931. Fresco. 93¾ × 74 in (238.1 × 188 cm).
LARRY RIVERS
The Last Civil War Veteran. 1959. Oil and charcoal on canvas. 82½ × 64⅛ in (209.6 × 162.9 cm).
WILLIAM ROBERTS
The Cinema. 1920. Oil on canvas. 36 × 30 in (91.4 × 76.2 cm).
ALEXANDER RODCHENKO
Composition. 1918. Gouache. 13 × 6⅜ in (33 × 16.2 cm).
AUGUSTE RODIN
Balzac. 1892–97. Bronze. 118 × 47 × 47 in (300 × 119 × 119 cm).
JAMES ROSENQUIST
Marilyn Monroe, I. 1962. Oil and spray enamel on canvas. 93 × 72¼ in (236.2 × 183.3 cm).
MEDARDO ROSSO
The Bookmaker. 1894. Wax. 17⅜ in (44 cm) high.
MARK ROTHKO
Light Red over Black. 1957. Oil on canvas. 91⅝ × 60⅛ in (232.7 × 152.7 cm).
GEORGES ROUAULT
The Bridge (Aunt Sallys). 1907. Oil on paper. 29½ × 41½ in (74.9 × 105.4 cm).

LUIGI RUSSOLO
Noise Intoner (Russolo and his assistant Piatti with the Intonarumori).
ANTONIO SANT'ELIA
Design for Station and Airport. 1913–14. Ink. 11 × 8¼ in (27.9 × 20.9 cm).
EGON SCHIELE
Mother with Two Children. 1917. Oil on canvas. 59 × 62½ in (150 × 158.7 cm).
OSKAR SCHLEMMER
Bauhaus Stairway. 1932. Oil on canvas. 63⅞ × 45 in (162.3 × 114.3 cm).
KARL SCHMIDT-ROTTLUFF
Landscape, Lofthus, Norway. 1911. Oil on canvas. 34¼ × 37¾ in (87 × 96 cm).
NICOLAS SCHÖFFER
Spatial Dynamic Sculptures. Not dated. Mixed media. 42 × 35 × 29 in (107 × 90 × 75 cm).
KURT SCHWITTERS
Das Haarnabelbild (The Hair Navel). 1920. Oil on board with painted relief wood, cloth, earthenware and hair. 35¾ × 28½ in (91 × 72.5 cm).
Merzbau. Third version. Elterwater, Westmoreland, 1947. Wall removed from Elterwater in 1965 to the Hatton Gallery, University of Newcastle-upon-Tyne. Wall is of local slate. Three-dimensional collage using miscellaneous materials. Approximately 135 sq ft (12.54 sq m).
PETER SEDGLEY
Yellow Attenuation. 1965. Acrylic on board. 48 × 48 in (122 × 122 cm).
GEORGE SEGAL
Walk Don't Walk. 1976. Plaster, cement, metal, painted wood and lights. 104 × 72 × 72 in (264.2 × 182.9 × 182.9 cm).
GEORGE SEURAT
The Bridge at Courbevoie. 1886. Oil on canvas. 18¼ × 21¾ in (46.4 × 55.3 cm).
GINO SEVERINI
Dynamic Hieroglyphic of the Bal Tabarin. 1912. Oil on canvas, with sequins. 63⅝ × 61½ in (161.6 × 156.2 cm).
DAVID SMITH
Cubi XIX. 1969. Sculpture in metal. 112¾ × 58¼ × 40 in (286.4 × 148 × 101.6 cm).
JACK SMITH
Mother Bathing Child. 1953. Oil on board. 72 × 48 in (182.9 × 121.9 cm).
ROBERT SMITHSON
Spiral Jetty. 1970. Stone.
PIERRE SOULAGES
Painting. 1956. Oil on canvas. 76 × 51 in (194 × 129.9 cm).
CHAÏM SOUTINE
Carcass of Beef. c.1925. Oil on canvas. 55¼ × 42⅜ in (140 × 107.5 cm).
NICOLAS DE STAËL
Agrigento. 1953. Oil on canvas. 28¾ × 39⅜ in (73 × 100 cm).
FRANK STELLA
Kastura. 1979. Oil and epoxy on aluminium wire mesh. 115 × 92 × 30 in (292.1 × 233.7 × 76.2 cm).
Ossippee I. 1966. Fluorescent alkyd paint on canvas. 94 × 137 in (242 × 350 cm).
JOSEPH STELLA
Battle of Lights, Coney Island. 1913. Oil on canvas. 75¾ × 84 in (192.4 × 213.4 cm).
CLYFFORD STILL
1957-D No. 1. 1957. Oil on canvas. 113 × 159 in (287 × 403.9 cm).
GRAHAM SUTHERLAND
Christ in Glory. 1952–62. Tapestry. 74 ft 8 in × 38 ft (22.55 × 11.58 m).
Devastation, 1941: East End, Burnt Paper Warehouse. 1941. Oil in wood. 26½ × 44¾ in (67.3 × 113.7 cm).

TAKIS (TAKIS VASSILIAKIS)
Signal 'Insect-Animal of Space'. 1956. Sculpture in metal. 81⅞ × 9 × 9½ in (208 × 22.9 × 24.1 cm).
RUFINO TAMAYO
Animals. 1941. Oil on canvas. 30⅛ × 40 in (76.5 × 101.6 cm).
YVES TANGUY
Mama, Papa Is Wounded! 1927 Oil on canvas. 36¼ × 28¾ in (92.1 × 73 cm).
ANTONI TÀPIES
Large Painting. 1958. Mixed media including sand. 78 × 102 in (200.7 × 260.7 cm).
VLADIMIR TATLIN
Monument to the Third International. 1919–20.
JOE TILSON
OH!. 1963. Mixed media. 49 × 37 in (124.5 × 94 cm).
JEAN TINGUELEY
Baluba No. 3. 1959. Mixed media including electric motor. 56 in (144 cm).
VINCENT VAN GOGH
The Church at Auvers-sur-Oise. 1890. Oil on canvas. 37 × 29¼ in (94 × 74 cm).
GEORGES VANTONGERLOO
Construction in an Inscribed and Circumscribed Square of a Circle. 1924. Cement. 10 × 10 × 14 in (25 × 25 × 35 cm).
VICTOR VASARELY
Arny-C. 1966. Oil on canvas. 29½ × 29½ in (75 × 75 cm).
JACQUES VILLON
Little Girl at the Piano. 1912. Oil on canvas. 50¾ × 37¾ in (129 × 96 cm).
MAURICE VLAMINCK
The Bridge at Chatou. 1906. Oil on canvas. 52¾ × 20 in (73 × 50 cm).
EDOUARD VUILLARD
Interior with Madame Vuillard. c.1897. Oil on canvas. 17 × 25 in (43 × 63.5 cm).
ANDY WARHOL
Campbell's Soup Can with Can Opener. 1962. Polymer paint screened on canvas. 70 × 53 in (180 × 135.6 cm).
Marilyn. 1967. Screenprint. 35⅞ × 35⅞ in (91.1 × 91.1 cm).
TOM WESSELMAN
Bathtub Collage, No. 3. 1963. Mixed media. 84 × 106 × 18 in (213 × 270 × 45 cm).
WOLS (ALFRED OTTO WOLFGANG SCHULZE)
Composition V. 1946. Oil on canvas. 6 × 5 in (15.9 × 12.3 cm).

Index